Trails to Gold

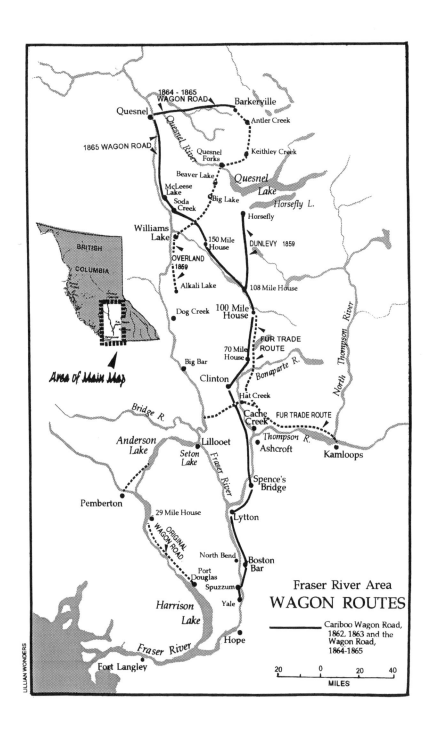

1864 - 1865
WAGON ROAD

Quesnel

Barkerville

Antler Creek

1865 WAGON ROAD

Quesnel
Forks

Keithley Creek

Beaver Lake

Quesnel
Lake

McLeese
Lake

Big Lake

Horsefly L.

Soda
Creek

Horsefly

Williams
Lake

DUNLEVY 1859

150 Mile
House

OVERLAND
1859

Alkali Lake

108 Mile House

BRITISH

COLUMBIA

Dog Creek

100 Mile
House

Area of Main Map

70 Mile
House

FUR TRADE
ROUTE

Big Bar

Clinton

Bonaparte R.

Hat Creek

Bridge R.

Cache
Creek

FUR TRADE ROUTE

North Thompson River

Anderson
Lake

Lillooet

Thompson R.

Seton
Lake

Ashcroft

Kamloops

Pemberton

Spence's
Bridge

29 Mile House

Lytton

ORIGINAL
WAGON ROAD

North Bend

Boston
Bar

Port
Douglas

Spuzzum

Fraser River Area
WAGON ROUTES

Harrison
Lake

Yale

Fraser River

Hope

Cariboo Wagon Road,
1862, 1863 and the
Wagon Road,
1864-1865

Fort Langley

20   0   20   40

MILES

Trails to Gold

by

Branwen C. Patenaude

Horsdal & Schubart

Horsdal & Schubart Publishers Ltd.
Victoria, B.C., Canada

Cover photograph at Cottonwood House by Leif Grandell, Studio Grandell, Quesnel, B.C.

Maps designed and drawn by Lillian Wonders, Victoria, B.C., from sketch maps and information furnished by the author.

Chapter-head drawings by the author.

This book is set in Galliard Book Text.

Printed and bound in Canada by Hignell Printing Limited, Winnipeg.

Canadian Cataloguing in Publication Data

Patenaude, Branwen C. (Branwen Christine) 1927-
Trails to gold

Includes bibliographical references and index.
ISBN 0-920663-35-4 (v.1)

1. Roads—British Columbia—History—19th century. 2. Transportation—British Columbia—History—19th century. 3. Cariboo (B.C.: Regional district)—History. 4. Cariboo (B.C.: Regional district)—Gold discoveries. I. Title.
FC3845.C3P37 1995   971.1'7   C95-910280-9
F1089.C3P37 1995

CONTENTS

ACKNOWLEDGEMENTS

I wish to acknowledge a much-appreciated Canada Council grant that got me started on the research in 1977; also special thanks to the staff of the British Columbia Provincial Archives during the last 20 years, and in particular Brian Young, Barbara McDougall, and Frances Gundry. From Heritage Conservation in Victoria my thanks go to Don Tarasoff, and to Chark Nipp, retired custodian of the vault at Legal Surveys. Many thanks also to Ken Mathers, at one time curator of the Barkerville Museum, and to the present-day staff and management of Barkerville Park, Brian Fugler, and Bill Quackenbush, who gave me access to their photographic collection, and more than once joined in my enthusiasm over solving a new piece of research.

Over the years there have been many interested pioneers and historians who took the time to assist me, some of whom welcomed me into their homes, and escorted me to the scenes of historical significance in their particular area. Among these, for Volume One, are:

Bob Norris of Lytton
Vashti and T.C. "Trav" Fisk of Venables Valley
Irene Stangoe and John Roberts of Williams Lake
Hilda Bryson of Lillooet
Earl and Jocelyn Cahill of Clinton
Gerry Andrews of Victoria
Bob Harris of West Vancouver

Branwen C. Patenaude

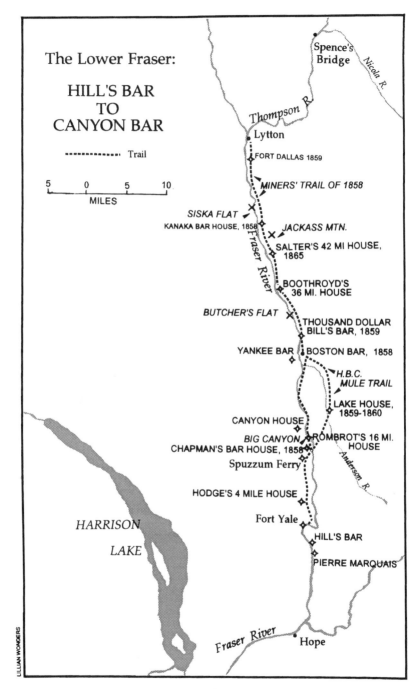

Map for Chapter One

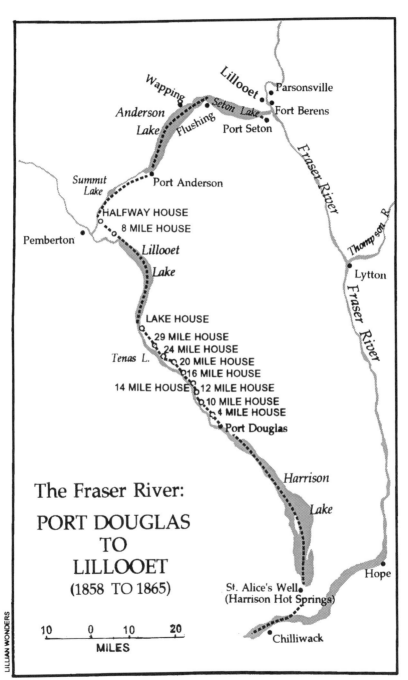

The Fraser River:

PORT DOUGLAS
TO
LILLOOET
(1858 TO 1865)

Map for Chapter Two

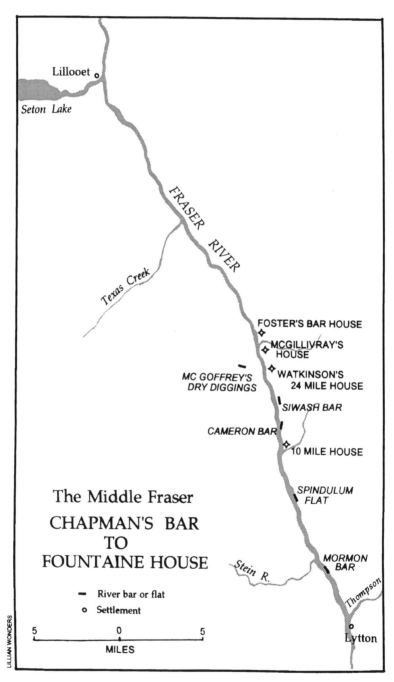

Lillooet o

Seton Lake

FRASER RIVER

Texas Creek

FOSTER'S BAR HOUSE

MCGILLIVRAY'S
HOUSE

WATKINSON'S
24 MILE HOUSE

MC GOFFREY'S
DRY DIGGINGS

SIWASH BAR

CAMERON BAR

10 MILE HOUSE

SPINDULUM
FLAT

The Middle Fraser

CHAPMAN'S BAR
TO
FOUNTAINE HOUSE

MORMON
BAR

Stein R.

Thompson

— River bar or flat
o Settlement

5   0   5

MILES

LILLIAN WONDERS

Lytton

Map for Chapter Three

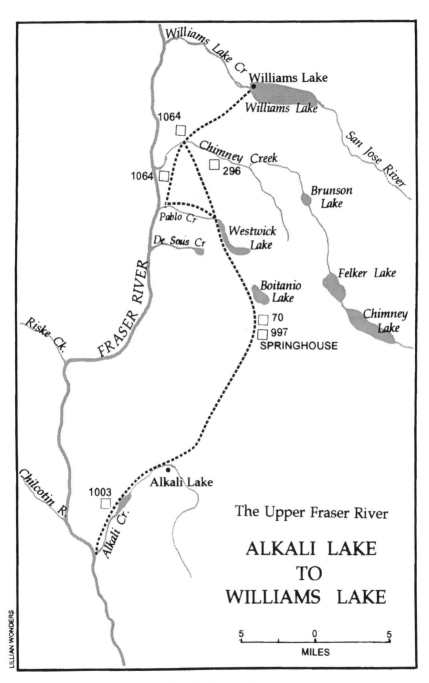

Williams Lake Cr

Williams Lake

Williams Lake

1064

San Jose River

Chimney Creek

1064

296

Brunson Lake

Pablo Cr

De Sous Cr

Westwick Lake

Felker Lake

FRASER RIVER

Boitanio Lake

Chimney Lake

Riske Ck.

70

997

SPRINGHOUSE

Chilcotin R.

1003

Alkali Lake

Alkali Cr.

The Upper Fraser River

ALKALI LAKE
TO
WILLIAMS LAKE

5   0   5
MILES

LILLIAN WONDERS

Map for Chapter Four

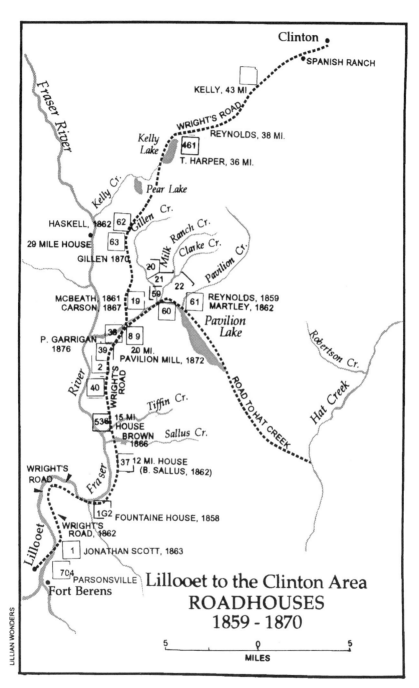

Clinton
● SPANISH RANCH

KELLY, 43 MI.

WRIGHT'S ROAD

REYNOLDS, 38 MI.

Kelly
Lake 461
T. HARPER, 36 MI.

Fraser River

Kelly Cr.

Pear Lake

Gillen Cr.

HASKELL, 1862 62

29 MILE HOUSE 63

GILLEN 1870

Milk Ranch Cr.

Clarke Cr.

Pavilion Cr.

20
21
59
22

MCBEATH 1861 19
CARSON 1867

61 REYNOLDS, 1859
MARTLEY, 1862

60

Pavilion
Lake

Robertson Cr.

P. GARRIGAN 38
1876 39 8 9

2 20 MI.
PAVILION MILL, 1872

River 40

WRIGHT'S ROAD

Tiffin Cr.

ROAD TO HAT CREEK

Hat Creek

53 15 MI.
HOUSE
BROWN Sallus Cr.
1866

37 12 MI. HOUSE
(B. SALLUS, 1862)

WRIGHT'S
ROAD

Fraser

1 G2 FOUNTAINE HOUSE, 1858

Lillooet

WRIGHT'S
ROAD, 1862

1 JONATHAN SCOTT, 1863

70 PARSONSVILLE Lillooet to the Clinton Area
Fort Berens

ROADHOUSES
1859 - 1870

5   0   5
MILES

LILLIAN WONDERS

Map for Chapter Five

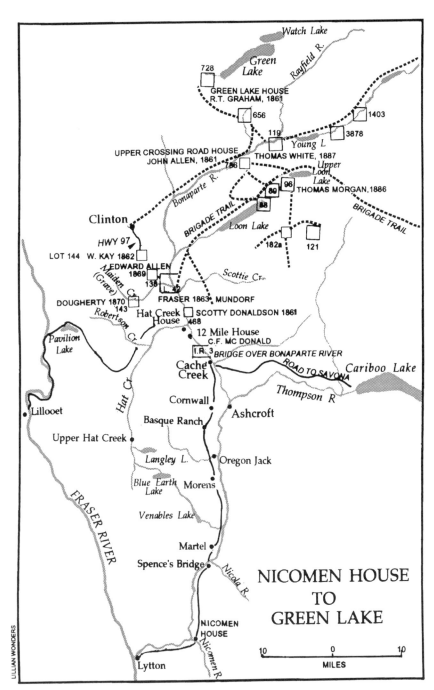

Map for Chapter Six

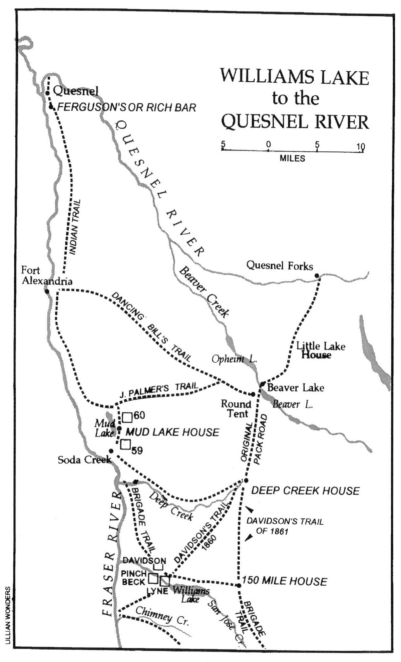

Map for Chapter Seven

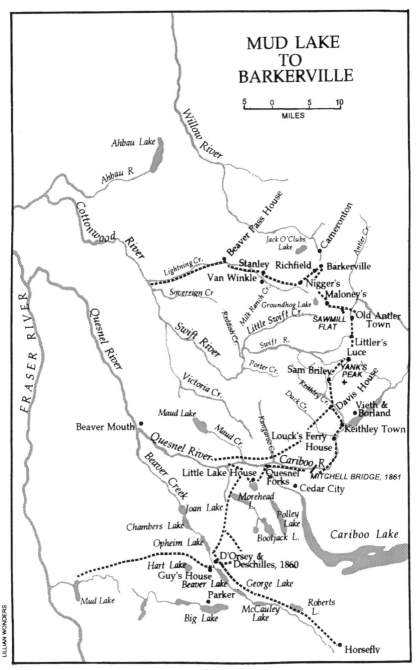

Map for Chapter Eight

INTRODUCTION

Less than 150 years ago the mainland of British Columbia was a virtual wilderness, inhabited by tribes of native Indians and a handful of Hudson's Bay Company fur traders. The arrival of 10,000 gold-hungry California miners in the spring of 1858 signalled the end of the monopolistic fur-trade era, and opened the country to settlement and development. Amongst the earliest of enterprises in the new colony was the operation of roadhouses.

Constructed in haste by opportunists who saw the need to supply food and shelter to the hundreds of travellers and their animals en route to the goldfields, a series of log cabins soon dotted the trails beside the Fraser River north and south of Fort Yale, and along the first trail built between Port Douglas and Lillooet. Even as these trails were constructed, hundreds of pack trains moved slowly north, travelling an average of only five or six miles a day. For this reason the earliest roadhouses were built within a few miles of each other. Once permanent roads were established and horses became the common means of transportation, roadhouses were located at ten- to 15-mile intervals, depending on the terrain. One exception was in the Lac La Hache area, between the 100 Mile and 150 Mile points, where there were more roadhouses per mile than in any other section of the Cariboo Road. This was due to the moderate climate, open meadow land, and easy access to water. Settled early, the land there developed into many self-sufficient ranches where housewives made themselves a steady income by taking in overnight travellers.

Situated on a convenient flat close to water and pasture, the first wayside houses, referred to at this time as "restaurants", were crude log shacks, offering limited services. The dimensions of those early public facilities were usually so small that with the close proximity of numbers of unwashed bodies, they became unbearably hot and smelly. Most roadhouses consisted of a single room with perhaps a small window and a door; a stone fireplace at one end was used for cooking, and provided the only source of heat and light. Almost the only piece of furniture was the bar, where liquor was sold at 25¢ a "shot". The sale of spirits, legal or illegal, was at first the main source of income for the roadhouse-keeper. At night, while miners and pack-train operators rolled up in their blankets on a dirt floor in front of the fireplace, the bar-keep slept on top of his liquor supply, to prevent any pilfering.

While the term "roadhouse" later came to refer to public houses in rural areas, even the first so-called "hotels" in communities such as Yale or Lillooet were no more sophisticated than those on the trail: a saloon, with sleeping loft above.

The supply of food at those primitive roadhouses was entirely dependent on the expensive pack-train delivery system. This was particularly true for the roadhouses between Port Douglas and Port Pemberton, where for the most part the rocky, mountainous terrain prevented the cultivation of gardens. With the cost of freight at almost 50¢ a pound, fresh produce was seldom seen, leaving the traveller with little choice but the usual fare of bacon and beans, bread, flapjacks or bannock, coffee, and tea, for which they paid a dollar at Yale, and $1.50 at Lillooet. Needless to say, the absence of running water and sanitation facilities made it difficult to maintain any degree of cleanliness.

As land was pre-empted, and where the first roads ran through private land, a roadhouse with a store often made its appearance. Operated as part of the farm, these self-sustaining enterprises offered a menu quite different from their counterparts in isolated, mountainous areas. By supplying their own meat, dairy products, fruit and even home-produced wine, farmers were able to keep their costs low, providing meals with a variety equal to any hotel or restaurant in San Francisco. For this reason roadhouse farms were much more likely to succeed through periods of poor economy than those without that support.

In the goldfields, entertainment came early to the roadhouse, the first social centre of a community. With each new gold strike came the establishment of a camp with a store and roadhouse, frequented by gamblers, travelling musicians, and prostitutes, all seeking a share of the miners' gold. Even in the most inaccessible areas of the Cariboo, hand organs known as "hurdies", pianos, and billiard tables appeared in the roadhouses, transported on the backs of mules all the way from San Francisco.

Competition between roadhouses was fierce, and prior to the completion of the wagon roads, properties changed hands frequently, for a variety of reasons. In the Cariboo, where the first recession occurred in 1864, several ambitious roadhouse-keepers lost their properties to dishonest money lenders. In other instances, the freight company that delivered supplies to the roadhouses foreclosed when overdue bills were left unpaid. When farmers from the Cariboo established stores and hotels in the Omineca during the short-lived gold rush of the early 1870s, several went bankrupt as a result of over-extended credit.

Not all travellers frequented the roadhouses; some could not afford the cost, choosing instead to camp out and cook their own meals, purchasing supplies along the way from the stores which were often part of a roadhouse complex. Others slept outside because they found the roadhouses infested with lice and bedbugs, carried from house to house in the clothing of the unwashed. This affliction was everywhere, and impossible to cure; in fact it was most unusual to find a roadhouse without the pests.

As the building of two wagon roads began in 1862, one from Lillooet, and the other from Yale, road makers erected markers to indicate the mileage. Roadhouses between Yale and Clinton took on the names of the land owners, such as "Boothroyd's", or "Cornwall's", and those between Lillooet and the 150 Mile House adopted the name of the closest mile post, for example, the 70 Mile House, the 115 Mile House, and the 150 Mile House.

The wagon roads brought a new era of sophistication to the roadhouses. With regularly scheduled stagecoach routes established in 1864 by Francis Barnard of Barnard's Express, women and families began to travel, and for this reason roadhouse-keepers began to divide their premises up into separate rooms. By the late 1860s, two-storey roadhouses contained a dining room, kitchen, ladies' sitting room, and private bedrooms equipped with spring mattresses and fresh linen. While most roadhouses were still of log construction, some were being built of lumber, cut by hand, or sawn in local mills. During the early 1900s, one or two roadhouses were known to have been assembled from prefabricated kits, purchased from Eaton's catalogue.

By the late 1870s there were a number of very large roadhouses with as many as 20 bedrooms. Hat Creek House, the Clinton Hotel, and the 150 Mile House are examples. These were not always operated by their owners, but by proprietors who leased them on a yearly basis. Supervised by a manager who employed a cook and other necessary staff, this type of roadhouse was the forerunner of today's hotels. Cooks came from a variety of ethnic backgrounds—French

Canadian, Chinese, black and European—and depending on their training and ability, commanded a high wage. Many of the earliest cooks were miners, especially the French Canadians and Chinese, who took on winter employment at the roadhouses. Girls from nearby Indian reserves were often hired to clean, and to assist the cook.

Following the establishment of stagecoach services to Barkerville, Barnard's Express, or the B.C. Express Company as it became in 1867, signed contracts with certain popular roadhouse farms to supply meals and accommodations for their passengers on a regular basis. Other ranchers along the road took contracts to board the stagecoach horses. Those farms which could supply enough good hay and grain got the contracts, sometimes only for the summer and at other times all year. These contracts were important to the farmers and roadhouse-keepers, assuring them of a steady income.

With the building of the Canadian Pacific Railway, and later the Canadian National Railway, through the Thompson and Fraser canyons in the mid-1880s, many sections of the original wagon road between Spence's Bridge and Yale were put out of service, and with them the roadhouse business in that area. In 1927 when a new road opened, most of the remaining roadhouses in established communities such as Spence's Bridge, Lytton and Boston Bar had become hotels. While the railroad practically ruined the roadhouse business north of Yale, it brought growth and prosperity to a new town at Ashcroft, 78 miles north. By 1890 Ashcroft had become the new centre of business in the upper country, causing a resurgence of traffic on the Cariboo Road and expanded opportunities for road-house-keepers in the north. At this time the government attempted to adopt a new set of mileage numbers on the road north of Ashcroft. This meant that all the old traditional roadhouse numbers would also have to be altered. Although the mile posts were renumbered, very few roadhouse-keepers accepted the change.

Prior to 1910, when fireplaces, wood-burning stoves, kerosene lamps, and candles were the only sources of heat and light, fire was the dreaded enemy of the roadhouse. Fear of fire made most people extremely cautious, but in public buildings, where there was little control over the actions of guests, the possibility of fire was even more extreme. Most fires were started by overheated stovepipes igniting tinder-dry shakes on the roof. The older the building, the drier the logs, and for this reason most roadhouses eventually burned down.

The years between 1886 and 1910 may be thought of as the heyday of the roadhouse era, and although there were more roadhouses than ever during this period, very few were any more sophisticated than those of the 1870s. While competing roadhouse operators vied for trade by providing finer furnishings, fancier meals, and better service, there were no noticeable improvements until the 1920s when electric lights, running water, and indoor plumbing became available. It would be safe to say that very few roadhouses ever provided any of the above. By this time cars were replacing the horse and buggy, and trucks carrying freight travelled for long distances without stopping. For these reasons the roadhouses became redundant.

While roadhouses in towns and communities became hotels, by the 1930s most roadhouses between towns had closed their doors to the public. Those that continued altered their focus to become guest ranches and holiday resorts. Although most of the original roadhouses are gone now, a handful still remain: Alexander Lodge between Spuzzum and Boston Bar, Cornwall Lodge and Hat Creek House near Ashcroft, Pollard's roadhouse north of Clinton, the 137 Mile House north of Lac La Hache, Moffat House and Anders' House below Quesnel, and Cottonwood House between Quesnel and Barkerville. Of these, Hat Creek House and Cottonwood House have become Provincial Historic parks, where during the summer visitors enjoy guided tours of the old roadhouses, and discover the fascinating history of the area.

Hat Creek House and ranch, CA 1890s. (COURTESY BCARS)

CHAPTER ONE

THE LOWER FRASER: HILL'S BAR TO CANYON HOUSE

WITH the decline of gold production in California in the early 1850s, American prospectors drifted north into British territory, searching for new sources of the precious metal. While a small deposit of quartz gold had been discovered on the Queen Charlotte Islands in 1850, the earliest reports on the mainland came from Fort Alexandria, where Hudson's Bay Company Chief Trader Donald McLean procured samples of Fraser River gold from the natives in 1853. Before long, it was realized that the yellow metal existed in many areas of the mainland, not only on the Fraser river and its tributaries, but also on the Skeena and Nass rivers to the north. Further discoveries of gold on a tributary of the Thompson River in 1856 attracted increasing numbers of Americans into British territory by way of the Columbia River. In many cases they were met with violent opposition from native Indians, who resented the outsiders taking what they considered to be their gold. As reports of larger and richer gold on the bench land above Lytton spread south in the fall of

1857, only the approach of winter prevented further escalation of the excitement. Early the next spring, American newspapers reported a shipment of 1,000 ounces of gold sent from Fort Victoria to London, England, aboard the sailing ship *Princess Royal*, which triggered a gold rush on the Fraser River:

> "The electrifying news was swiftly taken up in the pioneer press, namely the *Olympia Pioneer & Democrat* of March 5, 1858 and the *San Francisco Evening Bulletin* of March 19, 1858." [1]

During the first year an estimated 20,000 prospectors, mostly from California, entered British Columbia. While some travelled overland to reach the upper Fraser at Lillooet, the greatest number arrived by ship from San Francisco at Fort Victoria on Vancouver Island. Faced with yet another 80 miles to the mainland, the miners built boats and set sail across the treacherous waters of the Gulf of Georgia, heading for the mouth of the Fraser River. While many drowned en route, lost their way or were killed by hostile Indians, thousands found their way, and were soon rewarded with signs of gold, from Murderer's Bar, three miles below Fort Hope to Fort Yale, over 100 miles upstream.

HILL'S BAR.

Hill's Bar, a narrow strip of land a mile and a half south of Fort Yale, proved to be the richest and longest-worked bar on the lower Fraser. Of the 15,000 miners working between Hope and Yale in October 1858, 400 were mining at Hill's Bar. During the summer they lived in tents, as they had in California, but by fall, the cool, wet, climate of the area prompted them to chop down trees and build cabins. By June there were as many as 40 log buildings on the rise above the river, and by September a townsite was laid out.

One of the first buildings at Hill's Bar was a roadhouse and saloon, built in June 1858 by a French Canadian, Pierre Marquais. Not long afterward a boarding house was built by Kerrison and Company, to house the miners of their consortium. The great wealth of gold extracted from the lower Fraser River allowed the miners to live well, even extravagantly, on canned oysters and canned beef, with cases of champagne, whisky, and rum. As the population continued to increase that first summer, it caused a great shortage of food and supplies, and not even the Hudson's Bay Company stores at Fort Langley, Fort Hope, or Fort Yale could handle the demands. In response to this a number of independent merchants opened stores, without any objections from the Hudson's Bay Company, which had exclusive rights until November 1858.

FORT YALE, B.C.

Built originally as a stopover point along a new fur-brigade route in 1848, Fort Yale was immediately abandoned in favour of Fort Hope, 15 miles south. With the arrival of thousands of gold miners in the spring of 1858, Fort Yale came into use once more as a townsite and supply centre on the lower Fraser. In July that summer, when a reporter from the Victoria *Gazette* wrote about Yale, he pictured it as rather a pleasant place to live:

"There are about 700 or 800 people here, nearly all of whom are miners living in canvas tents, waiting for the river to fall. There are five or six log houses in the place, and the inhabitants are orderly and everything is peaceable and quiet. A number of miners are at work on the river bank with rockers, and most are making a living by washing the loose dirt and cobblestones." [2]

Also mentioned was the first restaurant, or roadhouse, at Yale:

YORKE'S HOUSE, YALE, B.C., 1858.

"There is but one public eating house in the town, and invariably the diet is bacon, salmon, bread, tea and coffee...the charge is $1.00 a meal. No milk or butter is ever seen. It is kept in a miserable log hut partly barked over, and with a dirt floor. Everything is done in the same room—which is no more than 12' X 14' and consequently cramped for space, and as hot as an oven.... At night miners sleep on the floor before a roaring fire at one end of the room." [3]

This account of Thomas Yorke's restaurant at Yale is probably the first written description of the interior of a public roadhouse on the mainland of British Columbia. Yorke's House on Front Street continued in operation until it was destroyed in one of two large fires that swept through the original part of Yale in the early 1880s. Thomas Yorke, entrepreneur and pioneer of Yale, was described by an early traveller in 1862:

"Known to be one of the wealthiest and principal owners of land in the area, a rough but honest Yankee collier known as 'Old York' left the coal mines in the States for those of Vancouver Island. With the gold discoveries he emigrated to the interior of B.C., investing all his earnings in the purchase of land in strategic places. His speculations proved correct, and his fortune secured. Even after this he continued to wear the same style of dress as when he was a collier—still the open necked buttonless blue shirt without cuffs, thick boots, bare head and tight moleskin pants noticeably short of the ankles." [4]

July 1858 saw the arrival of the stern-wheeler *Umatilla*, the first steam-driven vessel to reach Yale, and the first express service, The Pioneer Fraser Express, instituted by William T. Ballou, a character of some renown. The agent for Ballou's express in Yale was William Higgins, a journalist who spent a short time in the frontier settlement. In his book *The Mystic Spring*, written many years later, Higgins portrayed the eventful and sometimes tragic lives of the pioneers of Yale and Victoria. Also mentioned are several of the earliest hotels in Yale.

WILLIAM POWER'S HOTEL AND RESTAURANT, 1858.
Captain William Power, a well-respected young Irishman, and his bright young German wife opened their hotel on the flat at Yale in 1858. Soon regarded as the best in town, the hotel enjoyed an appreciative clientele. As a leading citizen of Yale in 1861 Power was one of a delegation of three to approach Governor Douglas with a petition to have the Cariboo wagon road start at Yale, rather than at Hope.

In November 1862, a miner, James Thomson of Edwardsburgh, Upper Canada, journeying south from the Cariboo, reached Yale, where he expected to board a steamer the next day for New Westminster. Accommodations were hard to find, for the town was full of miners going south for the winter. Thomson spent the first night in Yorke's Hotel, but when low water again delayed the steamer, and a second night's lodgings were required, it was ten o'clock before he found a room at California House.

CALIFORNIA HOUSE.
Still operating in 1880 when Sarah Crease and her husband, Judge Henry Crease, stayed overnight, the California Hotel "Kept by Tuttle", received mixed reviews in Mrs. Crease's estimation:

Thomas Yorke. (COURTESY BCARS)

"House dirty, occupants all men, but self, dined in saloon, waiter thoughtful and attentive—no sitting room—went to bedroom as soon as we could get a light." [5]

With the building of the Cariboo Road from Yale in 1862, the town became the main shipping point to the interior and the headquarters of several transportation and mercantile companies. For a few months in 1866 Yale had its own newspaper, the *B.C. Tribune*, and within its pages appeared an advertisement for yet another hotel.

COLONIAL HOTEL.
Built by two Frenchmen, Perrier and Letremouillere in 1862, the Colonial Hotel was visited by Dr. Cheadle and Lord Milton late in the fall of 1863.

A year earlier the doctor, as travelling companion and physician to Viscount C.W. Wentworth Fitz William, Lord Milton, a slender young English aristocrat prone to epilepsy, had left England with Milton for Quebec where they set out on a gruelling but adventurous journey across Canada. In his diary Dr. Cheadle mentioned this amusing incident:

"We arrived at Yale about four o'clock in the afternoon, and immediately ordered the best dinner they could give us at the

Colonial Hotel. The House was kept by a Frenchman, who excelled himself on this occasion, and provided a meal, which to us who had not eaten anything deserving the name 'dinner' for at least eighteen months, appeared perfection. The champagne, however, and sundry drinks with fraternising miners caused us to wake with tremendous headaches the next morning. Some of the visitors at the bar amused us greatly. One tall Yankee, considerably intoxicated, was possessed with the idea that he was Lord Nelson, and associating the great admiral in some way with cucumbers, ate several in succession, to prove his identity." [6]

By February 1859 Richard Hicks, Gold Commissioner at Yale, had been relieved of his duties pending an investigation of charges of bribery and corruption. In his place was Chartres Brew, appointed in 1858 to inaugurate the first police force in B.C. As it had been from the start of the gold rush, the collection of mining fees and liquor and trading licences continued to be a problem. In the spring of 1859 Chief Inspector Brew sent two constables, John Haynes and William Cox, on a journey from Yale to Lytton in an effort to collect delinquent fees. In a report of their findings, written on their return ten days later, Cox mentioned several of the earliest roadhouses in operation along the west bank of the Fraser. Leaving Yale early on the

Sarah Crease. (COURTESY BCARS, G.R. FARDON COLLECTION)

morning of April 21, the officers, with three Indian packers began their journey:

> "The morning was fine, and although the snow on neighbouring mountains was fully three feet deep, our trail on the west bank was pretty good. During the day we walked about 12 miles and on our way we passed three 'stop houses', at each of which I presume the illegal sale of spirits is carried on. As yet we have no ocular proof of such being a fact. In the evening we arrived at 'California House', (Spuzzum) close to the ferry and were detained the following morning until almost 12 o'clock by a heavy fall of snow. When the day brightened up we resumed our journey and came to the Canyon House at 6.00 pm. after a march of about 14 mls. We staid there the night much fatigued, as the trail had been very indifferent indeed." [7]

THE 4 MILE HOUSE, 1859.

Watson Hodge, an American miner associated with J.J. Hunt, kept a roadhouse and store on the river trail four miles above Yale. Late in April that year Hodge and Hunt were convicted of selling liquor without a licence, and fined $80 plus another $80 in costs, so it would seem that the constables, Haynes and Cox, had indeed found some "ocular proof" of their guilt.

While he was at Yale in June 1860, the Reverend George Hills, first Anglican Bishop of British Columbia, rode upriver, calling in at "Hodge's wayside house". In his diary Hills mentioned the food they enjoyed, and the generous attitude of the operator:

> "where we got some fried bacon, potatoes and coffee. When I offered to pay, they would take none." [8]

Apparently the lure of recent gold discoveries in the Cariboo was too much for Hodge to resist. In July that summer someone found the following notice on the locked door of Hodge's roadhouse:

> "My whisky's gone, and credit too,
> And I've put out for Cariboo
> So if you want rum or rye or ale,
> You'll have to get it down at Yale.
> (And pay for it.)
> HODGE" [9]

By 1864 Hodge had returned, no richer but a lot wiser, to the site of his former roadhouse. There he found that the former owner, Emmerson, had taken over the property. It was not long before Hodge preempted land a mile north, at the mouth of Canyon Creek, where he ran a competing store and restaurant for the next several years.

PIERRE MARQUAIS HOUSE, 1858.

In a letter to Governor Douglas in May 1858, Hudson's Bay Company factor Orvid Allard of Yale described the fast-moving developments of the area, and the fact that Pierre Marquais had built two roadhouses with stores, one at Hill's Bar, and the other "about five miles beyond the fort". While journeying upriver in the spring of 1861 to look over preparations for the building of a wagon road, James Douglas visited this establishment:

> "Two Frenchmen have selected a beautiful spot where they have built a kiosk, and laid out the grounds with taste. It is planted with native flowers, watered by a brook fed from neighbouring hills. They keep refreshments of all kinds, even to capital good claret." [10]

FRANK WAY'S CALIFORNIA HOUSE, 1858.

At Spuzzum, an Indian name meaning "little flat", about 11 miles upriver from Yale, a permit to construct and operate a rope ferry across the Fraser River was at first awarded to Harrison P. Eayres in September 1858 by Magistrate Richard Hicks, but when Eayres refused to give Hicks a share in the profits, the permit was cancelled. By September that year, when the miners' trail to Lytton first opened, the permit was awarded to Franklin Way, an American who had arrived in the area during the great rush of 1858. Not inclined to physical work, Way had no success at mining, but was known to be a very shrewd businessman. In addition to building a rope ferry, Way also established a roadhouse at Spuzzum, sometimes known as California House.

In June 1860, on the first of several yearly treks to the interior of B.C., Bishop Hills visited Frank Way's facilities. It had been a very warm day as he and his companions, the Reverend Crickmer and "William", the bishop's servant, neared what he referred to as "the Spuzzum riverside hut". As darkness fell, a summer storm sent flashes of lightning to reveal a large, single-storey log house, built close to

Bishop George Hills. (COURTESY BCARS)

Spuzzum Creek. Leaving their horses tied under the shed roof of an open stable, the three men fought against strong winds and driving rain to reach the roadhouse. The continuous storm and the fact that their two Indian packers had not yet arrived, persuaded the bishop to remain overnight. "An excellent supper was speedily provided us by the cook," wrote Hills in his diary, after which he launched into a long description of the sumptuous meal served by none other than Mrs. Hicks, wife of the disgraced magistrate at Yale.

> "She condoned her husband's discrepancys and informed us [that] during his term of office he had made $5000 on speculation, and that had he known all he learned afterwards, could have made much more." [11]

There were several other travellers at the roadhouse that night: an expressman, a packer, and several miners—indicative of the steady traffic crossing the river on Frank Way's ferry. Following an evening service conducted by the bishop, they all retired for the night:

> "The room in which we slept, on the ground of course, there not being a 2nd. storey, or indeed even a second room, was partitioned off from a small kitchen. There was also an

outhouse called the Bakery, where some slept. Our room was that where liquor was sold. My bed consisted of blankets laid upon a straw mattress. On one side of me was Mr. Crickmer, on the other, within arm's length, was a box filled with a cat and her kittens, so I was safe from rats coming to my face! William and three other men were lodged in different parts of the same room. I confess, tired though I was, I could not sleep much—principally owing to the heat of the room. I would gladly have seen the doorway open to the fresh air. It rained in torrents most of the night, and gave our beds some drops of the cool shower." [12]

The next day was the bishop's 44th birthday, and he awoke thinking how strange it was to find himself on the floor of a log hut in the "wildest, most inaccessible recess of the Cascade Mountains". After a "comfortable" breakfast of tea, coffee and ham, the party prepared to leave:

"Nothing could induce the good people of the House to take a single farthing for supper, lodging, or breakfast, which had been served to my party of three. They only regretted that accommodations and fare had been so poor. In passing on the ferry, when two Indian packers were added to my party, Mr. Way still declined to take anything. The fare across being three shillings for each person, it was no small addition to the suppers and breakfasts." [13]

In contrast to the bishop's testimony to the virtues of Frank Way were the remarks of David Higgins, the journalist, who had known Way personally:

"Frank was a droll character, a man without much education, but as bright as a new sovereign, and as keen edged as a fox rasor. To this day Yaleites relate the story of his pranks, some of which were not nice, and could not safely be related. During the gold rush he made barrels of money ferrying miners and their effects across the Fraser River at 50¢ a head. He told me that one day he filled a tin bucket full of silver and gold. On another occasion, following an accident, the ferry capsized in a riffle, drowning all the passengers, and only Frank survived. When interviewed by a reporter from the *Colonist* on the matter, the reporter asked... 'and was there much loss?', to which Frank replied, 'Oh no, I always collect the fares in advance'." [14]

While at Yale in June 1860 Bishop Hills also

"went to see the works being carried out to form a wagon road through the canyon, a narrow gorge of the mountain through which the Fraser converges. A party of Royal Engineers, assisted by others are at work blasting the rocks. The work is one of great magnitude—dangerous and arduous of execution". [15]

This was the start of the first six miles of road north of Yale, built by the Royal Engineers "around the frowning cliffs" and beside the wild waters of the Fraser. That fall, while surveys were carried out for the proposed route of the road between Spuzzum and Boston Bar, Sergeant William McColl, with a party of sappers, was dispatched to select a site for a bridge over the Fraser River. The spot chosen was a mile upstream from Frank Way's ferry, which spelled the end of Way's enterprises at Spuzzum. Anticipating his future, he sold the roadhouse and ferry complex to Thomas Yorke of Yale.

FRASER RIVER ROUTES, SUMMER, 1858.

As spring wore on in 1858 the thousands of miners expecting to gain access to the upper Fraser by way of the river faced many problems. To begin with, shortly after their arrival in April, the river rose in its annual run-off making it impossible to mine the bars, or to travel upstream for about six weeks. Overland routes were limited and dangerous. Of considerable help was the Douglas Portage, a 13-mile horse trail which had been built in 1848, skirting the first canyon to rejoin the river at Spuzzum, where in 1858 a ferry carried passengers and freight to the east bank. There the trail continued north to Chapman's Bar, turned uphill to a plateau some 2,500 feet above the river, and ran along a ridge to the Anderson River and Boston Bar.

While this route avoided the six or eight miles of the treacherous Upper Canyon, it was blocked with snow for most of the year. In spite of the terrible dangers, miners continued to use the Upper Canyon route, but not all survived. Established centuries before by the Indians of the Couteau tribe, there were actually two trails. The lower trail, a pathway leading over jagged boulders beside the river, could only be used while the water was low. When the river covered the trail it meant climbing, sometimes on hands and knees, to the upper trail, a narrow, irregular footpath between perpendicular cliffs rising to heights of 800 feet above the river. This was accomplished by moving from ledge to ledge along the Indian "ladders", a network of deer hide and fibre ropes suspended on poles, "like the shrouds of a sailing ship". [16] One false move or sudden dizzy spell could unbalance a man, sending him hundreds of feet to his death on the rocks below.

In June 1858 when John McLean, a miner from California, prepared to travel upstream from Yale, the river was at its height, and too dangerous for a canoe. It was also too early in the year to take the old Hudson's Bay trail up the mountain. Faced with no alternative, John and his three companions shouldered packs of over 70 pounds each and made their way through the Upper Canyon to Boston Bar. From there they crossed the river on a rope ferry to Yankee Bar, on the west bank, where they staked claims in a neighbourhood known today as North Bend. In August when their provisions ran low, the McLean party returned to Yale by the same route. Yale at this time was filled with miners who, fearful of Indian attacks, were fleeing from their claims above Yale. Due partly to poor treatment by the Americans, especially those on Hill's Bar, the Indians living in the

John McLean. (COURTESY QUESNEL AND DISTRICT MUSEUM)

canyons retaliated by raiding the isolated mining camps upriver. Dozens of miners were killed, and their decapitated bodies stripped and flung into the river, where they floated downstream past Yale.

Undaunted by the gravity of the situation, the McLean party replenished their supplies at Yale and prepared to return to Yankee Bar. By August the river had dropped, enabling them to travel by water, and as they paddled their canoe past Cross's Bar, a few miles upstream, they pulled three bodies from the water. At the end of August, when the safety of all miners seemed threatened, an army of several hundred miners, including John McLean, marched upriver from Yale to face the Indians of the Upper Canyon in a battle that raged for three days. Both sides suffered casualties, but finally when a peace pact was made, it allowed the miners to return to their work with some degree of safety. At Yankee Bar, where the McLean party remained all winter, they built a log cabin, and kept a roadhouse for passing travellers. One of these was Francis J. Barnard, who often stopped by on his way up and down the river delivering mail.

CANYON HOUSE, 1859.

As mentioned in Constable William Cox's report of April 1859, on a trip upriver to investigate delinquent liquor licences, Canyon House, on the west bank of the Fraser River, was located in the Upper Canyon, about 14 miles above Spuzzum. Lieutenant Mayne, on his map of 1859, marked the site as being on both sides of a sizable creek running into the Fraser, above the present-day Hell's Gate canyon. Nothing more is known of this roadhouse, which seemed to fade from view with the building of a wagon road on the east side of the river.

CHAPTER TWO

THE HARRISON ROUTE: PORT DOUGLAS TO LILLOOET

BY May 1858 Governor Douglas was becoming very aware of the problems facing hundreds of miners on the lower Fraser. Rising spring waters had made it impossible for them to reach their claims on the bars above Fort Yale, but in their determination to reap the first harvests of gold, many had gone overland, far from any source of supply, and were starving to death. Realizing that a reliable supply route to the upper Fraser must be built before winter, Douglas met with an assembly of miners in Fort Victoria to discuss the matter.

Certainly the Fraser Canyon route was not the immediate solution. The country's funds to develop trails and roads were very limited, but the governor knew that with the discovery of gold would come the resources to develop British Columbia. To solve this dilemma a company of 500 miners agreed, with certain concessions and supervision, to provide the labour to build 65 miles of trail, four feet in width, along a route well known to the Hudson's Bay Company, from the north end of Harrison Lake to the Fraser River at Lillooet.

Started in late July, the work was completed by winter. Governor Douglas, delighted with this accomplishment, wrote to his superiors in London:

> "I have the satisfaction of announcing that a supply route from Harrison's River to a part of the Fraser beyond the mountains is now finished, and a great many mules are already upon the trail." [1]

The convenience of this trail immediately reduced the cost of freight to the interior from 46 1/2¢ a pound to 18¢ a pound. As the hundreds of pack trains loaded with thousands of tons of food and supplies moved slowly up the trail, they prompted the building of many roadhouses along the route.

PORT DOUGLAS, 1858.

To reach Port Douglas and the start of the Harrison-to-Lillooet route, travellers took a steamer from Fort Victoria to New Westminster, and continued up the Fraser to the mouth of the Harrison River. Ten miles upstream they reached Harrison Lake, a deep body of water 45 miles in length. At the far end, on a short spit of land, stood the town of Port Douglas. Named in honour of Governor Douglas by the miners when they first arrived in 1858, the little supply depot soon blossomed into a community of storekeepers, hoteliers, packers, and several hundred transient miners. Taking advantage of the heavily timbered mountains surrounding Port Douglas, a sawmill equipped with a planer was soon in operation. Even in full production in 1861, the mill could not begin to supply the demands for lumber, some of which was used in a wagon factory established in Port Douglas. Merchants bought the wagons to transport supplies to Bridge River, north of Lillooet, the scene of a gold strike.

Among the leading entrepreneurs in Port Douglas in 1859 was Gustavus Blin Wright who, with his partner Thomas Davidson, ran a freighting business in the area. These two were soon to play a major role in the development of roads and roadhouses in the Cariboo.

Of the several "hotels" in Port Douglas, as roadhouses in the first communities were called, the most notable were The Hotel de France, Charles Florence, Prop.; the Columbia House and Restaurant; the Douglas Hotel, J.L. Smith and Co., Props.; and the William MacDonald Hotel and Saloon.

ROADHOUSES ON THE PORT DOUGLAS-TO-LILLOOET ROUTE.
Anxious to profit from the heavy traffic passing through the area, entrepreneurs hurriedly constructed rough cabins, where they provided liquor, food, and shelter for travellers. In just three months, at least a dozen such facilities appeared, scattered along the three portages, and by 1860 when the trail became a wagon road, several others were added. The crude nature of those first roadhouses was captured in comments made by Lieutenant R.C. Mayne, R.N., as a result of a tour of inspection he made in May 1859:

"I have mentioned the fact of there being 'restaurants' all along the Lillooet portages. All such places in this country are called 'restaurants', although they are simply huts, where travellers can obtain a meal of bacon, beans, bread, salt butter, and tea and coffee, for a dollar; while if he has no tent with him, he can select the softest plank in the floor to sleep on. Of course these places vary with their situation. At those restaurants on the lower Fraser, meals can now be had for 50 cents, and sometimes eggs, beef and vegetables can be got. On the other hand, at those far up the river I paid a dollar and a half for the bare miner's fare of bacon, beans and bread. Miners suffer a great deal from inflamed mouths generally attributed to their constant diet of bacon." [2]

The rocky, mountainous terrain between Port Douglas and Port Pemberton did not lend itself to farming to any extent, making roadhouse operators in that area dependent on the pack trains for food supplies. While the packers made big profits off the roadhouses, they also suffered losses. Caught in the act of robbing a freight wagon, the proprietors of the 24 Mile House, James Joice and his partner, were arrested during the summer of 1862. Operators had reportedly been losing supplies and liquor for some time, but had not discovered the thieves. While gaining a reputation for serving excellent meals at the roadhouse, Joice and his partner had been robbing the freighters regularly.

Of the thousands who journeyed to the goldfields by way of the Harrison route, only a few kept diaries, or left accounts. Of these, the most colourful was one kept by Dr. Cheadle. Arriving in Victoria from their across Canada adventure in September 1863, Cheadle and Milton decided to visit the goldfields of the Cariboo before returning home. Having already seen the Fraser Canyon, they took the

Dr. W.B. Cheadle. (COURTESY BCARS)

Harrison route. In his original journal Dr. Cheadle mentions many early roadhouses, not only on the Harrison route, but in several other areas of their journey. Where deserved, high praise is given, but on several occasions strong criticism is equally bestowed. Of Port Douglas, where they arrived on Friday, October 2, aboard the steamer S.S. *Hope*, Cheadle wrote:

> "A vile hole—put up overnight at MacDonald's, a wretched supper of pork and liver—miners gambling and drinking... Yankees pondering the scarcity of women." [3]

Anxious to get started on the first leg of their journey, Lord Milton and his doctor had expected to use the local stagecoach, but on finding that it meant a two-day delay, they sought out the local magistrate for advice on alternate transportation. In consulting J. Boles Gaggin, "a regular jolly Irishman from Cork", they were offered the loan of a horse, for Milton. When a second horse was not forthcoming, Dr. Cheadle grudgingly paid ten dollars to rent a mule named "Yank". Following "sundry beers and procrastinations" the three set out on the road, Gaggin having decided to accompany them as far as Port Pemberton "to inspect the roads" as he said. The journey had not progressed far before it became obvious that Gaggin,

Lord Milton. (COURTESY BCARS)

the agreeable, entertaining magistrate, was "a whale for drinks", stopping at almost every roadhouse for "refreshments". Dr. Cheadle began to wish they had waited for the stagecoach.

THE 4 MILE HOUSE.

Mentioned in the diary of Arthur Bushby, clerk to Judge Begbie, in April 1859, the proprietor of this roadhouse was Mr. Hancock, "a polite elderly gentleman who had seen better days" wrote Bushby. By spring of 1861 the 4 Mile House was operated by Mrs. Hannah and her brother, who prepared a breakfast of beefsteak pie for Bishop Hills and his companions, the Reverends Garrett, Pringle, and Knipe.

THE 10 MILE HOUSE.

An original roadhouse of 1858, the 10 Mile House was operated for several years by a German named Perrin, at least until 1863, when Lord Milton and Dr. Cheadle stopped by. Having gained an admirable reputation for good meals and excellent service, Perrin attracted such notables as Governor Douglas, Judge Begbie, and High Sheriff Charles S. Nicol.

THE 12 MILE HOUSE.

In his diary of September 1, 1860, Governor Douglas mentions the 12 Mile House and the proprietor, Mr. Gowan who, in spite of poor health, kept a clean and "prosperous looking restaurant". A creek in this vicinity now bears the name of this pioneer.

THE 14 MILE HOUSE.

Established in 1860 by a French miner "Chapais" and his compatriot, the roadhouse here was of secondary importance to the owners, who were busy making ten dollars a day mining on a paying bench nearby.

THE 16 MILE HOUSE.

Noted on Lieutenant H.S. Palmer's map of 1859, this roadhouse was also mentioned in Dr. Cheadle's diary of 1863 as being "kept by an old Scotch ship's carpenter, Mr. Waite. Finding it late we resolved to stay the night at the House, and ride forward in time for the steamer in the morning." [4] At the end of a long day's ride Dr. Cheadle and his companions relaxed before retiring for the night. Although the doctor constantly criticized Gaggin's drinking he did not mind admitting: "Gaggin and I had two jugs of mulled wine together, which made us sleep like tops." [5]

THE 20 MILE HOUSE.

At first named "St. Agnes Well" by Judge Begbie in 1859, this site became more commonly known as "the Hot Springs" where William Stein built a roadhouse and bath house on top of the hot spring. W. Champness, a tourist of 1862, also mentioned this roadhouse, and the hot springs:

"After eating a plain meal of bacon and beans we enjoyed the hot springs, the only really cheap comfort obtainable in B.C." [6]

This site is not to be confused with "St. Alice's Well", also named by Begbie, at the foot of Harrison Lake, the site of the present-day Harrison Hot Springs resort.

By June 1863, when young Harry Jones, a Welsh miner, came by, the 20 Mile House had been sold to entrepreneur Joseph L. Smith, who also owned the Douglas Hotel in Port Douglas. In his diary Jones mentions:

"We headed for the hot springs where a stopping place was kept by a man named Smith. We laid our blankets on the floor of Mr. Smith's bar room and slept comfortably." [7]

STANISLAUS HOUSE, THE 24 MILE HOUSE.

Established in 1860 and operated by James Joice and his partner prior to their arrest in the summer of 1862, the 24 Mile House was taken over by William Stein, former owner of the 20 Mile House. Stein renamed his roadhouse after the Stanislaus River in California, where he had mined in the early 1850s:

> "Stanislaus House. Near the 24 Mile post on the Douglas Portage about 5 miles from the lake. W. Stein, prop., formerly of the Hot Springs House. Wines, liquors, & Cigars. Good comfortable beds, 50¢. each, good accommodation for stock." [8]

While travelling to Lillooet in 1863, Cheadle's mule fell lame in the area of the 24 Mile post, so while Milton and "the judge" remained to regale themselves (once again) in the saloon there, Cheadle walked on with the mule, agreeing to meet them at the 29 Mile House on Tenas Lake by noon, in time to catch the steamer for Pemberton.

THE 29 MILE HOUSE.

Established in 1859 by a Mr. Williams, the 29 Mile House became the southern terminus for the steamboats S.S. *Marzelle*, and later S.S. *Prince of Wales*, that carried freight and passengers to Port Pemberton at the north end of Lillooet Lake. By 1863 Joseph L. Smith and his partner Tom Marshall had become owners of the 29 Mile House, one of several roadhouses they acquired between Port Douglas and Clinton. In May 1866 *The Cariboo Sentinel* of Barkerville ran the following advertisement:

> "29 Mile House...Douglas Portage.
> This House fitted up for the accommodation of travellers to the Bridge River Mines. Good beds, stabling for horses, horse feed, etc. A stage runs twice a week between this House and Port Douglas on the arrival of the steamers from below, and connects with the lake boats for Lillooet. J.L.Smith & Co., Props." [9]

Having walked five miles with the lame mule, Dr. Cheadle arrived at Tenas Lake an hour before the steamer was scheduled to depart. There was no sign of Milton or Gaggin, and while he waited Cheadle had lunch at the roadhouse, and then went down to the dock where the steamer was about to leave. Twice Dr. Cheadle persuaded the captain to wait another few minutes for his delinquent companions, but eventually the steamer could wait no longer, and left without them. The doctor was most annoyed, for time was of the utmost importance if he and Lord Milton were to reach the Cariboo mines before winter snows made travel impossible. Cheadle's diary indicates the measure of his frustration:

"...the steamer at last starting and leaving us in the lurch...much annoyed at thus losing another day." [10]

Cheadle and his companions were not the only ones to have missed the steamer, for not long after this the stage from Port Douglas arrived, bringing Hardy Curry, part owner of a rich mining claim on Williams Creek, and Flinn, the owner of a farm and operator of a ferry at Lillooet. Flinn was generous enough to provide Cheadle with a horse to ride across the portages. At long last, at about four p.m. Milton and Gaggin arrived, with the excuse that Gaggin had met friends at the 24 Mile House, with whom they shared another half a dozen ale. Having missed the steamer the trio had no choice but to remain overnight at the roadhouse. Cheadle was

"View of Lakes on Douglas Route" showing 29 Mile House, CA 1865. (COURTESY BCARS, GENTILE COLLECTION #2)

most impressed with the "nice clean beds" provided by the Irish housekeeper, Mrs. Marshall, whose husband Tom was part owner of the roadhouse. The next morning the steamer from the north brought two prostitutes, one black and one white who, having had a profitable season in the gold camps of the Cariboo, were now headed for warmer climates. The S.S. *Prince of Wales* took two hours to reach Port Pemberton, during which time Gaggin continued his drinking, but Milton and his doctor abstained.

LAKE HOUSE, 1858, 1859.

On Lieutenant H.S. Palmer's map, "New Westminster to Fountain, B.C." printed in 1859, the words "Lake House" are marked on the east bank, at the southernmost end of Lillooet Lake. As the trail builders reached this point in September 1858, entrepreneurs constructed several buildings, supposedly the start of a town. The site was abandoned shortly afterward in favour of another at the north end of the lake, where Port Pemberton was established. At the abandoned site, which in 1859 was known as "Lillooet", a building known as "Lake House" remained for a short time. While there is no documentation as to its use, the name suggests a roadhouse. Lieutenant R.C. Mayne's map of 1859 also marked this site, and several other buildings, beside the creek connecting Little Lillooet and Lillooet lakes.

PORT PEMBERTON, 1858.

Established as a settlement and supply depot for the trail builders of 1858, Port Pemberton became a jumping-off place for the second portage on the Harrison-to-Lillooet route. As miners, packers, and merchants scrambled to reach the new goldfields of Cayoosh Creek and Bridge River, a large volume of traffic passed through the port. By the following year, five or six log cabins dotted the lakeshore, catering to boatmen and travellers who sought shelter and food. Among the first of these was a roadhouse known as "Mr. O'Brian's store", where in April 1859 Judge Begbie and his clerk, Arthur Bushby, enjoyed an excellent meal, for which they paid a dollar each:

> "Oh, how we did just peg into it, after living for a month on bacon and beans." [11]

The more arable nature of the area was reflected in the variety of food served at the roadhouses in Pemberton and along the portages to Lillooet. The building of the trail in 1858 had opened the way for farmers to settle and work the rich meadow land just north of Lillooet Lake. As early as 1859, a year prior to the introduction of the Pre-emption Act, Judge Begbie was issuing seasonal permits for land use in this area.

PEMBERTON HOUSE.
With the increase in traffic, a second roadhouse opened in Pemberton, advertised in the Victoria *Gazette* of 1860:

"Mr. Drinkall's Pemberton House, where travellers can meet with every comfort at reasonable prices." [12]

The land on which this roadhouse stood had been pre-empted early that year by packers Peter Smith and John Shaw. By 1862 Mr. Drinkall had sold out to Smith, who advertised in the *British Columbian*, noting the new management:

"Beds & Liquors. Having engaged the best cooks on the Pacific coast, we are prepared to furnish the travelling public with all the comforts and luxuries of a 1st. class hotel at greatly reduced prices. P. Smith & Co., Props. Sept 12, 1862." [13]

Hired as bar-keep and clerk for $60 a month at Pemberton House in 1863 was young Richard Alexander, an "Overlander" in the Cariboo the year before. The roadhouse changed hands again in 1864 when it was acquired by Joseph Smith and Tom Marshall. Once again, Pemberton House was advertised in the papers, announcing the new owners and drawing attention to the "family rooms" and "Bagatelle Table" in the bar-room. The proprietors Smith and Marshall were still operating Pemberton House in May 1866.

Reaching Port Pemberton on October 6, Dr. Cheadle and Lord Milton bade farewell to Magistrate J.B. Gaggin and started on horse-back in company with Curry and Flinn over the 24 miles of the Pemberton portage, bound for Port Anderson.

THE 8 MILE HOUSE, PEMBERTON PORTAGE.
In his book *Vancouver Island and British Columbia*, published in 1865, the Reverend Matthew Macfie included part of the anonymous diary of a traveller to the Cariboo in 1863. The journey, made by

way of the Harrison route, included an overnight stay at a roadhouse just north of Pemberton:

"At Pemberton we took the wagon road and travelled eight miles the same day. About twenty of us slept on the floor of the 8 Mile House in the usual style, being very kindly invited by the landlord." [14]

The landlord was Peter Dickinson, who had pre-empted the land on December 19, 1862, where he built the 8 Mile House.

HALFWAY HOUSE, 1859.
Halfway House, a roadhouse farm established by Peter Dickinson in 1859, was situated along the portage just south of Summit Lake, the highest point on the route. In his diary of April 1859, Arthur Bushby described the trail, and the hospitality at Halfway House:

"...on the road we passed a small frozen lake 9 miles from Port Anderson. The trail is a good natural one. We stopped at Halfway House and had some bread and treacle—how we pitched into it." [15]

By 1860, after the introduction of the Pre-emption Act, Dickinson made application for his land:

"Having been in possession of a piece of land midway between this and Port Anderson for more than a year, and having laid out money for improvements to the said land to the extent of $2,000, I now apply for possession rights to the land, in all 160 acres. I have erected a House known as Halfway House, and a barn 60 X 35 ft., as you will see per plan attached. Peter Dickinson." [16]

Barely a year later Dickinson was offering his Halfway House and farm for sale, a move he would soon regret:

"Ranch For Sale.
Halfway House, situated between Anderson and Lillooet Lake on the Harrison to Lillooet route. Property of 160 acres including 1 large 2 storey House and kitchen together with a barn to hold 75-100 ton of hay and accommodation for 75

animals. Also a warehouse for storing goods. The grass is Blue Top. The ranch is fenced. 2 good plough horses, 75 hogs, 100 chickens. Contact J.L.Hughes & Co., agents on the premises, or Edgar & Aime, Wharf St. Victoria." [17]

As they proceeded northeast towards Lillooet on October 7, 1863, Dr. Cheadle and his party stopped at Halfway House. Although they did not stay long, the doctor learned a lot about the new owner and the reasons for the sudden departure of Peter Dickinson.

"For dinner we stayed at the Halfway House, owned by a Virginian of the name Ketterel. He had only been there a year— there is a fine open flat of, I suppose 100 acres partly under cultivation—such good land is rare. He [Ketterel] bought it for $2,000, and the first year's crop has paid the purchase. The settler, [Peter Dickinson] was led away by the Bentinck Arm Excitement, went there, and then thru' Cariboo, and eventually returned to set up the opposition House within a mile of his old quarters—but no good land!" [18]

The "opposition House" was of course the 8 Mile House.

During the 1870s the Halfway House and ranch were owned by Thomas Poole, a widower who lived alone with his two children. Known to be a hard-working and responsible land owner, Poole was found murdered at Halfway House in April 1879. The roadhouse had been set on fire, and the bodies of Poole and his 11-year-old daughter, Mary, were discovered in the remains of the basement by passing Indians who had noticed the smoke rising from the burning building. Poole's eight-year-old son Perry was never found: only his cap, dangling from the branch of a tree out in the yard. On investigation a coroner concluded that the victims had been shot, but for what reason was a complete mystery. At first the atrocity was thought to have some connection with Poole's involvement in a botched, government-funded cattle-trail project between Lillooet and Burrard Inlet from 1873 to 1877. Poole and his neighbours had taken contracts to service the road builders, for which Poole supplied many head of beef cattle. After $38,000 was spent over a period of four years, the three-foot trail was still unfit for use.

Two of Poole's neighbours were charged with murder and tried at Clinton by very prestigious legal men, but without conclusive evidence, both were acquitted. The trials caused the financial and

Ketterel's Halfway House, photographed by Charles Gentile. (COURTESY BCARS)

social ruin of the accused, and brought about great resentment and animosity between the settlers in the Pemberton meadows area. In 1883, after the conviction of two Indians for the murder of several Chinese in the Chilcotin, the Victoria *Colonist* reported that these same men were thought to have also murdered the Poole family, believing them to have a large cache of money in Halfway House, from the sale of cattle to the road builders.

During the 1890s William Vader settled in the area, taking over the Poole place. While his tenure was short, Vader began building a second Halfway House and a barn to accommodate 25 animals. In 1900 Ronald Currie and his sister, Anne McIntosh, children of John Currie, an early pioneer, bought the property and kept a roadhouse for a few years. The house was small, but when there were not enough beds, mattresses and blankets were laid out on the floor. In 1912 while railway-survey crews were at work along the portage, Halfway House became home to the Spetch family; Elizabeth Spetch and her daughters were known to have served 42 lunches in one hour. At the start of the First World War an Englishman named Law and his young wife lived at Halfway House, owned at that time by Dr. T.V. Devy. Prior to Law's enlistment and departure overseas, his wife gave birth to a baby girl, the first child born at Halfway House. Law was killed in battle.

As Dr. Cheadle and his companions rode on from Halfway House on October 7, 1863, they passed downhill through dense woods toward Anderson Lake, 800 feet below Summit Lake. From the edge of the timber they viewed a wide expanse of lake with snow-capped mountains rising up on both sides, to a height of 5,000 feet. Anderson and Seton lakes, each about 16 miles in length, were at one time a single body of water, separated eons ago by a landslide that formed a neck of land a mile and a half wide.

ANDERSON LAKE HOUSE.
That night Dr. Cheadle and his party stayed over at a roadhouse at Port Anderson:

> "Port Anderson, where we slept in a nice clean House kept by a Frenchman, meals, beds, and accommodation each cost $1.00." [19]

The Frenchman's roadhouse stood close to the lake, just behind the public access and wharf. It was here that Bishop Hills held a service of worship in June 1861, attended by a congregation of ten, among whom were several Indians and a Mexican. Out in the back yard was the grave of a Mexican packer, shot to death in a brawl at the roadhouse.

Port Anderson, Anderson Lake, from the ILLUSTRATED LONDON NEWS, *1864.*
(COURTESY BCARS)

Anderson Lake House was still catering to the public in 1866, operated by proprietor Franklin Roberts, who advertised his facilities in the *British Columbian*:

"ANDERSON LAKE HOUSE,

Franklin Roberts,
Proprietor.

This House is pleasantly situated at the
foot of Anderson Lake, on the
DOUGLAS-LILLOOET ROUTE,
And affords excellent accommodation.
Meals at all hours, and the best of
Liquors constantly on hand
Charges moderate and no pain spared
to merit public patronage." [20]

Following their overnight stay at Anderson Lake in October 1863, Milton and Cheadle boarded the slow-moving side-wheeler S.S. *Lady of the Lake*, taking three hours to reach the other end. Across the mile and a half portage between the lakes was a wooden tramway built in 1861 by Peter Smith and his associates, who charged a toll to transport passengers and freight along the track in a horse-driven cart.

From the western end of Seton Lake the travellers boarded a much larger and faster steamer, the side-wheeler S.S. *Lady Seton*, to reach Seton Portage. The awesome beauty of Seton Lake in the fall of the year inspired Dr. Cheadle to write of it in his diary:

"The scenery on this lake is finer than the others, the mountains being higher, steeper, and more rugged, descending nearly perpendicularly into the water...the brilliant yellow and red autumn tints contrasting with the dark green and black of the pines and the bright greens of the poplars, together with the varied shades of the rocks, were more beautiful than I ever saw before." [21]

SETON LAKE HOUSE, 1861.
Bishop Hills, who had travelled this same route in 1861 left an interesting reference to a roadhouse on the eastern end of Seton Lake. In his diary the bishop wrote:

"This evening, in company with Mr. Brown and Mr. Knipe I rode over to Mr. Calbraith's [*sic*] at Seaton [*sic*] Lake. He is the owner of the steamboat, and an American. They had prepared dinner. Our party consisted of Mr. Calbraith, Mr. Taylor, a partner in the steamboat, and several men engaged on the premises. Mrs. Calbraith is a particularly pleasing and ladylike person. She is descended from the Cherokee Indians...though with seven parts of white blood." [22]

A year later, in 1862, John Calbreath was to become closely involved with the contractor Gustavus Blin Wright in the building of the Cariboo wagon road from Lillooet to Alexandria.

THE DEMISE OF THE HARRISON-TO-LILLOOET ROUTE.

Between the years 1858 and 1863 the bulk of traffic making its way to the mines of the Cariboo went by way of the Harrison-to-Lillooet route. As a result of political lobbying by merchants, roadhouse-keepers, and steamboat operators along the route, great amounts of public money were spent to improve the original trail, and finally to build a wagon road, completed in 1861, to Lillooet.

With the start of road building through the Fraser canyons and the Thompson River valley in 1862, business along the Harrison route began to fade. The slow, cumbersome transportation system across the several lakes and portages could not compete with the more direct passage from Yale. Although a number of roadhouse farms north of Pemberton continued to operate through the early 1900s, by 1866 most roadhouses along the Douglas portage had closed.

The Reverend A.C. Garrett, one of Bishop Hills' clerics, declared the route abandoned in 1865. While on a missionary tour to the Cariboo that year, Garrett described in his diary the dilapidated houses in Port Douglas where he, like Milton and Cheadle in 1863, was entertained with "genuine hospitality" by Magistrate J. Boles Gaggin. Greatly reduced in population, Port Douglas still contained a blacksmith shop, a saloon, and a store, but Garrett noticed particularly the church, which had fallen into disrepair, and the bell atop the steeple, rusty from lack of use. At the 20 Mile House where Garrett enjoyed the hot spring, the proprietor was out of food, and at the 29 Mile House he was forced to wait three days for a steamer to Port Pemberton.

CHAPTER THREE

CHAPMAN'S BAR TO LYTTON AND LILLOOET

AS hostilities ceased between the miners and the Indians of the Fraser canyons in September 1858, miners returned to their claims above Yale.

ALEXANDER'S HOUSE, CHAPMAN'S BAR, 1858.
Lot 1B, G.1., Yale.
One of the largest and richest bars on the east side of the river was Chapman's Bar, two miles above Spuzzum, where dozens of miners were washing from one to four ounces of gold each, per day. Among this large community of miners, William L. Alexander opened a restaurant and store beside the mule trail which, at that time, ran close to the river.

The following summer, while searching for a route for a transcontinental railway line, Walter Moberly, an engineer, explored the formidable canyons of the Fraser River. Working his way south on foot from Boston Bar, he took two days to reach Chapman's Bar, a distance of 12 miles. There he found Alexander's House, a little log hut about 15 feet by 25 feet, where he enjoyed a "good meal of slap-jacks, bacon and coffee." [1] The meal made him sleepy, and as he rested in a nearby cabin he awoke suddenly to find a pig making off with one of his boots. Although he chased it for some distance, the animal eluded him, and eventually disappeared into the woods. The loss of the boot was serious as he had still many miles to walk over the rough trail to Yale. In desperation Moberly put on a boot that he found, which had to be stuffed with moss to make it fit. By the end of the day he was suffering intolerable agony, the boot having worn the skin right off his foot.

Bishop Hills in 1860 also mentions the stopping house at Chapman's Bar:

"At Chapman's Bar I found a respectable storekeeper, a young man named Alexander. He had been a miner, a pleasant person from Indiana. We spoke about the Sunday observance, and he said that miners did not work on Sundays, but spent the day washing clothes and baking bread. He also spoke of the hardships and temptations of the miners." [2]

By 1864 a partner of Alexander's, Louis Waigland, had purchased 32 acres of land beside the Cariboo Road near Chapman's Bar, on which was built a large, two-storey frame roadhouse. The property was Crown Granted in June 1864. A good photograph of Chapman's Bar House, or Alexander's 14 Mile House, as it was also known, was taken by pioneer photographer Frederick Dally in 1867, showing three double wagon trains parked outside the roadhouse, pulled by many head of oxen and mules. Directly behind the roadhouse is the old Hudson's Bay Company trail of 1848, leading up the mountain to Lake House and Boston Bar. During the construction of two railway lines through the Fraser Canyon, in the mid-1880s, and early 1900s, much of the original property of the lodge was lost. When the highway was widened in 1952, crews moved the old building back another six feet, placing it on a cement foundation.

In the two small cemeteries located a little south of the lodge, ancient headstones and moss-covered iron crosses lie hidden in the grass. The roadhouse is known today as Alexandra Lodge, due to its proximity to the Alexandra Bridge that spans the Fraser River at Spuzzum, its original name having been forgotten. Recognized as one of the oldest stopping places on the road today, Alexandra Lodge

Chapman's Bar House, 1867, photographed by Frederick Dally. (COURTESY BCARS)

has continued to function on and off for many years as a hotel, restaurant, store, and historical attraction.

LAKE HOUSE, 1860.

From Chapman's Bar, in the early summer of 1860, Bishop Hills and his entourage took the old Hudson's Bay Company trail of 1848, climbing up to a ridge some 2,500 feet above the Fraser:

> "We had a very fine view of the river as we ascended.... flowers on all sides, amongst which were roses, wild Pansy, Columbine, and others." [3]

Travelling in a northerly direction for about ten miles they eventually reached Lake House, a roadhouse situated near a group of small lakes. Due to deep snow on the trail for many months of the year, Lake House was only open during the summer. In spite of this, business at the roadhouse flourished during the first two years of the gold rush. Not long after Bishop Hills' visit, Lake House was deliberately burned to the ground, on the orders of the local magistrate, Henry Ball. At this time the house was occupied by a Mr. Gibson, who was accused of selling liquor to the Indians; instead of arresting Gibson, the magistrate had the roadhouse burned. What was not realized was that although Gibson lived there, the building was owned by W.H. Wetherill, ferryman at Boston Bar. In a letter to Colonel Moody, Commissioner of Lands, in August 1860, Wetherill demanded an investigation of the matter. While there is no proof that he was compensated, it would appear so, for not long after the incident Wetherill was building a new house in Boston Bar.

ROMBROT'S 16 MILE HOUSE, 1861.
Lot 2, G.1., Yale.
In 1858 Claude Etienne Rombrot and G. Barraud, members of a company of French miners on Island Bar, opened one of the first stores in Boston Bar. In 1860, following the completion of an improved mule trail between Yale and Lytton, the partners pre-empted 160 acres of land "situated between miles four and five above Chapman's Bar, and eighteen miles south of Boston Bar." [4]

When Barraud left the partnership, Rombrot sent for his brother Vincent, who arrived from France in 1861. Between them they built a roadhouse on the pre-emption which became known as Rombrot's 16 Mile House. One of the first references to this hostelry appeared in June 1866 when two of F.J. Barnard's stage horses were drowned "at Rombrot's, where the river has inundated the wagon road." [5] During an economic slump in the late 1860s Claude Rombrot left the operation of the roadhouse to Vincent, while he returned to storekeeping in Boston Bar. On the death of Vincent Rombrot in January 1873, an obituary in the Victoria *Colonist* stated:

"We regret to hear of the death of Monsieur V. Rombrot of the 16 Mile House from Yale. Mr. Rombrot was a settler of 1861, and was much respected. He has been suffering for some time, and it is supposed the cause of death was inflammation of the mucous membrane." [6]

With his failing health, and the decline of business, Vincent Rombrot had not fared well during the last six years of his life. An account of his estate, which appeared in Judge Begbie's benchbook of 1873, revealed that Vincent had never married, and died without making a will, leaving assets of less than $1,500. As brother and former partner to Vincent, Claude Rombrot was able to take over the 16 Mile House property, where he continued to operate a roadhouse during the first half of the 1880s. An excerpt from the account of a travelling reporter expands on the excellence of Rombrot's cooking:

"... a few miles further on we come to the wayside inn of M. Rombrot, a true son of sunny France, hospitable, kind, and polite. Presently lunch is announced. Every article except the sugar and tea is produced locally. Biscuits are as light as a feather and white as the fallen snow, made of Kamloops flour from Mara & Wilson's mill; butter with the flavour of new mown hay, bacon sweet, and delicious beefsteak just off the bunch grass, tender and juicy; eggs newly laid, all farmed locally, a repast upon which a hungry prince would not turn his back." [7]

Rombrot's roadhouse was one of several to close during the mid-1880s when that area of the original Cariboo Road was virtually destroyed by the building of the Canadian Pacific railway line through the Fraser Canyon.

BOSTON BAR, 1858.
Named for a company of American miners who found gold at this point on the Fraser River in 1858, the community of Boston Bar was at first situated on a low flat beside the river where a rope ferry connected it with Island Bar, on the opposite shore. By 1860, long after the majority of miners had moved upriver, Boston Bar continued to grow as a supply centre. Bishop Hills, on his first journey in 1860, noted the five commercial buildings: "Two stores, a liquor shop, a roadhouse, and a blacksmith." [8] At the first store operated by Rombrot and Barraud, Hills was invited to take a glass of wine. When he declined, requesting water instead, the Frenchmen gave him a delightful raspberry drink, flavoured with syrup made from the juice of wild berries.

BRASSEY'S ROADSIDE HOUSE, 1860.
Another Frenchman, Brassey, also mentioned by Bishop Hills, operated a roadhouse and store in Boston Bar, where two black men did the cooking and waited on customers. Brassey's establishment was still in operation the following year, but with Chinese cooks in the kitchen.

THE INTERNATIONAL HOTEL, BOSTON BAR, 1863.
Lot 30, G.1., Yale.
With the building of a wagon road through Boston Bar, Alexander Coutlie filed an application to pre-empt 160 acres of land "near Boston Bar village", where he built a hotel for travellers on the new road to

the Cariboo. The pre-emption was actually on land reserved by the colonial government as a townsite in 1861. This fact was recognized in the pre-emption application, in which Coutlie agreed to possible expropriation at any time. Before long, Coutlie's International Hotel was considered among the best on the road, and "Boston Bar Alex", as Coutlie became known, enjoyed the distinction. All went well until 1866, when the government decided to sell the reserve land at Boston Bar, and Coutlie was forced to buy the land on which the hotel stood. That was bad enough, but when Coutlie was also charged $200 a year for an operating licence, it was more than he could bear financially. As a result the business was leased to Alex and William Charters for two years, after which Coutlie ran the following advertisement:

"International Hotel, Boston Bar.
The public are advised that this long and favourably known hotel has again come into the hands of the original owner, who will give his personal supervision to the establishment." [9]

Coutlie continued to operate his hotel for another five years until 1873, when the property was Crown Granted and sold to Edward Grove of New Westminster. Edward Grove was ill when he bought Coutlie's hotel, and died within the year. By 1876 H.B. Dart had taken over the International Hotel. While on a trip to the Cariboo in the autumn of 1880, Sarah Crease described in her diary their accommodations in Boston Bar:

"Rooms very small, but clean—comfortable soft bed. Next morning had excellent milk, porridge for breakfast—Mr. Dart has some good fruit, plums, pears, etc." [10]

Due to the extraordinarily heavy snowfall during the winter of 1893, the spring run-off of 1894 caused heavy flooding in most communities along the Fraser River. At Boston Bar, the village was completely gutted, and had to be relocated to a higher bench just north of the original site.

THOUSAND DOLLAR BILL'S ROADHOUSE, 1859.
THE 26 MILE HOUSE, 1862.
Lot 1A, G.1., Lytton.
Located on top of the first hill north of Boston Bar, this roadhouse received its name as a result of the proprietor's habitual remark, "I

bettcha a thousand dollars." Unfortunately "Bill" did not have legal tenure of the land, and lost it in 1863 to a Mexican, Lorazo Rocco, who pre-empted 45 acres of land situated at the 26 mile post, about one half mile north of Boston Bar. By 1939 this had become the site of an auto camp, and later a motel.

THE FRASER ABOVE BOSTON BAR, 1860.

As Bishop Hills and his party moved north from Boston Bar in June 1860, the trail along which they travelled lay close to the river, where groups of miners were at work on almost every bar. Today these names are mostly forgotten:

> "At Paul's Flat, a few miles beyond Boston Bar I spoke to two miners, a Frenchman and an Italian, who together were clearing $20 a day....At Ensley's Flat, between Paul's Flat and Fargo's Bar, we passed a store kept by a Frenchman. Close by here was a mining flume of several miles in length, carrying water to the 'diggings' on a bench 100 feet above the river." [11]

HALFWAY HOUSE, BUTCHER'S FLAT, 1860.

Approximately 32 miles north of Yale the bishop reached what he called the Halfway House. "Here we found a butcher's shop," wrote Hills, who also mentioned that he wished he had known of it earlier, for they had been "on salt provisions for some days." [12] Alfred Selwyn, a geologist involved in the Pacific Railroad Exploration Survey of 1870 referred to the area as "Butcher's Flat". In a report to the Geological Survey of Canada in 1871, he wrote:

> "Camped at Butcher's Flat 31.05 miles from Yale, on the edge of a dry, stony, gravel terrace, thinly clothed with pine trees, and sloping at an angle of 32 degrees, down to the swift and turbid waters of the Fraser, 100 feet below." [13]

BOOTHROYD'S FOREST HOUSE, 1861.
THE 36 MILE HOUSE.
Lot 3, G.1., Lytton.

The following record of sale for "land near Lytton", filed in Victoria on October 14, 1862, describes the location of Boothroyd's roadhouse and ranch:

"I Henry Hartnett, of Murderer's Bar, in consideration of $663.00 U.S., paid by George W. Boothroyd, have sold all those parcels of land on a flat of land about 22 miles south of Lytton, on the east bank of the Fraser River consisting of 1 Lot of 160 acres of pre-empted land, and 1 Lot of 50 acres of purchased land adjoining, together with the buildings and improvements, I.E. fences." [14]

While the actual sale did not take place until the autumn of 1862, it would appear that the Boothroyd brothers, George Washington and William Harrison, had been operating a road-house at this site since the fall of 1860. On a Royal Engineers map of 1861, showing the extent of an Indian reserve 14 miles above Boston Bar, the location of Forest House, a store and blacksmith shop, is noted to the east of the reserve.

Originally from England, the Boothroyd brothers left home for California in the early 1850s, where they mined for gold and managed a hotel, arriving on the lower Fraser in 1858. By 1859 William Boothroyd was teaching school in Yale, where he was said to have been the first paid teacher on the mainland of British Columbia. From a description of the land purchased in 1862, the property had already been developed to some extent, perhaps by Henry Hartnett, the vendor.

The first of many documented references to Forest House (Forest being the maiden name of Mrs. George Boothroyd) is found in the account of a travelling reporter from the Victoria *Colonist,* dated April 26, 1861, upon reaching "Forrest House" 11 miles from Boston Bar. In July 1866 another publication, the *Examiner*, of New Westminster, published the following advertisement:

"Forest House. 36 MILE POST between Lytton and Boston Bar. Travellers will find every accommodation at this Hotel. Excellent cooking. Good beds. Stabling for horses. Hay and Oats. Boothroyd Bros., Props." [15]

A classic photograph of "Boothroyd's hostelry" taken by Frederick Dally in 1867, shows a typical roadhouse farm, with the Cariboo Road running between the house and the several barns and outhouses. Parked in the yard are no less than nine freight wagons with accompanying teams of horses and mules.

Boothroyd's House. (COURTESY BCARS)

For nearly a decade Boothroyd's roadhouse and ranch flourished, gaining such renown that the whole area within a five-mile radius became known as "Boothroyd". During the early 1870s, while William Boothroyd was away at the Omineca gold rush, George Boothroyd ran into financial difficulties, forcing him to sell part of the original 210 acres of the ranch. On William's return in 1873 George sold out to his brother, and left with his family for Surrey, on the lower mainland. William Boothroyd remained at Forest House for another three years, until March 1876, when the *Mainland Guardian* published the following notice:

> "For Sale by order of the Mortgage, Boothroyd's Ranch.
>   Situated on the Yale-Lytton wagon road, between Boston Bar and Lytton. Consisting of 80 acres of land thereabouts, with the improvements and dwelling houses. Tenders for the purchase of the above property will be received up to May 15, 1876 by the undersigned to whom application can be made for further particulars. Alex E.B. Davie, Victoria, B.C. March 13, 1876." [16]

As far as is known, William Boothroyd, who had not communicated with his brother since their parting in 1873, returned to England shortly after losing the ranch, and was never heard from again. The reasons for the failure of the Boothroyd enterprises at the 36 Mile House have never been fully explored. Most self-sufficient roadhouse farms beside the wagon road, especially those in favourable climates, made a great deal of money during the gold-rush era and, with careful management, continued to operate successfully through times of economic hardships. Dr. M.S. Wade mentions that Boothroyd's roadhouse was not as popular as Salter's 42 Mile House, a few miles farther north. Even so, there must have been other reasons for George Boothroyd to have suddenly run into financial problems in the early 1870s. One may have been their financial investments in the Omineca gold rush. The over-estimation of its riches and consequently the short duration of the Omineca "rush" bankrupted many investors, ranchers, and store owners.

It was also well known that the brothers did not get along together, especially after George married a woman of native blood, producing a large family of dependants. An article in the Victoria *Colonist* of December 1862 revealed that there was also conflict between William Boothroyd and the local Indians:

The George Boothroyd family. (COURTESY BCARS)

"Indians at Boothroyd's Hotel attacked William Boothroyd, cutting him severely about the face and body, and would have killed him, had not another white man interfered." [17]

With his strong English upbringing, William had apparently not been able to overcome his prejudices against anyone who was not British. Boothroyd's roadhouse and ranch did not sell for some years, and was managed in the meantime by the creditors. In 1882 it was sold to Oliver H. Evans of Ashcroft. Today, the site of Boothroyd's ranch is part of a small airport.

THE 42 MILE HOUSE, 1861.
Lot 14A, G.1., Yale-Lytton.
Past Boothroyd's the trail rose slowly for six miles, to a small flat at the foot of Jackass Mountain. Known as the 42 Mile post on the wagon road, the roadhouse there was built in 1861 by George Salter, an American miner. "Salter's House", a two-storey log structure facing the road, catered mostly to freight-wagon drivers, rather than stagecoach passengers. Built as it was, at the foot of the steepest incline on the Cariboo Road, the house served as a hostel for freighters who lodged there, sometimes for several days, while they drove their loaded wagons up Jackass Mountain. A photograph of the 42 Mile House, taken by Charles Gentile in the late 1860s, shows a collection of shake-roofed buildings on the west side of the road, set against a backdrop of steep, forest-covered mountains.

Prior to his retirement to the lower mainland in 1873, George Salter sold his roadhouse to W.A. Johnston, a later resident of Quesnel. Three years later Salter suffered a heart attack and died at his home in New Westminster. By 1877 the 42 Mile House had become the property of A. Stevenson and W. Tinline.

In 1882, while Mr. and Mrs. Benton ran the roadhouse, a terrible accident occurred on the road two miles south of the 42 Mile House. William Jones, the operator of a nine-horse freight team, was transporting a wagon load of blasting powder to various railway construction sites along the Canadian Pacific line. William's father, J.T. Jones, the former principal of the Cache Creek Boarding School, accompanied him. They had started from Yale that morning, and as they climbed the hill at Tilton Creek, the 5½ tons of powder blew up, killing two of the horses, and blowing William and his father right off the road. Severely burned and suffering from concussion, the two men were found wandering in a dazed condition by another freighter, who escorted them to the 42 Mile House. While Mrs. Benton put them to bed, her husband Thomas rode to Lytton to summon the doctor. For two days the father lingered on, passing in and out of consciousness, but finally he succumbed to his injuries on the third day. William Jones, a healthy young man, recovered after a few days rest.

JACKASS MOUNTAIN.

As Bishop Hills and his party advanced upriver toward Lytton in June 1860 they started up Jackass Mountain, the highest point on the old trail. The following excerpt from Hills' diary records the occasion for which the mountain was named:

> "The trail is frequently dangerous. We ascended to great heights on the almost perpendicular side of the mountain gorge, on which one false step would mean certain death. Today we met a man with a pack train, in a gloomy mood. He had just witnessed one of his mules rolling over and down the mountain, being dashed from crag to boulder until the mighty torrent below received it and carried it away." [18]

Two years later, when Hills passed through the same area, men were blasting the rocks in preparation for the road that was built that year. Waiting until work had ceased for the day, Hills and his party started through, but soon found the way blocked with debris and rock. Choosing what they thought to be a detour, they found themselves on a narrow, winding trail less than a foot wide, about 800 feet above the river. Suddenly the path disappeared completely, leaving them no alternative but to turn the horses, one by one, back up the trail. This was no easy task, for the animals were very nervous:

> "By God's great mercy we succeeded in turning each horse, and after considerable exertion and anxiety managed to regain the road." [19]

KANAKA BAR HOUSE, 1859.
Lot 4, G.1., Lytton.
Gold was first discovered at this point on the Fraser River in 1858 by Kanakas, natives of Hawaii, and former employees of the Hudson's Bay Company. In what was reported to be a very rich area in 1859, there were

"...two sluice companies at work, with nine men making an average of $7.00 each per day. They have built a ditch over 4 miles long from the upper flats to supply water for mining." [20]

Two of these miners, Eugene Combe and a partner, Charles Sadoux, settled at this site, each acquiring ten acres of land. Many years later, a historian and superintendent of the B.C. Express Company, James Leighton, wrote of these enterprising and industrious Frenchmen:

"They opened a stopping house and had a liquor licence, as they all did along the Cariboo Road. They sent home to France for alfalfa seed and planted it at Kanaka. By 1865 they had a good field of it. They supplied all the stage horses, also the freight teams that stopped there overnight." [21]

Kanaka Bar House, the store, and Barnard's livery stables continued in operation for many years. Following the death of Combe in May 1870, it was apparent that he had become financially indebted to Lytton businessman Louis Hautier, to whom the property fell.

THE 50 MILE HOUSE.

Siska Flat, a grassy bench overlooking the Fraser River about 50 miles from Yale, was once the site of an early roadhouse. Bishop Hills, in his journal of 1860, writes of Siska Flat, where he entered the store of a French miner, Paillard, who did not speak a word of English. A drawing made from a survey of the area by the Royal Engineers in 1861 marks M. Paillard's store and mining claim, which borders an Indian reserve.

During the 1940s Bruce Hutchison wrote a newspaper article describing the ruins and the location of an old roadhouse at approximately this site:

"On leaving the highway, cut through an old orchard planted by the H.B.C. Behind this and between two broken down snake fences you will see the original narrow Cariboo Road, clinging to the brink of the river. It winds down the 50 Mile hill along a steep grade and across an old rotten bridge which many years ago spanned the 50 Mile Creek. There on the bluff which falls down to the river you will come upon the remains of the old 50

Mile House. All that is left now is a log cabin, its roof fallen in, its great chimney a heap of stones and crumbling mortar. Close by are a few broken pieces of rusty iron, a broken wagon wheel, and a few horseshoes, the only other mementoes left to tell of the days when oxteams and stage coaches climbed the 50 Mile hill towards Lytton." [22]

SISKA LODGE, 1927.
Many years later, in 1927, when a new road opened between Yale and Spence's Bridge, Siska Flat became the site of a very popular stopping place operated by Allen Gaugh, his wife Helen, and son Allen. Far below the highway, on the same level as the original Cariboo Road, the builders of the modern lodge came across many artifacts, including mule and ox shoes. When a fire destroyed the lodge in 1933, a second one was built, which proved to be a popular holiday spot during the 1930s and '40s. In the large dining room, where many a thick steak was served, the windows looked out on an inspiring view of the Fraser Canyon and the twin railway bridges. During the 1950s, following the sale of the business to the president of B.C. Electric Company, the lodge burned down again. When a third Siska Lodge was built in the 1960s, the main buildings were beside the present highway, with cabins built at lower levels. At that time Siska Lodge was operated by Fred and Florence Lindsay of Quesnel.

LYTTON, 1858.
Rumours of larger gold nuggets on the upper Fraser were true. At Lytton, where gold was found on the river bars and on the benches above the river, it was common to find nuggets weighing up to one-third of an ounce. As a supply point for hundreds of miners at the confluence of the Thompson and Fraser rivers, the little community, known first as The Forks, received the name Lytton after Sir Edward Bulwer-Lytton, Secretary of State for the Colonies. Where the community emerged, on a dry, open flat above the river, the wind blew constantly, stirring the light, sandy soil into clouds of dust. Lieutenant R.C. Mayne, who passed through in the summer of 1859, was obviously not impressed with the site. Complaining of the constant wind that filled his eyes with grit, he described Lytton as:

"An irregular row of some dozen wooden huts, a drinking saloon, an express office, a large Court House—as yet unfin-

Lytton, CA 1860. (COURTESY LYTTON HERITAGE SOCIETY)

ished—and two little buildings near the river which had once belonged to the H.B.Co. but which were now inhabited by the district magistrate." [23]

GLOBE HOTEL, LYTTON, 1862.
Lot 5, Block X.1., Townsite of Lytton.
One of the earliest hotels, and certainly the best known in Lytton's history, was the Globe which opened in the summer of 1862. The following is an advertisement which appeared in the *British Columbian* in July 1866:

> "L.V. Hautier & Co's Hotel and Billiard Saloon. Lytton City.
> This House is furnished in the best style, and a stock of excellent liquors and cigars are kept constantly on hand. The billiard tables are unsurpassed in the colony. The charges are moderate." [24]

The Globe Hotel was operated by the Hautier family for over 40 years. Louis Vincent Hautier, a Belgian, with his wife Josephine Dubois Vanderbrook, had arrived in Lytton in 1860 with two small children. Married in San Francisco, Louis and Josephine moved to Victoria in 1858, where Josephine, an actress and well-known opera singer, performed in many concerts. That summer while a pregnant Josephine and little Louisa remained in Victoria, Louis made his way up the Fraser River to The Forks where he came across many French-speaking prospectors. Among these were Eugene Combe and his partner Charles Sadoux, who were mining on Kanaka Bar, below Lytton. When Combe and Sadoux opened their roadhouse there, Louis turned from mining to his real calling as cook, herbalist, and amateur physician at Kanaka Bar House. On his return to Victoria in the spring of 1860 Louis convinced Josephine of the golden opportunities awaiting them at Lytton, where he intended to open his own hotel.

Reaching Yale by steamer, the little family made the remainder of the journey on foot. Indian bearers accompanied them, and a native woman, Lasha, carried the baby Alphonse, and helped three-year-old Louisa along the trail. By 1862 the Hautiers had acquired Lot 5, Block 10 of the recently surveyed townsite, where they opened the Globe Hotel later that summer. A large kitchen garden, grown to supply the needs of the hotel, was located on a pre-emption of land two miles south of the town.

Madame Hautier, a gourmet cook, presided in the kitchen and worked hard to establish a reputation for serving the best meals in town. With the completion of the wagon road to Lytton in 1862, business flourished at the Globe Hotel, where many well-known gold-rush personalities met. Alphonse Hautier, a child at the time, later recalled Judge Begbie and his excellent bass voice, which could be heard from his room at the hotel, as he performed his daily ablutions. Sir Matthew, as he became, recognized Madame Hautier as the young woman who had sung with him at the miners' benefits in Victoria in 1858.

In 1862 while Governor Douglas was a guest at the Globe, he sought the advice and services of Louis Hautier in the removal of several stubborn corns on his feet. Hautier guaranteed to rid him of six corns for five dollars each, but when it came time to pay, Douglas gave Louis only $25. On his return some time later the governor complained that one corn had grown back. "Ah hah!" retorted Hautier. "That was the one for which you did not pay!" As a herbalist, Louis Hautier cured many people of their ills, especially children. While he grew some herbs on the pre-emption, he gathered others such as bark, roots, and wild plants from the nearby hills. These were turned into medicinal concoctions by Louis, who was very secretive about his recipes.

Over the years Hautier was constantly involved in one business scheme after another, some of which resulted in court cases, the most serious involving a shooting. During the 1860s when Hautier and a partner, Ellerd, opened a meat market in Lytton, they were opposed by another local butcher, Patrick Kilroy, who was jealous of the competition. One night in Hautier's saloon Kilroy was heard to insult Madame Hautier, and a fight broke out between the hot-tempered little Belgian and the burly butcher Kilroy. When Kilroy grabbed Hautier's cane and proceeded to knock him about the head, Hautier pulled a gun, and fired at Kilroy, wounding him only slightly. In the trial before Judge Peter O'Reilly, the charge of intent to kill against Hautier was reduced to common assault, to which Hautier pleaded guilty, and paid a fine of $50. Kilroy, on the other hand, a known troublemaker, was fined $400 for inciting the fracas. This incident and several others involving Louis Hautier were partly the result of his over-indulgence in liquor, a problem common to most notables in gold-rush communities. Despite their many ups and downs, Louis and Josephine Hautier raised a family of five children while operating the Globe Hotel, until 1880, when Josephine fell ill from overwork, depression, and an excess of liquor. That fall, as Sarah Crease passed through the area with her husband, she mentioned in her diary:

Louis Vincent Hautier. (COURTESY BCARS)

"Reached Lytton about 6.00 p.m., went to Hautier's, every-thing the picture of misery and decay (liquor the cause) Mdme. Hautier very fine spoken woman—singer, actress and cook—the poor man." [25]

Shortly after this Louis Hautier turned the hotel over to his eldest son Alphonse, and retired with Josephine to the farm at Kanaka Bar. On Sarah Crease's return to Lytton three weeks later, she mentioned the changes that had taken place at the Globe Hotel:

"Found the rooms cleaner and more comfortable than before, but the cooking not so good." [26]

At Kanaka Bar, where she visited the Hautiers:

"Found Mdme. Hautier very ill on a wretched bed...did our best to help her." [27]

Josephine Hautier died on September 13, 1881, at the age of 44, and was laid to rest in the family plot on their original pre-emption, south of Lytton. Louis Hautier lived on until January 3, 1886, and was buried close to his wife and infant son Willie, who had died at the age of three in 1869.

The Globe Hotel was operated by the sons Alphonse and Albert Hautier, until 1896, when it was sold to a veteran hotelier and saloon-keeper, Samuel Adler. Alphonse Hautier remained as manager of the hotel until 1900, when he retired to his ranch at Texas Creek. The hotel burned to the ground in a disastrous fire that swept through Lytton in 1937, and was not rebuilt.

BAILLIE HOTEL, LYTTON, 1868.
Lot 5, Block X, Township of Lytton.
Built by William McWha and his associates in 1868, this hotel was taken over by George Baillie in 1872. Originally from Edinburgh, Scotland, Baillie had travelled to the goldfields of the Cariboo in 1862 where he mined and played the violin in Alex Hardie's dance hall in Cameronton. While operating his hotel in Lytton, Baillie also ran a saloon and dance hall in Lillooet until his death in 1887. By 1912 the original Baillie Hotel had been torn down, and in its place was built the first Lytton Hotel. Destroyed in the fire of 1931, the Lytton Hotel was replaced by the New Lytton Hotel, built by Anton Medori.

THE FRASER RIVER ABOVE LYTTON.

Upon their arrival at the confluence of the Fraser and Thompson rivers in 1858, some miners turned northeast up the Thompson, while the majority continued up the Fraser to Lillooet, a distance of 45 miles. Within that distance miners found rich deposits of gold on both sides of the river. During the summer most miners lived in tents at the site of their diggings, but where they remained longer, they built log cabins, some of which became roadhouses.

CAMERON'S BAR, TEN MILES SOUTH OF FOSTER'S BAR, 1858.

Named for the discoverer, John A. Cameron, known later as "Cariboo" Cameron, Cameron's Bar above Lytton was among the richest. In May 1859 a reporter from the Victoria *Gazette* mentioned:

> "...on Cameron's Bar, an area 300 yds wide by half a mile in length, a company of miners were hard at work. They had thoughtfully surrounded themselves with those solid comforts so essential to health, a large log house, scrupulously clean, with a nice clay roofed bake oven near at hand." [28]

TEN MILE HOUSE AT CAMERON'S BAR, 1860.

Lot 81, G.1., Lillooet.

By 1860 Cameron's Bar had become the site of a roadhouse operated by two Mexicans, Antonio Guerriera and Jose Tressierra. While returning south from his journey to the Lillooet area in 1860, Bishop Hills and his party stopped here for dinner. Apparently the Mexicans squatted on this land until 1869, when they made application to pre-empt 160 acres each.

FOSTER'S BAR HOUSE, 1858.

Jack Foster, one of a company of miners from Whatcom County, Washington Territory, opened a roadhouse and store in 1858 beside a very large, rich mining bar about 22 miles north of Lytton. The roadhouse was still there in 1865 when a miner, Brown, charged with claim jumping, and four of his companions took refuge at Foster's Bar House. When the law arrived to arrest him, Brown resisted, and was shot, forcing the party to surrender.

WATKINSON'S 24 MILE HOUSE, FOSTER'S BAR, 1866.

Lot 84, G.1., Kamloops.

By the mid-1860s when stagecoaches travelled the road, Joseph Watkinson and his family kept a roadhouse at the 24 Mile post, the halfway point between Lytton and Lillooet. Arriving in California from his home in Cornwall, England, in 1858, Watkinson was met with the news of a gold rush on the Fraser River, a destination he reached soon afterward. At Hill's Bar near Yale, Watkinson met Thomas Harris, a Welsh miner, and together they travelled to the Cariboo. Later, Harris and Watkinson returned to the Lillooet area, where in 1864 they joined with entrepreneurs F.W. Foster and Richard Hoey in building the first flour mill at Lillooet, on Cayoosh Creek. By 1866 Watkinson, a married man with two children, had settled down to farming and roadhouse-keeping, an occupation he continued until his death in 1914.

While the original roadhouse burned in 1912, a second house, still standing, was built soon afterward. Close by is an original barn from the early 1900s. No longer a roadhouse in the true sense of the word, the Watkinsons' comfortable farmhouse receives many visitors each year, royally entertained by Mrs. Edith Watkinson, an English war bride. Fred Watkinson, the fourth generation of this pioneer family, still works the farm.

McGILLIVRAY'S HALFWAY HOUSE, 1913.

Lot 83, G.1., Kamloops.

Archibald McGillivray of Ontario arrived in the Lillooet area in 1890, to supervise the workings of a gold dredge on the Fraser River. By 1913 McGillivray and his wife, Josephine, had purchased the John Roberts farm, just south of Watkinson's land, where they established a roadhouse known as the "Halfway House" on the Lytton-to-Lillooet road. The large, two-storey log house facing the road continued to serve the public for many years, managed by succeeding generations of the McGillivray family. During the 1940s Alexander McGillivray sold out to the Buckerfield Seed Company, which hired him to work for them. While occupied by foreman C. Dohler during the winter of 1948, Halfway House was completely destroyed by fire.

THE BIG SLIDE, 1859.

Just north of Foster's Bar, the mule trail to Lillooet was often blocked by big slides, where rocks and soil fell from high cliffs onto the narrow trail beside the river. When this occurred travellers were forced to use an alternative route, from Foster's Bar up through a high mountain pass to Fountain, a community eight or nine miles northeast of Lillooet. During the 1860s Judge Begbie, whose official duties required him to travel through the area at least once a year, complained bitterly of the slides:

> "I have had to unload three animals, one at a time, on a path not 2 feet wide, and 1000 feet above the Fraser without even a bush to break the fall—Last autumn I had to do it alone, as the packer could not get past." [29]

Almost 130 years later, slides still occur on this stretch of road.

LILLOOET, 1859.

Situated at the northern terminus of the Lillooet River route to the upper Fraser, the little community, first known as Cayoosh Flat, became Lillooet in 1859, while it was the central point of mining activity. In 1862 with the building of G.B. Wright's wagon road to Clinton, Lillooet became mile zero of the Cariboo wagon road. By 1863, with a population of 1,600, there were hotels and shops of every description, built along the one dusty street.

STAGE HOTEL, LILLOOET, 1860.

Prior to the completion of the wagon road from Yale, and while the Harrison route was still popular, this hotel was advertised in the *B.C. & Victoria Directory* of 1863:

> "Stage Hotel, J.Herkimer, Prop.
> This House is furnished in the very best style, and the table is supplied with the choicest viands. Stages connecting with the steamers for New Westminster leave daily." [30]

First opened in the spring of 1860, the Stage Hotel was visited in 1862 by Overlander R.H. Alexander and his companions, who were on their way south for the winter. At the hotel Alexander was delighted to find two former companions, Alfred Handcock and Johnnie Brown, working there.

> "...had supper and stayed the night there. Lillooet is quite a small town. There is one street in it and a church. The Stage Hotel is a first rate House." [31]

The proprietor of the hotel, Herkimer, offered Alexander and his friends a job cutting wood at $2.50 a cord, which at first they gratefully accepted. When it was realized that the wood, a very knotty yellow pine, was impossible to split, they were forced to turn down the offer.

"When we came to settle up with Mr. Herkimer he treated us very well, giving us $5.00 more than we earned by a good way." [32]

Other notable guests at the Stage Hotel were Dr. Cheadle and his companion, Lord Milton, on their way to the Cariboo in the fall of 1863. Having reached Lillooet on October 8, they remained there for two nights while awaiting the stagecoach. Their sleep was disturbed on both nights, once when the doctor's bed collapsed, and again when inebriated miners tried to occupy their bedroom at two o'clock in the morning. Dr. Cheadle also found out that pioneer hotels did not always provide overnight shoe-cleaning services.

PIONEER HOTEL, LILLOOET, 1862.
Opened by Charles Nelson in 1862, this became the Excelsior Hotel in the early 1900s. It was destroyed by fire in the summer of 1930.

INTERNATIONAL HOTEL, LILLOOET, 1866.
This hotel, built by Spelman and McKenzie, opened in May 1866, when it was advertised in *The Cariboo Sentinel* of Barkerville. Thomas Spelman, an Englishman, also owned saloons in Lillooet, and was for a while the government agent and registrar.

VICTORIA HOTEL, LILLOOET, 1892.
Built by Dan Hurley of Lillooet in 1892, the Victoria Hotel was operated for a time by William Allen and his wife, Jane. The bar of this hotel was the gathering place for miners of the Bridge River country, which was developing at that time, and Allen was always ready to grubstake a prospector.

BILLY BARKER ON CANADA BAR, 1860.
Following his arrival in Lillooet, Bishop Hills spent several days visiting local Indians, and talking to miners. At French Bar on the west side of the Fraser, just north of the community, a ferry crossed over to Fort Berens, an abandoned Hudson's Bay post of 1859. Adjoining French Bar were Canada Flat and Canada Bar, where the

bishop met with several miners. Among these was one William Barker, who "struck it rich" in the Cariboo in 1862:

"...Canada Flat, where amongst others is a company of seven Englishmen. They live in two log huts. An elderly man named Martin is their captain. They had all worked in California. One of these miners on Canada Flat is named Barker, he comes from Norfolk, a bargeman on the river between Cambridgetown and Lynn. The railways put him out of work and sent him, he says, to America..." [33]

PARSONSVILLE HOUSE, 1862.
Lot 1, and Lot 704, G.1., Lillooet.

By 1861 the site of the abandoned Fort Berens had become a supply depot for pack trains destined for the Cariboo goldfields. From its small beginnings the depot grew into a community known as Parsonsville, named for Otis Parsons, a packer on the Harrison-to-Lillooet trail of 1858. One of the more substantial buildings in 1862 was a roadhouse known as Parsonsville House, built and operated by Crawford and Matheson. None of these early developments had any legal tenure. Alexander Kennedy pre-empted the site of Parsonsville in 1863, and within two years had acquired 620 acres of very desirable farmland, which he sold to Jonathan Scott, an American from Winchester, New York. Scott, an enterprising farmer, grew and processed the first tobacco crops in the interior of British Columbia, which found a ready market in the goldfields. Scott spent the rest of his life at Lillooet, where he died in 1882. A memorial to this pioneer was erected in the 1950s, by M.L.A. George Murray, of Lillooet, on the site of the tobacco press.

BRIDGE RIVER HOUSE, 1859.

At the Bridge River, a milky stream flowing into the Fraser north of Lillooet, Bishop Hills found the Indians of the Hoystien tribe busy picking wild raspberries which, when dried, were used in the making of pemmican.

Named for the bridges built there by the Indians over several centuries, the Bridge River gained attention in 1858 when Europeans discovered rich deposits of coarse gold at its mouth. As a result, a small town sprang up around the mining camp, where a roadhouse and store were said to have been operated by two miners, Fraser and Davis. By May 1859 there were as many as seven businesses at the town of Bridge River. One of these, a transportation company, was operated by Gustavus B. Wright and his partner Thomas Davidson, who had built a new 60-foot toll bridge over the river. An interesting comment made by Lieutenant R.C. Mayne reveals the fact that the Indian bridges, over which the natives had freely travelled for hundreds of years, had been torn down by whites, who built a new toll bridge and proceeded to charge everyone, including the Indians, 25¢ to cross. The gold at the mouth of the Bridge River lasted only a few years, and by 1865 the little community had virtually disappeared. At this same time good prospects were being found on Gun Creek, a tributary of the Bridge River, 50 miles upstream.

FOUNTAIN OR FOUNTAINE, 1858.
An area known as the Fountain, at the junction of several trails from Lillooet, Lytton, and Fort Kamloops, became an important supply centre for miners in 1858. Situated eight miles north of Lillooet on a high, grassy, terrace above the Fraser River, it was named by French Canadians for the natural springs that came bubbling up out of the ground. These springs turned the semi-arid terraces into an oasis of highly productive agricultural land.

FOUNTAIN HOUSE, 1858.
Lot 1, G.2., Lillooet.
In view of these natural advantages an Italian miner, Lorenzo Latora, took up land at the Fountain, where he opened a roadhouse in 1858. Sending back to his native land he sponsored three of his countrymen to work (under contract) for three years in the development of his roadhouse farm. Grape slips imported from Italy were planted in nearby fields, and within a few years Latora was serving a good rich wine at the roadhouse while exporting casks of wine to other centres. Raisins were also sold to the miners, who took them along in their packs. In addition to these luxuries, fresh milk, beef, and vegetables, all produced on the farm, were served at the roadhouse. These were much appreciated by Bishop Hills and his companions when they stopped there for lunch in the summer of 1860:

"At the Fountaine [*sic*] there are three houses, one a store and restaurant kept by an Italian Lorenzo Littora [*sic*]. Mr. Elwyn and Mr. Sheepshanks accompanied me. Lorenzo gave us luncheon...bread, cheese, radishes, raisins, and a good Claret. He would make no charge." [34]

Latora did a roaring business, especially in 1861 and '62, during the height of the gold rush. With the completion of the wagon road from Yale to Barkerville in 1865, business began to fade, prompting Latora to advertise in *The Cariboo Sentinel*:

> "Fountain House. Lorenzo Latora, Prop.
> This House affords every accommodation for the comfort of travellers. The table is furnished with all the delicacies of the season. The Bar is stocked with the choicest of wines, Brandy, and Cigars. Good stabling for horses. Hay, barley and oats on hand at low prices. Newly milled flour for sale cheap." [35]

Lorenzo Latora had pre-empted the first parcel of land in the Fountain district in 1861, to which he added an adjoining 160 acres in 1872. This hard-working and enterprising pioneer remained at the Fountain for the rest of his life. Shortly after his death in December 1888, the Victoria *Colonist* wrote:

> "The late Lorenzo Latora died in his 70th year. Owner of one of the finest farms in the region, his hospitality was unbounded. He was the earliest settler in the area." [36]

Following Latora's death, Nicolas Colanda, one of the Italians he had hired in 1858, took over the farm, where he also remained until his death. Following the First World War this became part of the Fountain Indian Reserve.

CHAPTER FOUR

LILLOOET TO ALKALI LAKE AND CHIMNEY CREEK

WHILE the majority of miners remained to work the profitable ground between Lillooet and the Fountain in 1858, miner Aaron Post of California made a daring expedition of exploration up the Fraser to the mouth of the Chilcotin River, about 90 miles north. On his return to Fort Victoria in July, Post exhibited samples of the gold he had found, and gave details of his extraordinary journey in an article published in the Victoria *Gazette*. Later that year, as a result of Post's findings, a number of miners worked their way upriver from Lillooet. They also found gold, but without adequate supplies, they were forced to return.

THE FRASER RIVER ABOVE LILLOOET, 1859.
Early the next spring, following the arrival of an additional 3,000 miners on the river, the race to find richer gold gathered momentum. The river was the only access into the vast wilderness of the northern interior, for until the building of overland routes from Lillooet, there

were only Indian trails, and the Hudson's Bay Company brigade routes to Fort Kamloops and Fort St. James.

Among the vanguard of adventurers were Peter Dunlevy and his four companions, James Sellers, Thomas Moffitt, Thomas Menefee and Ira Crow. While mining on the lower Fraser in 1858 Dunlevy heard of Aaron Post's findings, but it was the spring of 1859 before they travelled north to reach the mouth of the Chilcotin River. There they found gold so fine, it was hard to save. A chance meeting with Tomaah, a native runner for the Hudson's Bay Company, revealed to Dunlevy and his men the existence of more plentiful, larger gold on a creek many miles to the northeast. A month later, at Lac La Hache, where the Dunlevy party met with members of Tomaah's tribe, they were guided in to Little Horsefly Creek where they found a large deposit of "gold like beans". [1] While Dunlevy's strike heralded the start of the Cariboo gold rush, the event was equally significant to the history of roadhouses in the area. By 1860 the Dunlevy party, rich from their mining ventures, was investing in the most lucrative enterprises of the time, freighting and roadhouse-keeping.

Even as Dunlevy and his partners discovered gold at Horsefly, other parties of prospectors, including Benjamin MacDonald of Cape Breton, and John Rose, an American miner, had travelled upstream from Lillooet. At Fort Alexandria where they paused to rest, the

Peter C. Dunlevy. (COURTESY BCARS)

factor's daughter advised MacDonald of gold found by the natives up the Quesnel River, 30 miles to the north. Setting off immediately they found the mouth of the clear green stream described to them, and none too soon, for they were immediately followed by hundreds of gold-hungry prospectors, swarming up the river. Fast on the heels of the MacDonald party was John McLean, who claimed to have reached the mouth of the Quesnel on June 12, 1859.

Having spent the winter of 1858 at Yankee Bar, on the lower Fraser, McLean and his companions left in February, to travel upstream. At that time of the year there were still many stretches of the river where the ice had not melted, but by mounting runners on the loaded canoe they were able to push it over the ice to the next stretch of water. At Lillooet, where rich finds of gold tempted the party to remain, they decided to travel on before the river rose in its annual flood.

To remark casually, as in the account of the MacDonald party, that these men "travelled upstream" on the Fraser River for a couple of hundred miles, is to grossly underestimate the enormity of the feat. In John McLean's account (taken from notes made by E.O.S. Scholefield in 1910) the extreme dangers involved in such a journey, even in low water, are vividly described. To pass safely through the many canyons, rapids and whirlpools along the way demanded great skill in navigation, cool heads, and nerves of steel. Of prime importance was the choice of a canoe. A northern Indian canoe with a shovel front was far safer than the "Chinook" canoe, whose "cutwater", or straight bow caught the current, making it difficult to handle in rough water. Even with the best of canoes, McLean was in the river more than once. On one occasion above the mouth of the Chilcotin River, while the canoe was being pulled through a bad spot McLean, who had remained in the canoe, was suddenly thrown overboard and sucked under in a whirlpool. After what seemed an eternity he reached the surface, and was able to discard his heavy hip waders. When the current eventually carried him to shore, the high, steep river bank prevented him from climbing out of the icy water. Fortunately McLean's companions had anticipated this predicament, and rescued him with ropes.

While the great hordes of miners raced upstream to keep up with the initial discoveries, some were content to remain along the way, to work their claims, and open trading posts and roadhouses. With only a few mule-train operators venturing over the wretched trails above Lillooet, the transport of goods by river, in spite of the dangers, continued for some time.

A map entitled "Rough Sketch of Cayoosh District", drawn by Corporal J. Conroy of the Royal Engineers in 1861, shows the names of many creeks and river bars mined in 1858 and '59, between Foster's Bar, below Lillooet, and Alkali Lake, north of the Chilcotin River. Named usually for the discoverer, each mining camp included several log cabins, and a few tents. Following the arrival of mule trains in the summer of 1860 there were no less than seven trading posts within the area. While several of these locations grew to become communities and villages, most were abandoned and

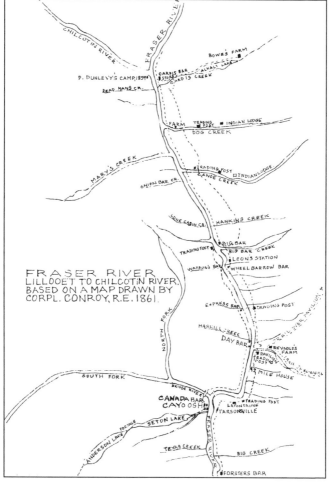

Lillooet area, based on Corporal Conroy's map, drawn by Branwen C. Patenaude.

forgotten as soon as the gold ran out. Above the Fountain were Haskell's Bar, Day Bar, and Express Bar, where John McLean and his party found rich diggings. It was a very large bar, worked by many miners, where in 1859 a ferry was established to carry passengers across the river to a roadhouse and trading post on the east bank. From here a trail connected with Cut-Off Valley, 50 miles to the northeast.

LEON'S STATION, 1859.

Thirty miles above Lillooet, on the east bank of the river, a miner, Leon, kept a store, livery stable, and roadhouse. Mentioned in several diaries of 1862, Leon is presumed to have been an American black. From here trails on both sides of the river led to Big Bar, about 18 miles north. While at Leon's Station John McLean and his party witnessed the destruction of a large Chinook canoe loaded with nine men and their supplies. The river at that point takes a sharp turn, where for about a hundred yards a series of swift currents and whirlpools cannot be avoided. Before going through, the men, all Italians, stopped to talk to the McLean party, who advised them to portage around the rough water. At this the Italians only laughed, and climbed back into their canoe. Sure enough, as soon as their craft hit the whirlpool, it capsized, drowning three of the men, and scattering their supplies upon the water. Gathering up what they could salvage, the remainder of the party were forced to abandon their journey, and return to Lillooet.

THE RED DOG SALOON AND ROADHOUSE, 1861.
Lot 220, G.1., Lillooet.
In a report of mining at Big Bar, published on September 30, 1859, the *British Colonist* mentioned:

> "...many companies of miners who intend to winter there, [where] they were building boats to ascend the river the next spring....The country about Big Bar is flat and thickly wooded with pine and fir; back from the river are extensive tracts of prairie and beautiful grazing lands." [2]

With such glowing reports it was not suprising that a miner, Joseph Haller, settled at Big Bar in the early days of the gold rush. Having made good money mining, Haller and a partner opened a combination store, saloon, and roadhouse known as Red Dog.

House, which operated for several years, until the gold ran out, and the population declined. Next Haller turned to packing with a train of 12 mules, transporting goods between Lillooet and Alexandria. While packing was amongst the most lucrative of trades, the operator was subject to many risks. During the long winter of 1861 Haller lost all of his mules, forcing him to start over again. By 1869 he was married and settled on a ranch at Big Bar Creek, where he and his wife raised a family of nine children. This self-sufficient and enterprising family of German Canadians was typical of a hardy breed of pioneers, so essential to the permanent settlement of a new country.

MOUNTAIN HOUSE, JESMOND.
Lot 137, G.1., Lillooet.

Philip Grinder, an American miner on Cardis Bar (Alkali Lake) in 1859, mined in the Cariboo before returning to settle on pre-empted land, first at Alkali Lake with Herman Bowe in 1861, and then at Big Bar Creek in 1868. With several partners Grinder developed a ranch and operated a two-storey roadhouse of log construction known as the Mountain House, on the stagecoach run between Clinton and Dog Creek.

By 1914 this enterprise was owned and operated by Harry Coldwell, a carpenter from the lower mainland, and his wife Louise. At this time the stage, driven by Joe Place, often with several passengers, remained overnight at the roadhouse. It was not long before the Coldwells became well known for their good meals and genuine hospitality. Over the years they raised two girls, Elsie and Evie, and a son, Pete, on the ranch. When a post office opened in the roadhouse in 1919, the name chosen was Jesmond, after Harry Coldwell's home town in England, Jesmond Dene, near Newcastle on Tyne. The original log roadhouse built by Grinder was destroyed by fire in 1921, but was soon replaced by another of similar construction, across the road. At that time the building served as a lodge for summer guests at the ranch. With the new house came the installation of a telephone. When the post office closed in 1960, a small store, built in 1927, continued operating until Harry's death in 1970. As his father grew older, Pete Coldwell took over the work of the ranch, to which he added a hunting camp and facilities to accommodate a growing tourist trade. Pete married Joyce Chapman, a local school teacher at Big Bar, and together they raised a third generation of ranchers and big-game hunters.

DOG CREEK, 1861.

Dog Creek, an oasis in the midst of a semi-arid area south of Williams Lake, had for centuries been the wintering place of native peoples of the Chilcotin tribe. An explanation of the name Dog Creek is found in a prize-winning essay written in 1862:

"At Dog Creek there lived in times past an Indian Chief, a favourite of the Hudson's Bay Co. packers, who gave him the nickname of 'Le Petit Chien'." [3]

So pleasant were the winters in the Dog Creek area that a number of Mexican and French packers of the Hudson's Bay Company built cabins there and became permanent settlers. Among these were Raphael Valenzuela, Jose Tressierra, Antonio Mondada, and the Basque packers Jean and Pierre Caux. Following the initial rush of miners in 1859 some Europeans remained to settle the land, where they raised beef for sale to the mining camps up and down the river. Among the first were the French aristocrat, Le Comte de Verespeuch, more commonly known as Verespeuch Gaspard, and S.L. Charles Brown, who pre-empted land and built a grist mill at Dog Creek in 1861. During the 1870s the population doubled when Chinese miners discovered pockets of gold in "clay bedrock" high above the river. Employed to dig the miles of ditches neccessary to supply water to the mines, dozens of Chinese labourers lived in the attics of four Chinese stores built at Dog Creek. These buildings also housed saloons, gambling rooms, and brothels, all designed to entertain the miners. In competition was another saloon and restaurant, operated by a white man, Carlyle, at the foot of the long, steep brigade trail leading out of the valley.

DOG CREEK HOUSE, 1886.

Lots 141, 142, G.1., Lillooet.

When Dog Creek House was destroyed by fire in March 1966, it meant the loss of one of the oldest original buildings of the Chilcotin district. Predating the gold rush of 1859, the main entrance of the roadhouse was a log cabin built by the Mexican packer Raphael Valenzuela. When Joseph Smith Place arrived in Dog Creek in 1886 he bought Valenzuela's 300 acres where he began to develop a cattle ranch. To the original cabin Place added a second storey and a lean-to kitchen, where he operated a store, roadhouse and licensed saloon. In the kitchen, Chinese cooks worked over large, wood-burning stoves

Dog Creek House. (COURTESY BCARS)

to prepare meals for stagecoach passengers, freight drivers, ranch hands, and cowboys, who sat together at one long dining table. The cowboys of those early days were a colourful lot with their angora chaps, silver spurs, hand-tooled leather saddles, and gaily coloured saddle blankets, inherited from their Mexican ancestors. In the saloon run by Joseph Place, where no woman dared to enter, men wore six shooters and indulged in wild antics and coarse language.

Prior to Place's marriage in 1887 to Jane Beaumont, of Yorkshire, England, the roadhouse was considerably enlarged with the addition of a two-storey "L", containing a ladies' sitting room, two bedrooms, a new kitchen and a laundry room.

Over the next ten years three sons and a daughter were born to the Places, all of whom learned to accept responsibility at an early age. Almost before they could walk the boys became familiar with horses, riding, and overseeing the care of a growing herd of cattle and prize horses. Jane Place and her daughter Annie maintained the roadhouse, and supervised the cooking. While Chinese cooks freed her from the kitchen, Mrs. Place was kept busy raising a large flock of poultry and growing a big vegetable garden, which was important to the meals served at the roadhouse. By late fall of each year the shelves of the cellar were lined with bottled vegetables, sweet pickles, sauerkraut and corned beef. Wild raspberries, blueberries and currants, picked by local Indians, were turned into wine, preserves, and jams. It was only during the winter, when the work subsided to some degree, that the family engaged in social pursuits.

By 1912 Joseph Place had built an empire at Dog Creek. Aside from the steady enlargement of the ranch, which by this time included 7,500 acres of deeded land and 2,000 acres of leased land, Dog Creek House had grown to the proportions of a hotel, with 22 bedrooms and a large basement. At this time the store and post office, located for years in the roadhouse, were moved to a new, two-storey building across the road. Beside it were a large new barn and a modern dairy. Lumber to complete these renovations and new developments were manufactured on a small, water-powered sawmill located on the ranch.

There had been a plan behind these extensive developments. Joseph Place, in touch with the proposed route of the Pacific Great Eastern Railway line, speculated on its passing up the Fraser River from Lillooet, where it would run close to, if not right through, the Dog Creek valley. When completed, however, the route was 40 miles away. At this same time Place's son-in-law, Frank Lindsay, persuaded him to back the purchase of a fleet of Winton 6 limousines, for use on the stage route between Ashcroft and the 150 Mile House. This last expensive venture was short-lived, for roads in the Cariboo at this time were hardly suitable for horse and coach, let alone heavy, seven-passenger automobiles. Before long it became obvious that Place's debts, the result of his poorly judged speculations, had placed the future of the ranch and Dog Creek House in jeopardy.

In the meantime, Charles R. Place, youngest son of Jane and Joseph Place, married Ada Halstead of Yorkshire, England. Although small in stature, (she was scarcely five feet tall, and might have weighed 100 pounds) this young lady, possessed of large and spirited ambitions and even larger personality, proved to be a strong force in the future of Dog Creek House. Over the next few years two sons were born, Charles Geoffrey at Ashcroft, and Hilary in England, while Ada was visiting her parents. It was 1919 before the family came to realize the full impact of the debts of 1912, when the mortgage holders took possession of the ranch. In an effort to maintain financial stability Joseph Place became a stage driver on the weekly run from Ashcroft. To make matters worse, Jane Place became seriously ill, and although an operation was performed, she did not recover, and died in Victoria. Following his wife's death Joseph Place also took ill, and died in 1924.

Jane Place and her daughter-in-law, Ada Place. (COURTESY BCARS)

In spite of losing control of the Dog Creek ranch, the sons of Joseph Place, Frank, Joseph Jr., and Charlie, remained in the area, taking up land nearby. With hard work and tenacity they hung on until 1930, when they reclaimed the homestead and 1,500 acres at a reasonable price, and on attractive terms. It was a proud moment when Charlie and Ada Place, with their two sons, moved back into Dog Creek House.

Ranching was never easy, and during the depression years, when top steers, driven to Williams Lake, sold at two cents per pound, it was almost impossible to survive economically. Fortunately the road-house trade was able to help out. In an effort to attract visitors to Dog Creek House Ada Place advertised overseas, and before long had a clientele of guests from all over Europe and the United States. Aside from her gracious hospitality and good food, Mrs. Place kept her visitors amused and entertained with "Open House" afternoon teas once a month, to which all the neighbours were invited. At other times there were tennis matches, organized hikes, piano recitals, and stage plays, put on by the visitors. For nearly 20 years the guest book at Dog Creek House included the names of aristocrats, business tycoons, movie stars, clergymen, and political leaders. Perhaps the most regular of these were the churchmen, both Anglican and Catholic, who remained overnight following services at the roadhouse and on the Indian reserves nearby. Of these, Father Thomas and the Reverend Basil Resker were the favourites. The Canadian artist A.Y. Jackson was also a guest at Dog Creek House, where he remained for several days, painting the unique landscape of the Dog Creek valley. During the Second World War when the Government of Canada maintained an emergency airport and weather station atop the plateau near Dog Creek, the staff spent many off-duty evenings at Dog Creek House. On these occasions Mrs. Place played her piano, led sing songs, showed movies, and provided refreshments to the men and their families. At this time it was not unusual to serve weekend suppers to 30 or 40 guests.

While many of the original furnishings of Dog Creek House were retained over the years, Mrs. Place was constantly redecorating, especially the bedrooms, each with a different colour scheme accented with matching bedspreads, drapes, and paper-flower arrangements on the tables. Running water and electricity were installed in the 1940s. At this time the old bar-room became the bathroom, and Mrs. Place's passion for music boxes became evident when she installed a musical toilet seat that played "God Save the King" when one sat down. Beside it was joke toilet paper that was a source of great amusement as it was unrolled.

By the 1950s both Ada and Charlie Place were showing the effects of years of struggle. During this time Mrs. Place survived a spinal operation, but Charlie died in February 1956, leaving her alone, save for the companionship of A.J. Drinkall, longtime bookkeeper at the ranch. Although her sons tried to persuade her to move to Williams Lake, Mrs. Place remained at the old roadhouse. In 1961, when a fire gutted the store and post office, those services were returned to the roadhouse. That same year Mrs. Place sold the Dog Creek ranch to George Demming, and when that sale fell through, sold it again, to Gerald Weingart and family. Early on the morning of March 4, 1966, in a howling easterly gale, Dog Creek House burned to the ground as a result of faulty wiring in the attic of the old house. Ada Place was never aware of the sad ending to her historic home, for she had died in September 1963.

ALKALI LAKE HOUSE, 1860.
Lots 6,7, G.3., Lillooet.
Beside the Fraser River about 17 miles north of Dog Creek are Cardis Bar and Cardis Creek, where Lewis Cardis, a miner from California, discovered fair diggings in the spring of 1859. Among

that first group of miners was Herman Otto Bowe, who took note of the hundreds of acres of arable land behind Cardis Bar prior to his departure for the mines of the Cariboo. On his return in 1860, and with the arrival of pack trains in the area, Bowe operated a temporary trading post, saloon and roadhouse beside the river trail, just north of Cardis Bar. The following year Bowe and a partner, Philip Grinder, pre-empted 360 acres of rich farming land at the head of Alkali Lake. Here Bowe constructed a few small log buildings, in one of which he accommodated travellers on the overland trail to Williams Lake. One of these was young Harry Guillod, who wrote in his diary:

"Made 17 miles [from Dog Creek] to Alkali Lake House without adventure. Had a good meal, lots of milk, and all kinds of fresh vegetables." [4]

In 1863 the following advertisement appeared in the *B.C. & Victoria Directory*:

"WILLIAM BOWE
ALKALI LAKE RANCH
British Columbia
This ranch is situated on the
RIVER TRAIL, on the DIRECT ROUTE
to CARIBOO, within an easy day's
ride of WILLIAMS LAKE.
The very best accommodations for TRAVELLERS
The BAR well supplied with
WINES, LIQUORS, & CIGARS.
Constantly on hand, large quantities of
HAY and GRAIN." [5]

Born in Hamburg, Germany, in 1834, the son of liquor distiller John Bowe and his wife Elsbe, Herman Bowe, more often known as William, or Bill, left home as a young man for the California gold-fields, where he worked in the Tuolumne area until his arrival on the Fraser River in 1858. Bowe was said to have got his start in cattle ranching in 1862 when three men from Oregon arrived with a herd of longhorn cattle bound for Barkerville. The drive of several weeks had taken its toll on the animals, many of which had died beside the trail. Fearing the outcome of a further journey, the cattlemen, believed to be L.W. Riske and the two Witherow brothers, sold their cows to

Bowe. Fed on nutritious bunch-grass, natural to the rangeland of the Chilcotin area, the cows survived and flourished. Those that were sold the following year brought $100 a head.

The need for a stopping house at Alkali lasted only a few years, until perhaps 1865, when the wagon road from Yale provided a more direct route to the goldfields. In July of that year Magistrate Henry M. Ball remained overnight at Bowe's roadhouse, and made this remark in his diary: "Bowe's at Alkali....Dirty House." [6] The original roadhouse, a cabin beside a large log barn, still exists today, used as a storehouse.

Following Bowe's marriage to Caroline Belleau, daughter of the Alkali Lake chief, a larger home was built. Having visited the ranch in 1886, a reporter wrote of H.O. Bowe's "comfortable home", one of several residences on the ranch. Of the four children born to Bowe and his native wife the favourite daughter was Emma, for whom a piano was transported by freight wagon, all the way from New Westminster. When the Alkali Lake ranch was sold in 1909 to C. Wynn Johnson, it included the piano. When the ranch was sold again in 1939 to Mario von Riederman, the piano remained, until it was donated to the Williams Lake Museum in the 1970s. Herman Otto Bowe retired from Alkali Lake in 1909, leaving the ranch in the care of his son John. He died at New Westminster on July 22, 1912, in his 78th year.

Alkali Lake Ranch, with H.O. Bowe's cabin, and a barn dating from 1891.
(COURTESY BRANWEN C. PATENAUDE)

The Overland Trail from Alkali Lake to Chimney Creek.

From Alkali Lake the overland trails used by the pack trains of 1860 led to Spring House, in a prairie-like area about 14 miles north. Here the trail separated, one branch going east to Chimney Creek, while the other led north to Williams Lake, where it met the Hudson's Bay brigade trail to Fort Alexandria. The name Spring House was derived from "St. Peter's Spring", the name given to a natural spring by Father Modeste Demers, an Oblate Catholic missionary, who ministered to the Indians at this site in the 1840s.

Harry Guillod, who passed by the site, wrote in his diary of August 8, 1862:

> "We camped at a place where there was a little spring, where somebody had put up on a tree close by, a cross with the words 'St. Peter's Spring', executed in red chalk." [7]

Spring House, 1862.
Lot 70, G.1., Lillooet.

Traditionally, the only name associated with Spring House is that of the Boitanio family, and in particular Augustine Boitanio, who purchased the property in 1886. There had in fact been much earlier settlers at Spring House.

As Bishop Hills made his way south from Williams Lake in September 1862, he described in his diary the journey to St. Peter's Spring:

> "Left Williams Lake at 9 a.m., camped at St. Peter's Spring at 6 p.m., distance 26 miles. For some distance the road was an ascent out of the basin of Williams Lake, and then along a country abounding in grass, thinly timbered forest and open prairies with lakes. After about 7 miles we descended a steep pitch into Chimney Creek, where farming operations were being successfully carried on. The road then lay by prairies and lakes, the former abundant in grass, the latter in wild fowl, of which we got two pair from King's [the packer] gun. We observed hay being cut in several places, and a Cornishman who had taken up a considerable tract, and was building a House." [8]

That there had been a roadhouse at this location in the early 1860s is confirmed in an advertisement of January 27, 1863.

"For Sale Cheap.

One third interest in the Spring House on the Centre Trail, between Alkali Lake and Williams Lake, consisting of a House and store containing Bar Room, etc, etc, also a dining room 19 X 29 stocked with liquors and provisions ready for the spring trade. 620 acres or thereabouts of good prairie land. A good stable capable of accommodating horses, plough horses, etc. The House is situated about 20 miles from Williams Lake." [9]

During the summer of 1863 in the vicinity of Spring House, two Italians, Lazaro Monteverde and his companion, Balance, were murdered by four Indians on horseback. The two men had been en route from Lillooet by way of the river trail, bound for Chimney Creek, where Monteverde had planned to open a roadhouse and trading post. Following an overnight stay at Spring House, the travellers were attacked by the Indians, who robbed them, shot them dead, and left them on the trail. It was suspected that the attackers somehow knew that Monteverde was carrying a considerable amount of gold. The culprits were later captured and convicted in a trial held at Williams Lake before Judge Begbie. All were executed.

Having operated a pack train for many years between Lillooet and Barkerville, Augustine Boitanio was no stranger to the Spring House ranch when he purchased the property in 1886. Leaving Italy while still a boy, Boitanio had worked in the California goldfields prior to his arrival on the Fraser River in 1858. Travelling first with the Hudson's Bay Company packers, transporting goods between Lillooet and Williams Creek, he was soon operating his own pack train, consisting of many mules.

Over the years Spring House received many guests, and in 1901 was visited by young Arthur Crease, son of the eminent Judge Henry Crease, and his friend Joe Pemberton, who bicycled up from the coast to Barkerville. Of the Boitanios Crease wrote:

"Found good road to Augustine Boitanio's...large family, all sizes. After supper they brought out the violins and we had a wonderful dance, quadrilles, etc. I ordered a pair of gloves from Cecilia Boitanio, a gifted glove maker." [10]

Cecilia Boitanio, daughter of Augustine and his wife Magdelin Mary Kutslip, was one of four children in the family. Augustine Boitanio died in 1914, leaving his sons Antoine and Clifford to operate the ranch.

CHIMNEY CREEK HOUSE, 1862.
Lots 10,11, G.4., Cariboo.

One of the earliest roadhouses on the trail from Alkali, Chimney Creek House was operated by Amadee Isnardy, a French packer and trader of the early 1860s. By 1868 Isnardy had acquired by preemption and purchase 314 acres of arable land "near the mouth of Chimney Creek", [11] where since 1862 he had operated a roadhouse and store close to the junction of two trails, ten miles south of Williams Lake. The saloon of Isnardy's roadhouse was for years a popular gathering place for miners and travellers who used the river trail from Lillooet.

Long after it had ceased to be a roadhouse, the old two-storey, hand-hewn, squared-log structure with dove-tailed corners remained at the site, looked upon as a landmark by local inhabitants. During the early 1900s a new two-storey frame house was built beside the old structure. In the 1970s when the old building began to lean into the newer house, it was torn down.

Chimney Creek House. The two-storey squared-log house was the original home of the Isnardy family. (COURTESY BCARS)

CHAPTER FIVE

G.B. WRIGHT'S ROAD: PARSONSVILLE TO CLINTON

BY early spring 1862, the flats of Parsonsville, across the Fraser River from Lillooet, resembled a tent town, where road contractor G.B. Wright had gathered an army of labourers to build a wagon road to the Cariboo.

In March newspapers carried this advertisement:

"500 Men Wanted.

To work on a Wagon Road from Lillooet to Mud Lake. No one will be hired for a period less than 2 months. If they wish they can engage until the full completion of the road. Wages will be paid in cash on the road at the expiration of the time for which men are hired. Any persons desirous of taking sub contracts for sections of the Road, not less than 5 miles, will have an opportunity to do so. Application is to be made to the undersigned, at Port Douglas or Lillooet. G.B.Wright & Co., Port Douglas. March 24, 1862." [1]

The assembly of over 250 men had been broken up into three camps, composed of ground clearers, road builders, and ditch, culvert, and bridge builders. Each camp had its own cook, who served meals from a chuckwagon, similar to those used in the cattle drives of the old west. On the job each man would carry his own personal belongings, while tents and tools would be transported by wagon. Road-making tools at this time consisted of picks, shovels, mattocks, hammers of several weights, pronged forks, and black powder for blasting. Wheelbarrows, which were also used, bore the closest resemblance to anything mechanical.

At a time when men worked from dawn to dusk, wages for white labourers were $1.50 a day, with foremen receiving $2.50. Chinese and Indian labourers were paid a dollar a day. Work began in late April, but it was another month before the first reports of the road were published:

> "The G.B.Wright & Co. road is progressing well. The firm
> has 275 men working and packers should be able to haul goods
> to the summit of Pavilion Mountain by June." [2]

Road building had reached the 12 Mile point from Parsonsville before Sergeant John McMurphy of the Royal Engineers reached Lillooet to begin his assignment, to direct and approve the route, inspect the bridges, file reports, and measure the completed mileage of Wright's wagon road. Armed with an impressive record as a veteran of the Crimean War, McMurphy had more recently been involved in the building of the Port Douglas-Lillooet road of 1858. In a journal he kept between May 1862 and August 1863, the building of Wright's road is traced, and many of the roadhouses mentioned.

THE 15 MILE HOUSE.
Lot 536, G.1., Lillooet.
It was mid-morning of October 10, 1863, when the stagecoach finally pulled out of Lillooet, crossed the Fraser, and headed north over a narrow road cut out of the mountainside. The four horses struggled uphill with nearly a ton of freight and several passengers, including Dr. Cheadle and Lord Milton. By evening the travellers had reached the 15 Mile House where they remained overnight, the doctor complaining bitterly about the accommodations:

"Wretched place. No fire, no beds. Milton slept under the counter, I along side of it, and Hall on the top, with four or five miners along the floor." [3]

The settler at the 15 Mile ranch and roadhouse, William M. Brown, lived there for many years before pre-empting the land in 1872. A Crown Grant for 320 acres issued in 1900 was registered in the name of Elizabeth Keatley, a granddaughter of William Brown.

THE 20 MILE HOUSE, 1870.
Lot 38, G.1., Lillooet.
At the 20 Mile post near Pavilion Creek, 100 acres of land were pre-empted in 1862 and 1863 by Michael McCarty and John McComb. While these were abandoned soon afterward, the land was taken up again in 1870 by Michael Gillen, a miner on Day's Bar in 1858. Gillen and his wife operated a roadhouse and store at this site for a year before selling out to Philip Garrigan. Garrigan and a son, Pete, both blacksmiths, continued to operate the business, transporting supplies with their own freight wagons.

McMurphy's diary of June 25 and 26, 1862, describes how, after inspection, each mile of the road was marked:

"Rode into Parsonsville to chain the road out to Pavilion. Started out 7.00 a.m., chained the road fourteen miles. Putting up Mile 'marks'. The contractors will fix boards on them with the Miles painted on them. We have two men with us to cut the posts, and dig holes to fix them. Corporal Woodcock and I used the chain from Parsonsville to the bridge across Pavilion Creek, being twenty two miles. Gave a certificate with a guarantee to G.B. Wright." [4]

THE 22 MILE HOUSE.
Lots 60, 61, 58, 59, 56, 22, G.1., Lillooet.
Mentioned as a popular stopping place, the 22 Mile House, operated by the Martley family in 1862, was not actually on the route of Wright's wagon road, but on the Marble Canyon trail to the Bonaparte River. In his diary of June 17, 1862, Sergeant McMurphy explained:

"Explored the face of Pavilion Mountain in hopes of bringing the road nigh to Captain Martley's ground, but there is not the shadow of a chance, and to go up the valley and come back again with the road would cause an unnecessary amount of labour." [5]

Nevertheless the stagecoach carrying Dr. Cheadle and Lord Milton in 1863 stopped at Martley's ranch before backtracking to where Wright's road started up Pavilion Mountain. Development of the land at Martley's ranch began in 1858 as was mentioned by Lieutenant R.C. Mayne:

"Just beyond the Pavilion Lake we passed a log hut, near which a farmer was ploughing with two horses." [6]

Occupied by an American, David Reynolds, the farm had been in operation for a year when Mayne passed through in 1859 and already there were 20 acres under cultivation, irrigated by water from nearby Pavilion Creek. Governor James Douglas and Bishop George Hills who visited Reynolds' farm and roadhouse in 1861 both left glowing accounts. Douglas remarked:

"Reynolds has barley, oats, potatoes, wheat and other vegetables. One turnip weighed 26 lbs!" [7]

Bishop Hills, who was there ten days later, made mention of a dairy of 26 cows attended by Mrs. Mallon, an Englishwoman from the Isle of Man. Reynolds' establishment was of one the earliest documented examples of the growing roadhouse/farm industry in the interior of B.C. While marketing his produce in and around Lillooet, he also supplied meals and accommodation to passersby at very little extra expense.

In spite of the introduction of the Pre-emption Act in 1860, Reynolds, who was only 22 miles from Magistrate Thomas Elwyn's office in Lillooet, made no formal application for his land at Pavilion Creek. In 1861, when this and adjoining lands in the immediate area were pre-empted by Captain John Martley, Reynolds, who was legally only a squatter, gave up his land.

A year later, when Bishop Hills returned to the Lillooet area, he and Reverend Knipe visited the new owners of the Pavilion ranch, now known as "The Grange":

"Mr. Knipe and I rode early to Capt. and Mrs. Martley's where we partook of a hospitable breakfast. Delicious strawberries and rich cream with fresh butter were in contrast to my daily pan of beans and bacon. We observed a goodly show of cows and about eighteen pigs. Some fifteen acres were under cultivation and many more fenced in. A stream flows through the property and there can be no doubt it will prove a productive farm." [8]

Captain John Martley, a decorated veteran of the Crimean War, arrived in the Lillooet area with his wife and two step-children in May 1861. As the recipient of a land grant awarded to veterans of Britain's armed forces, Martley had decided to settle near Pavilion, where he acquired 1,440 acres of arable land. When Maria Martley and her children arrived on the farm in the spring of 1862 they moved into the log cabin built by Reynolds. For someone who was about to operate a farm kitchen Mrs. Martley knew very little. Fortunately, David Reynolds' housekeeper, Mrs. Mallon, agreed to stay on to help her get started. Maria Martley soon adapted to the strenuous life of a pioneer wife, cooking for freighters and farm workers, and raising a second family. Located off the beaten track, the Martleys' roadhouse catered mostly to freighters and individuals passing along the Marble Canyon trail. To augment his income Captain Martley invested in several freight outfits. In later years his son Arthur drove many a load of farm produce over the various routes out of Lillooet.

Martley's freight wagon, between Lytton and Lillooet. (COURTESY LILLOOET DISTRICT HISTORICAL SOCIETY)

Arthur Martley, son of Captain John Martley. (COURTESY BCARS)

With the building of a wagon road through the Marble Canyon to Hat Creek in the late 1880s, traffic along that route increased dramatically, benefitting the roadhouse business. It was at this time that a new roadhouse was started at the Martley farm, built by Arthur Martley. The large, two-storey log house, situated close to the hillside, faced southwest, its windows allowing for a magnificent view of a wide valley and open river benches high above the Fraser River.

While Mrs. Martley, her daughters, and son Arthur were well liked by the local community, Captain Martley could make no such claim, as he was known for his arrogant manner and pompous behaviour. At one point in his long tenure he decided to run as a candidate in the general election of 1882. Among the several contenders was Ned Allen, an ex-boxer and convict whom Martley did not consider as serious opposition. When the votes were counted Ned Allen was the winner, with Martley's name at the bottom of the list. At Clinton, where Martley heard the results, he immediately mounted his horse and set out for home. After going only a few paces he wheeled about and announced in a grandiose manner to the crowd gathered outside the schoolhouse: "Gentlemen, I thank those who voted for me, but it is evident that the people of Lillooet prefer to go to the penitentiary for their members!" [9]

Following Captain Martley's death in 1896 Mrs. Martley moved to Lillooet, but Arthur, who never married, continued to live on the farm with his sister Alice and her husband William Manson, a well-known big-game hunter and guide. For several seasons Alice acted as hostess in the new house which served as a lodge for Mr. Manson's hunting parties.

By 1899 Martley's farm had been sold to John B. Bryson and his partner John C. Smith, blacksmiths at Ashcroft. At first the partners attempted to operate both the farm and the blacksmith business together, but after two years of frustration they split up, with Bryson operating the farm, and Smith remaining in Ashcroft. An energetic young man, Bryson made many improvements to the ranch, including the completion of the two-storey roadhouse started by Arthur Martley. In due time he courted and married Minnie Carson, a daughter of Robert Carson of Pavilion Mountain. In addition to raising a family of six children, this hard-working couple catered to the steady comings and goings of stagecoach passengers and freight-team operators for many years. While Minnie Bryson cooked and saw to domestic needs, John kept the wagons and stagecoaches in good repair. By the time the Bryson children were grown, many changes had taken place on the highways of the Cariboo. By 1915, and as the roads slowly improved, horses were replaced by automobiles, signalling the demise of the road-house, and consequently the need for blacksmiths. For the Brysons, who were essentially farmers, it had little effect except to lessen their contact with the outside world. Following the deaths of John and Minnie Bryson in the early 1940s the farm was operated for a few years

John Bates Bryson house, CA 1901. (COURTESY LILLOOET MUSEUM)

by their sons, but was sold in 1949. The roadhouse at The Grange caught fire and burned down shortly afterward.

THE ROAD OVER PAVILION MOUNTAIN, 1862.

By June 15, 1862, Wright's wagon road from Lillooet had reached the 22 Mile post near which a bridge was built across Pavilion Creek. Here the road began its sharp ascent by way of several switchbacks for nine miles up the side of Pavilion Mountain. At the top was a large plateau of land 5,000 feet above sea level. There had always been a trail of sorts across the plateau, and while it was safe enough in summer, the altitude there made it a treacherous place in the winter. In May 1861, a year prior to the building of the wagon road, the Victoria *Colonist* published the following account:

> "Tragedy On Pavilion Mountain.
> A dead Chinaman, half eaten by coyotes and crows, was found upon the plateau of Pavilion Mountain. The dead man, owner of a pack train, had started in February to see if it was possible to take his wagons across, but got caught in a blizzard and froze to death. He was armed with a revolver and a Bowie knife at the time of death..." [10]

Just why G.B. Wright chose such a difficult route for his road has always been a subject for conjecture. A much easier grade would have been the route followed many years later by the Pacific Great Eastern Railway from west of Pavilion Mountain, north to Kelly Lake and east to Clinton. Realizing that he was short of funds to finance his road-building project (by June he was already $40,000 over budget) it may be that Wright was influenced by land owners on the mountain who wanted a road past their farms.

From records of land pre-emptions and diaries it is clear that by 1862 most of the arable land in the Pavilion area had been settled. Bishop Hills, who travelled through that summer, mentioned:

> "There were bands of horses and cattle grazing, and extensive preparations were being made to fence in considerable acres of land." [11]

In October 1863, when Dr. Cheadle and Lord Milton rode the stagecoach along this route, they dined at a roadhouse on top of the mountain:

"We walked straight up the mountain side—awfully steep, and killing for the horses. Near the top we reached the 29 Mile House, where we got a fair dinner. Passed numerous returning miners and pack trains. Once past an extensive plateau of about fifteen miles we began the descent of the mountain known as 'Rattlesnake Grade', the most dangerous carriage road I have ever encountered. The narrow road turned six times, down which we rattled at a fearful pace. Had a wheel come off, or the brake given way, it would been certain death!" [12]

CARSON'S RANCH AND ROADHOUSE, 1867.
THE 26 MILE HOUSE.
Lot 19, G.1., Lillooet.

By 1867 the "plateau of rich grass" on top of Pavilion Mountain had been settled by a serious young man who spent most of his life there. Robert Carson had been taken as a child from Scotland to Ohio, U.S.A., where at the age of 19 he joined an immigrant wagon train headed west for Oregon. While en route the party came under Indian attack from which, according to Carson, he was the only survivor. So traumatic was this experience that it is said he would not talk about it for years. Hearing of the gold rush at Lillooet on the Fraser River, Carson headed north, following the old Hudson's Bay Company brigade trail through the Okanagan to Kamloops and Lillooet. There he acquired a string of horses and made a living as a packer for a few years. On exploring the flanks of Pavilion Mountain for horse pasture he discovered the plateau with its miles of grassland, a natural site for a cattle ranch. By 1867 he had amassed a sizable herd of cows, and built a log house, barns, and several outbuildings on land that had been abandoned by miners Haskell and McBeath. Over the years he pre-empted several hundred additional acres. With freighters and the stagecoach stopping at the door, Carson's cabin soon became a roadhouse, while his barns provided shelter and feed for teams of horses and mules. The writer Bruce Hutchison, who became a friend of the Carson family, in later years described Robert Carson and his achievements:

"With logs hauled out of the woods by horses and squared by his axe he built a cabin and barn. From Marble Canyon he brought limestone to make mortar for his stone chimneys. The fir trees of the area, so dry they could be burned as they were cut, fed his stove and kept his house warm when the mountain was swept by the blizzards, and snow blocked the trail." [13]

Due to the great distances and lack of roads, cattle sales in the Lillooet area were for many years limited to local markets. In 1877 Carson attempted to expand his market by driving a herd of 200 cows over a newly built trail from Lillooet to Burrard Inlet. While the trip proved a complete disaster, almost annihilating the herd, it took him to the coast where he met his future bride, Eliza Jane Magee of North Fraser Arm. They were married at the bride's home on April 3, 1878, and the trip back to Carson's ranch became the honeymoon, an arduous journey of two weeks. Almost immediately the bride showed herself to be a woman of strong character and conviction. Upon her arrival at Carson's roadhouse Eliza Jane sat down to a meal with her husband and the stage passengers. Placed on the table and sideboard of the dining room were several liquor bottles from which copious drafts were consumed by the host and his guests during the meal: everyone, that is, except the new bride. As the meal ended and passengers prepared to reboard the stage, Eliza Jane was seen putting on her coat and making for the door. "Where are you going?" asked her puzzled husband. Pointing to the liquor bottles she announced "Either they go, or I do." Whereupon Robert Carson took the offending objects outside and emptied their contents onto the ground. From that time on liquor was not served in Carson's roadhouse.

In further descriptions of Carson's ranch Bruce Hutchison elaborated on the roadhouse and its builder. Though Carson had been dead for many years, the writer was obviously moved by his lasting influence:

"Carson's signature was visible everywhere. The beams showed the scars of the broadaxe....On the floor by his chair were two grooves made by years of pushing back from the table. Under his hand the house never ceased to grow. From the original two-roomed cabin others continued to sprout as the family increased, so many galleries, stairways and passages that the house was no longer a creation of architecture, but a problem in geography. Long habitation, birth, death, and toil, the family of children, the strangers constantly stopping, the traffic moving up and down the road all gave the house a palpable feeling of life, carved it with wrinkles, and proclaimed it a sanctuary in the silence and loneliness of the mountaintop." [14]

The Carsons were used to strangers in their home, where hospitality was extended to travellers on the long journey between Lillooet and Clinton, and where almost every day, except in winter, the road brought its traffic. Politicians, families, churchmen, businessmen and bankers all enjoyed a meal, or lingered over coffee, exchanging news and views before departing the house—perhaps forever.

One important fact not mentioned by Bruce Hutchison was that the original roadhouse burned down in May 1887. It happened while Robert Carson was away freighting goods to Clinton. When he returned later that day he found the house a smouldering ruin, but the family safe, living in the dairy house. There they remained until a new home was built later that year. There were ten children in the Carson family, five girls and five boys, all born on the ranch. Mrs. Carson, in her determination to have them properly educated, was instrumental in the building of the first Pavilion school, a mile and a half from the ranch. To help raise the funds the Carson boys milked a herd of cows, from which their mother and sisters made mountains of butter, for sale in several locations in the interior. Later Mrs. Carson saw to it that her children went on to attend college in the lower mainland. Her persistence paid off. Although neither parent lived to see it, two sons, Robert Henry and Ernest Crawford, became members of the provincial legislature, representing Kamloops and Lillooet. During the 1940s Ernest Carson became Minister of Public Works, and Bob, the Speaker of the House.

Following the deaths of Robert Carson in 1911 and Eliza Jane in 1931, the family retained their many acres and varied interests in the Pavilion district for some time, but finally sold out in the 1940s to Colonel Victor Spencer. A more recent owner was J. Edward (Ted) Termuende, who encased Carson's log house in a modern frame building, leaving one wall of the old house open to the living room. The great hand-hewn, squared logs, with wide bands of mortar in between, made an interesting feature wall. Unfortunately, as do almost all log buildings, the house burned down in October 1986.

Haskell's 29 Mile House, 1861.

On their return to settle in the Lillooet area in 1861 many of Captain Day's company of miners, Frank McKay, Lloyd Haskell, Maxwell McBeath, Jesse Davis, James Maxfield, William Smithson, and John Harvey, took up land on Pavilion Mountain, where they farmed in a co-operative group. Land in the vicinity of the 29 Mile post was first pre-empted on August 14, 1861, and a roadhouse operated by Ella Haskell was built on an open meadow where the road crossed Pavilion Creek. Opposite the house were two large barns. Known as "Haskell's" in 1863, the 29 Mile House was a regular stage stop en route between Lillooet and Clinton, mentioned very favourably in several early diaries. In the Cornwall diary of 1863 there appears this entry:

> "Haskell & Co. have built a capital House there, and are making experiments in agriculture to see what will grow, it is 5000 ft. above sea level." [15]

By 1865, with the building of the Yale route to the Cariboo, both the roadhouse and the farm faded from view.

MICHAEL GILLEN'S 29 MILE HOUSE, 1871.
Lots 62, 63, G.1., Lillooet.
While some of Captain Day's associates returned to Pavilion Mountain in 1861, still others, such as Michael Gillen, remained in the Cariboo for a number of years. By 1870 when Gillen and his wife Mary returned, they pre-empted the abandoned land of early settlers at the 21 Mile post and the 29 Mile House farm. Following the sale of their roadhouse at the 21 Mile post in 1871, Gillen and his wife settled down near the 29 Mile post where they established another roadhouse on the site of Haskell's House of 1862. A family of four daughters grew up there, each of whom married into well-known Lillooet and Clinton families. This mountain-top roadhouse continued in operation until Mary Gillen's death in 1895. With the sale of the property in 1905, Michael Gillen retired to Vancouver. Today almost all signs of habitation have disappeared from the site, except for an old root cellar on the lower side of the road. While the roof has caved in, the cellar still boasts a double storm door at the entrance, facing Pavilion Creek. Where the roadhouse stood are still a few remnants, the shards of heavy, dark-green liquor bottles, the rusted iron parts of an antiquated bread-making machine, and the handle from an old-style water pail.

SERGEANT JOHN MCMURPHY'S DIARY, JULY 21, 1862.
By July 21, Wright's road had been completed down the nine miles of "Rattlesnake Grade" on the north side of the mountain, where the road makers found easy ground:

"All the difficulty on the road is mastered. Went around the little Lake, [which the Engineers named Pear Lake] where the country is level for about sixteen miles, which with a few men, a good road can be made in ten days. Rode ahead about twelve miles to look at country where the road will go—it is a fine grassy valley [Cut-Off Valley] where hay cutting is going on." [16]

THE 38 MILE HOUSE.
Lots 9, 10, G.1., Lillooet.
Following his departure from the 22 Mile post north of Lillooet in 1862, David Reynolds took up land at the 38 Mile, in the Cut-Off Valley. Once again Reynolds was a squatter, and probably a speculator. Verification of his existence at this site, where he operated a roadhouse in 1863, is found in a sketch accompanying Record No. 127, filed on February 17, 1863, which shows "Reynolds' House and farm" in relationship to four land pre-emptions to the east. This roadhouse was one of a number of "Good Stopping Houses" listed in the Victoria *Colonist* of March 9, 1863. By the mid-1860s this and other adjacent land between Kelly Lake and Mile 41 on Wright's wagon road had been purchased by Edward Kelly and his brother, George. For many years this was a part of one of the largest cattle ranches in the country. Miners on the Fraser River in 1859, the Kellys had been the first to settle inland at what became Kelly Creek and the Cut-Off Valley. By the early 1900s the ranch had been acquired by Frederick W. Foster of Clinton, with the exception of the site of the 38 Mile House, which in the 1880s became the property of Thaddeus Harper.

SERGEANT JOHN MCMURPHY'S DIARY, SEPTEMBER 25, 1862:

"We have a great many Canadians working with us that came overland by way of Lake Winnipeg and Red River." [17]

Having spent all summer travelling to reach the goldfields of the Cariboo, the first of the Overlanders landed at Quesnellemouth on the Fraser River in early September. Finding it was too late to complete their journey to the mines, they went south, hoping to find work on the Cariboo Road. An even later group, the Symington party, did not arrive until early October. Despite the effects of their long, harrowing journey they continued to travel, on foot, heading south. One of these, R.H. Alexander, mentioned in his diary:

"There are a lot of them, [Overlanders] at Bridge Creek, [100 Mile] some having taken subcontracts on Wright's wagon road." [18]

Remaining overnight at Clinton, Alexander and his companions proceeded on toward Lillooet by way of Pavilion Mountain. A few miles out, they came across a roadhouse in the Cut-Off Valley:

"About seven miles out [from Clinton] we came to a House kept by one Walker, who formerly farmed near Handereko, at Queenston." [19]

THE 40 MILE HOUSE.
Lot 273, G.1., Lillooet.
The 40 Mile House, built in the early summer of 1862 by William Walker and his partner, Thomas Fuller, was located on land beside which Wright's wagon road would soon be built. While it is certain that it operated for at least a year, nothing more is known of the roadhouse at this location. Having received a Certificate of Improvement on their land in May 1863, the partners sold out to Edward Kelly. A later owner was Frederick W. Foster.

THE SPANISH RANCH.
Lots 267, 268, 269, G.1., Lillooet.
About two miles southwest of Clinton, the wagon road of 1862 intersected an older mule trail used by the fur traders. At this point there is a ranch dating back to pre-gold-rush times that had been a relay station for several Mexican and Spanish packers working for the Hudson's Bay Company. Realizing the need to register their land, M. Garcin, B. Balencin, and T. Angula each pre-empted 160 acres at this site in October 1862. While some histories relate this property to the most famous of packers, Jean Caux, commonly known as Cateline, there is no documentation of his ownership. The property was Crown Granted in 1896 when it was acquired by F.W. Foster.

CLINTON, THE 47 MILE POST, 1862.
As the road builders neared the 47 Mile post on Wright's road, Sergeant John McMurphy mentioned in his diary:

"Mr. Watson left the Road Company this day, gone to build a House on his preempted land at the supposed junction of the roads, the Company has lost a faithful servant in him." [20]

Robert Watson, his brother, George, and a friend, Walter McKinnon, had been among the hundreds of miners in 1858 to travel up the Fraser River, where the Watson brothers did very well on what became Watson Bar, between Lillooet and Lytton. By 1861 they had gone into the packing business, transporting supplies for the road builders between Port Douglas and the Cut-Off Valley.

THE CLINTON HOTEL, 1862.
Lots 1, 2, 3, 4, G.5., Lillooet.
In spite of the government land reserve at the proposed junction of the Yale and Lillooet roads, Watson, his brother, and their friend McKinnon staked out several parcels of land which eventually became the site of Clinton town. On a portion of this, and beside Wright's wagon road, the partners built a roadhouse. During the 1862 season this facility, a one-room log cabin measuring 20 by 40 feet, catered to an increasing number of miners and pack-train operators. Once the actual junction of the road was determined, the partners built a large, two-storey log house 115 by 65 feet, consisting of three rooms on the main floor, with five bedrooms above. In the spring of 1863 the following advertisement appeared in the Victoria *Colonist*:

"WATSON & CO, of the 47 MILE HOUSE, situated at the junction of the Lillooet, Lytton & Alexandria Wagon Road Beg

The Clinton Hotel, CA 1865. (COURTESY BCARS, GENTILE COLLECTION #1)

To Inform The Travelling Public That They Have Erected &
Are Now Fitting Up Near Their Old Stand A Large &
Commodious House To Be Known As The Clinton Hotel." [21]

The advertisement, of considerable length, went on to describe the
large bar-room, private sitting room, bedrooms fitted up with "Pulu"
mattresses, free bunks for those who brought their own blankets, and
the expert cooking of the "culinary department". Prices were very
reasonable, with weekly board at $15, daily $2.50, and single meals
and beds at one dollar each. The stabling of animals was also one
dollar a night, with grain extra.

"Pulu" mattresses came into vogue in the early 1830s. Stuffed with
a fibrous material found in the base of the leaf stalks of the Hawaiian
fern tree, or pulu plant, these light-weight mattresses were a great
boon to the roadhouse keepers, who had to consider the cost of
freight. Pulu was later replaced by kapok, a similar light-weight
material, found to be verminproof and more resistant to moisture.

Once the Cariboo Road was completed in 1865, prices fell, with
most roadhouses charging only 50¢ each for beds, meals and
stabling. As proprietors of the hotel, Watson and Company engaged
Mr. and Mrs. James Uren to manage their facility, but it was Jane
Uren who operated the roadhouse, as Mr. Uren, a freighter on the
road, was seldom home. Jane Uren soon established a reputation as
an excellent housekeeper and cook, providing meals that included
such delicacies as fresh beef, vegetables, and fruit, brought in on her
husband's freight wagon.

By 1868 Watson and Company had sold their Clinton Hotel to
Joseph L. Smith, for years the proprietor of a number of roadhouses
along the Douglas Portage and at Port Pemberton. Upon taking
possession Smith and his partner, Tom Marshall, enlarged the hotel,
adding wings to either end of the original building. Here they established a billiard room, and a ladies' parlour. It was in Smith's billiard
room in 1868 that the first of many annual Clinton Balls took place.
Designed to relieve the mid-winter blues, the event was held soon
after the new year. Tickets were five dollars a couple, and included
not only bed and breakfast for two nights, but also stabling and hay
for four horses. So popular was the idea that revellers continued their
merry-making all winter, going from one community to another.

Following Joseph Smith's death his wife married his partner, Tom
Marshall. Mrs. Marshall was cook and housekeeper at the Clinton
Hotel for many years. Rough and ready by nature, she was known to

swear and smoke, and several diaries mention her habit of lighting a match on the sole of her shoe. In spite of this Mrs. Marshall knew how to treat her valued guests, as noted by Sarah Crease, an overnight visitor at the Clinton Hotel on September 9, 1880. In her diary Mrs. Crease gave Mrs. Marshall top marks for her accommodations, a pleasant change from her usual criticisms:

"Lovely drive into Clinton, reached Mrs. Marshall's at 6.00 p.m. cold and tired. House very clean and comfortable. Mrs. Marshall an honest talking, rough, kind hearted woman. Food very good, delicious butter and cream, bed soft and comfortable. Breakfasted on delicious oatmeal porridge and cream. At lunch Mrs Marshall brought me a plate of soup and entertained me with an hour's gossip about herself and her neighbours." [22]

While two other facilities were built in Clinton, the Dominion Hotel, which burned down in 1908, and the Palace Hotel, which became a boarding house in the early 1900s, (and still stands today), the Clinton Hotel was always considered to be the best, and for some years was the oldest hotel in B.C. In May 1958, just after the annual ball, the townsfolk of Clinton were awakened early to hear fire sirens wailing and people running toward the north end of town where the old hotel stood engulfed in flames. Three people, a man, his wife, and their child, died in the blaze; when the fire broke out, the manager had called all the guests personally, and although the little family had answered the call, they had gone back to sleep. The hotel burned to the ground, and was not rebuilt.

CHAPTER SIX

NICOMEN TO CLINTON AND GREEN LAKE HOUSE

RUMOURS of gold in the interior of British Columbia had circulated since 1852. A few years later it was discovered in several locations, at Fort Colville on the Columbia River, at Fort Hope on the Fraser, and in 1856 on the Thompson River, just south of Nicomen.

NICOMEN HOUSE, THE 68 MILE POST FROM YALE.
Lot 13, G.1., Lytton.
The gold rush near the Indian village of Nicomen prompted such a flurry of staking and increased population that by 1860 Nicomen had been included in the proposed route of a wagon road. On a tour of inspection that summer, Governor Douglas ate breakfast at Nicomen House, 12 miles east of Lytton. The community boomed again during the construction of the road in 1862 and Nicomen House flourished as a result. The gold rush faded by 1864 and with the establishment of Barnard's stagecoach route, Nicomen was bypassed.

During the 1870s, when optimism ran high over the proposed route of the Canadian Pacific Railway, Nicomen House was owned by John Clapperton, a tax collector at Spence's Bridge. By 1876 Clapperton had sold to George Coxon, storekeeper and freight agent at Nicomen, whose daughter, Alice, took over the operation of the roadhouse. Such was the situation when a young Englishman, Joseph S. Place, arrived to work for Mr. Coxon in 1877. Within the space of a few years Alice Coxon had married Joseph Place, borne him two children, and died giving birth to a third. Under these sad circumstances Joe Place left Nicomen, sending his children away to be raised by relatives. Following the death of his father-in-law, Place inherited Nicomen House. The property was Crown Granted in 1884, and sold shortly afterward.

With the arrival of the C.P.R. Nicomen became known as Thompson Siding, where a frame-built roadside house was located just south of the railway underpass. At this time the roadhouse was owned and operated by Mr. and Mrs. Art Clements, known to be a colourful pair. In the rough and boisterous atmosphere of those early days Mrs. Clements was more than able to hold her own. On one occasion while she was hostess at the house, a quarrelsome customer was forcibly overcome by the buxom lady, and had to be rushed to hospital in Lytton, where he was treated for concussion. Apparently the victim had been dealt a fearsome blow with a chamber pot.

COOK'S FERRY, 1861. THE 80 MILE HOUSE.
Lot 438, G.1., Kamloops.
Mortimer Cook and his partner, Charles Kimball, had been freighters for the Hudson's Bay Company when they started a ferry service in 1861, across the Thompson River about a mile south of the Nicola River. Close to the ferry a roadhouse, store, and blacksmith shop were built on the south side of the river. With Kimball's departure a year later Cook carried on alone, and the area became known as "Cook's Ferry".

Returning from their two-year expedition across Canada in 1863, Lord Milton and Dr. Cheadle spent a couple of days at Cook's Ferry, where they met the proprietor of the roadhouse, and enjoyed the culinary efforts of the black cook, John Jackson Ferguson:

"Met Mr. Cook, an Ohio man, the usual Yankee, but quieter. Had delicious supper, very clean and well cooked. Milton and I went to bed with headaches from three drinks of brandy during the day." [1]

While still at Cook's Ferry, Dr. Cheadle wrote in his diary the following startling information:

> "Before starting out this morning some Indians came in with the news that they had found a dead body stranded in the shallows of the river close by. When we went to look at it with Mr. McKay, [the Express man] from certain marks tattooed upon the arm, and from a published description, it was decided that this was one of Thomas Clegg's murderers in the crime committed near the 141 Mile House, [Cariboo Road] two weeks before." [2]

SPENCE'S BRIDGE, 1865.

By 1865 Cook's ferry had been replaced by Thomas Spence's bridge, built a little upstream of the ferry, and Mortimer Cook had disposed of his holdings to entrepreneur T.G. Kirkpatrick. Fortunately for the new proprietor the excellent cook remained at the roadhouse to serve many more fine dinners. As it happens, cooking was only one of J.J. Ferguson's talents. In a photograph of the 80 Mile House, Ferguson is seen seated on the steps, entertaining the guests by playing his fiddle. By this time "Spence's Bridge", as it was

The 80 Mile House, Cook's Ferry, (now Spence's Bridge), CA 1866, with John Ferguson playing the fiddle. (COURTESY BCARS)

The Cariboo Road north of Yale, showing how the road was disrupted by the building of the railway. (COURTESY VANCOUVER PUBLIC LIBRARY)

now known, had become a community with a hotel, post office, telegraph operator, blacksmith shop, and two general stores. In 1876 land that included the old ferry site, the bridge approach, and the roadhouse was acquired by S. Mard Nelson, one of four enterprising Nelson brothers.

In September that year Sarah Crease, on a trip to Barkerville with her husband, Judge Henry Crease, reached "Cook's Ferry", as she still called it, and mentioned in her diary:

> "...went to Nelson's House. Bed in little drawing room. Mrs. Nelson rough, smart, and fond of children. Had a good supper in dining shed—bed soft and clean...room covered with pictures of children in very low art!"[3]

When the original wagon road north of Yale was put out of service by the building of the railways in the mid-1880s and early 1900s, most traffic went by way of Lillooet. For almost 40 years business was curtailed at the roadhouses and stores through the Fraser and Thompson River canyons. Plans to restore the original route were largely implemented in 1926, but it was another year before the 22 miles of road between Lytton and Spence's Bridge were completed. Travel brochures of 1926 did not include Spence's Bridge.

THE 84 MILE HOUSE, 1869.
Lot 22, G.1., Yale.
As a result of the "Big Bend Excitement", as the short-lived gold rush on the Columbia River was known, activity increased along the Cariboo wagon road between Yale, Cache Creek, and Savannah's Ferry. By 1863 Pierre Morens, originally from southern France, pre-empted 163 acres of land on the west bank of the Thompson River, four miles above Spence's Bridge. Here Morens established a farm and roadhouse beside the wagon road. By 1873 he had run into financial problems, and was forced to mortgage his farm to Claude Biget for $2,000, a deferred payment with interest at one and a half percent per month. In default of payment the property was to be sold at auction, but fortunately, Morens was able to meet his obligations.

Pierre Morens died at his home in the spring of 1897, but his wife and family carried on and received a Crown Grant on the property on March 3, 1913. Always known for their friendly hospitality and good meals, several generations of the Morens family continued to operate the roadhouse. The land there was still held by the family in 1939, in the name of Leon Morens.

OREGON JACK'S HOTEL, THE 96 MILE POST, 1863.
Lots 788, 789, G.1., Kamloops.
"Oregon Jack", whose real name was John or Jack Dowling, had been a gold miner in 1858 before turning to the more lucrative pursuit of packing. By 1862 he and his partner, Dominic Gavin, had pre-empted land about 16 miles northwest of Cook's Ferry where they opened a wayside house beside the trail, at the top of a long hill. Catering mostly to packers and freight-team operators, this early hostelry was said to have been somewhat wild and unruly. A reference made to Oregon Jack by a passerby in the 1880s described him as a vile-looking man with a red face, bald head and bowed legs. His chief claim to fame was the fact that he had not drawn a sober breath since arriving in B.C. Despite this, he was said to have been pleasant and hospitable to his guests at the roadhouse. The reputation given Jack Dowling could not have been altogether accurate. In the diaries of their neighbours the Cornwall brothers, both Dowling and his partner Gavin appear to be responsible farmers and loyal friends. Gavin was one of the first to assist the Cornwalls in settling their land in 1862. For many years both Dowling and Gavin were Christmas dinner guests of the Cornwalls, which in itself says something, for the

Cornwalls did not have to tolerate undesirables in their private company. Dowling also knew how to reciprocate. An entry in Henry Cornwall's diary of January 15, 1865, reads:

"Houghton, Cudlip, and I drove over to Oregon Jack's for dinner and back again the same night—got home about 1.00 a.m. A warm night—pleasant drive—we were feasted in great style having really a fine dinner with excellent pastry and egg nog afterwards." [4]

However, there is no doubt there were some pretty wild shindigs at Dowling's roadhouse, also mentioned by Henry Cornwall:

"Oregon Jack gave a Squaw dance, at which everybody got very drunk, I believe!" [5]

Following the deaths of Dominic Gavin and Jack Dowling in the 1890s their properties became part of the nearby Basque Ranch.

THE BASQUE RANCH, AT THE 97 MILE POST, 1860.
Lots 14, 17, 18, G.1., Lytton,
Lot 375 G.1., Kamloops.
As early as 1852 parties of American prospectors had entered British territory by way of the Okanagan where they found deposits of gold on the Thompson River. Further incursions were thwarted by hostile native Indians who attacked the American miners as they crossed the border from Washington until 1858, when miners arrived en masse by way of the Fraser River. At this time a few of those earlier prospectors returned to the Thompson River, not to mine, but to farm the land. One of these was Louis Antoine Minnaberriet, son of a French aristocrat from the Basque area of France.

Leaving home for the California goldfields in 1849, Louis later raised cattle on a ranch in Oregon. As one of a party of prospectors on the Thompson River in the early 1850s Minnaberriet returned with others of his countrymen in 1860 to establish a farm and road-house on land that became the 97 Mile post on the Cariboo wagon road. On his decision to settle permanently in B.C., Minnaberriet returned to Oregon in 1861 where he collected all his possessions, including a large herd of cattle and horses, before starting back for his new home beside the Thompson River. During the journey of many weeks several of the animals died; when the wagon wheels wore out, he finished the journey on solid wheels cut from pine trees. By 1862 Minnaberriet and his associates—the three Baron brothers, Jean, Fermin, and Gratin; Francois St. Paul; Jean Amparient; and Dominic Gorgie—had between them pre-empted over a thousand acres of good farmland. With grain and hay as their main crops, they also grew grapes and made them into wine, served at the roadhouse. Known as the Basque Ranch, by the 1880s all of this had become the property of Minnaberriet. There were two families of Minnaberriets, a native family and later a white family. For many years they lived and worked the large farm and operated the roadhouse, which was also a stagecoach stop. With the prospect of the Canadian Pacific Railway line passing through the area in 1883, the Basque Ranch was sold to two English brothers, Leonard and Walter Langley. The sale included 2,000 acres of land, stock, buildings, and machinery, all of which changed hands for $40,000. Following this, Louis Minnaberriet returned with his second family to France, leaving his native family behind in the Spence's Bridge area.

CORNWALL'S ASHCROFT HOUSE, 1863. THE 104 MILE HOUSE. Lots 15,16,17,G.1., Lillooet.

Just north of the Basque Ranch and adjoining the Bonaparte valley was the Cornwall brothers' ranch, where a roadhouse known as Ashcroft House first operated in 1863. Sons of Reverend A.C. Cornwall of Ashcroft House, Gloucestershire, England, Clement Francis Cornwall and his brother, Henry Pennant Cornwall, were direct descendants of a long line of British aristocracy. Both Clement and Henry were graduates of Cambridge University, and Clement in 1862 had been accepted at the Inner Temple at London where he would study law. During the winter of 1861 the English papers had been full of reports of the fabulous gold finds in the interior of B.C. Reading these with great interest, Clement and Henry became caught up in the excitement, so much so that they decided to give up their sheltered lives in England to seek their fortunes together in the new colony.

Leaving Southampton in April 1862, the young aristocrats reached Victoria on June 3, where they remained only long enough to obtain the necessary horses and supplies for a journey to the interior. Upon reaching Lillooet by way of Port Douglas, the brothers sought out Magistrate A.C. Elliot for advice and direction. Possibly due to his information, the Cornwalls changed their minds about mining, deciding instead to look for land suitable for farming, an occupation with which they were already familiar. For further advice Elliot gave them letters of introduction to Captain Martley and Donald McLean, two responsible men who had recently taken up large tracts of land in the district. In his capacity as government agent, Elliot would also have acquainted them with the recently instituted pre-emption regulations, and the wagon roads being built through the country that year. Crossing the Fraser River at Lillooet the Cornwalls travelled northeast to Hat Creek, where they entered the Bonaparte River valley, and came across the old Hudson's Bay Company pack trail leading to Fort Kamloops. Along this route, 26 miles north of Cook's Ferry, on a "desirable looking flat watered by two streams with fine surrounding range for cattle" they pre-empted two adjoining parcels of land of 160 acres each, on July 1, 1862.[6] Situated in a semi-arid climate, these lands, with irrigation, proved to be some of the most arable in the district, but this was only the beginning. Within ten years the Cornwall brothers had developed the most progressive farm in the district, extending over 6,000 acres, on which were kept over 1,500 head of cattle, an operating sawmill, grist mill, a market garden, and a popular roadhouse. Fortunately the Cornwalls kept interesting and informative diaries, and from these can be traced the history of a roadhouse that operated continuously for 75 years.

The Cornwalls developed their enterprise with impressive speed. This was due in part to their ability to hire labour, but also they themselves worked unbelievably hard, seven days a week to begin with. Contrary to common belief, the brothers were not financially subsidized. Following the initial investment of $10,000 from their own accounts in England, they borrowed further sums from their father and a cousin in New Zealand, all of which were paid back. Any profits they made in B.C. came from their own endeavours.

The first house built at Ashcoft, a single-storey log building with a steep shake roof, was ready for occupancy by the end of October 1862, containing a kitchen, living room with fireplace, two bedrooms and an attic. The attic proved to be of immediate financial benefit. No sooner had the Cornwalls moved in, set up a kitchen stove, and hired a Chinese cook, than they began to accommodate overnight guests who slept in the attic. The approach of winter brought passing miners from the north, and packers with their animals heading into the Bonaparte valley, a traditional wintering area. By December the Cornwalls had decided it would be worthwhile to build a larger house, a "public" roadhouse, beside the trail where a wagon road would soon pass through their property. While the roadhouse would be built of logs, lumber would be needed for floors, ceilings, and finishing. Since there were no sawmills nearby, two men, Pringle and Nicoll, were hired to whipsaw 11,147 feet of lumber in ten weeks for four cents a foot, and their food. Left-over material would be used later in the construction of a water wheel.

January 1863 was extremely cold with below-zero temperatures at night. Henry had been away in Victoria since early December, leaving Clement with the hired men to experience his first winter on the ranch. In his diary Clement complained that the house got very cold at night, freezing his beard and moustache to the blankets. By the end of February two men, "Cutter & Holes" were engaged for $175 to construct the roadhouse, a building 40 by 20 feet, containing two rooms and a kitchen on the main floor, with an attic above:

> "It seems like a large sum, but some say they couldn't do it for that price. It should not take more than six or seven weeks." [7]

While the house was being built other men were kept busy "up on the hill," cutting shakes for the roof. In March, as the building of the new roadhouse progressed, traffic increased at the "upper", or original house where the Chinese cook served meals to passing miners, this time on their way north. Henry Cornwall arrived back at the ranch on March 14, bringing with him many necessary supplies including seed to plant the fields. As Clement ploughed, Henry harrowed, and in April they sowed timothy and clover and put in a field of oats and barley. With the crops planted they directed their efforts to the roadhouse. Having secured a liquor licence from Magistrate Henry Ball in Lytton, the Cornwalls opened their road-house on April 30, 1863, taking in $29 the first day. In the bar-room of the "public", as the Cornwalls referred to the second house, framed pictures hung on painted walls, and a large mirror reflected a varied assortment of coloured liquor bottles standing behind the bar. Here, in overstuffed leather chairs, guests relaxed and read the latest English papers, sometimes three months old. Obviously, the opening of Ashcroft House, and especially the saloon, was the cause of some neighbourhood jealousy, as Clement mentioned in his diary:

> "A man from above complained that he was nearly poisoned by liquor at the Roadhouse. Very odd considering that it was the best I could get in Victoria for our own consumption!" [8]

The operations of the roadhouse and saloon at this time were handled by hired managers, one of whom was Charles A. Semlin who later became Premier of British Columbia. Once the heavy spring traffic had subsided, the roadhouse was generally quiet. In light of this the Chinese cook at the upper house was dismissed for the summer and Clement and Henry ate in the roadhouse. Two notable visitors in June were Reverends Sheepshanks and Knipe, who held evening service at the house. On a trip to Lytton in June, Clement noted the fine job of road making done by the Royal Engineers around the Bluffs, 800 yards north of Cook's Ferry. At the Engineers' camp, where Clement was invited to dinner by Lieutenant Palmer, he very much enjoyed the concert given by the men, who kept their instruments with them wherever they were sent.

During the heat of August while the Cornwalls were frantically busy harvesting their first crops, a number of guests arrived at the farm, filling both houses for a day or two. The visitors were inspecting that portion of the Cariboo Road north of Cook's Ferry to Clinton, under contract to James Hood in 1863. With Hood were the government overseers of the work, Walter Moberly and members of the Royal Engineers. Also at the house was the Cornwalls' neighbour, Captain Venables, who disgraced himself the first evening when, in a drunken state, he started a fight with Sergeant Morey. In October, when Judge Begbie and his entourage remained overnight, he and Clement stayed up late discussing some of Begbie's latest cases. The roadhouse was very busy again, signifying the end of the mining season up north:

> "A good many men are going down and the 'Public' does a fair business, the consumption of food very large." [9]

By November the weather had turned really cold and, as it seemed impossible to keep the roadhouse warm, it was decided to close it for the meantime, as Clement wrote:

> "Moved all the things from the roadhouse, the job occupying all day. ...Shut up the House, it being far too cold for winter use." [10]

A few days before this Dr. Cheadle, Lord Milton, and one other stage passenger, Captain Harrison, arrived quite late at Ashcroft House. They were hungry, but the cook, who had already gone to bed, was not happy to see them:

"Got to Cornwall's Ranche about 9.00 o'clock—they have two houses, one wayside kept by an employee and their own home some half mile distant. The Chinaman cook had gone to bed and turned out very sulky to provide us with beef steaks. Our fellow passenger Capt Harrison would have toast, which added to his ill temper. The younger Cornwall (the elder being down at Victoria for supplies) sent word down that he would be glad to see us at the other house and Milton and I walked up there after supper—found a tall, regular, First Trinity man who received us very hospitably—he took his degree in 1859." [11]

Winter came with a vengeance in January 1864, but did not last long, and by February the snow was gone. Once again Clement wrote in his diary of the preparations to open the roadhouse:

"Finished painting in the roadhouse." [12]

Three days later word came that the wagon road, built the summer before, had fallen in at several places so that the wagon with supplies for the roadhouse could not get through. Despite this inconvenience the roadhouse opened on February 27:

"A bright sunny day ... a good many men on the road up, and the House is full." [13]

Among that company was a band of Cornish miners who sang and performed at the "public". However, there were other visitors who did not meet with Clement's approval:

"An awful specimen of a woman at the roadhouse tonight." [14]

A new Chinese cook arrived at the roadhouse on March 4, but the very next day Clement reported:

"The new cook got dead drunk in the afternoon....Henry started out at 11.00 pm up to the Junction [Cache Creek] to overtake "Owen" the China Cook we had last year." [15]

A couple of days later Clement's diary mentioned that Henry had rehired the old cook, but only by promising him higher wages. Spring of 1864 had come a lot earlier than the year before and with the warm weather and balmy breezes Clement's attitude was one of optimism for the new season:

"Beautiful day, young grass springing rapidly all about. Lots of travel, and the road looks quite lively with waggons, pack trains, buggies and pedestrians. We hauled out some rails and slabs to the Public today, where we are about to build a new kitchen." [16]

Thus ended a full year of operation at Ashcroft House.

By 1865, having developed their ranch to a point where they could relax a little, the Cornwall brothers established a racetrack on the field beside the roadhouse. A year later, on October 29, 1866, the *British Colonist* reported the Fall Races at Cornwalls' ranch which included the Ashcroft Derby, the Lytton Steeple Chase, and the Yale Steeple Chase. To this most prestigious event came local horse breeders and entrepreneurs from all over the colony. The Cornwalls themselves competed, having by this time raised a few thoroughbred horses of their own. The meets, which went on for years, were always held on the manor grounds where they brought business to the roadhouse. During the 1870 Fall Races as much as $1,500 was taken in throughout the two-day event.

Over the years Cornwall's roadhouse was advertised in various newspapers. One of the earliest of the ads appeared in *The Cariboo Sentinel* in the spring of 1866. The unique wording, so different from the usual exaggerated descriptions of roadhouses, would suggest that it had been composed by the Cornwalls themselves:

"Ashcroft House.
Messrs. Cornwalls.
    At this well known House, halfway between Spence's Bridge and Clinton, on the Yale Route, Travellers will find Good accommodation, of living, liquors and of wine. Fresh butter, milk, and vegetables. Good stabling and cheap feed." [17]

While Clement Cornwall served as district magistrate in 1867, Ashcroft House became the site of the first court case in the area. The first post office in the Bonaparte district also opened at Ashcroft House, on July 1, 1865, with Clement Cornwall as postmaster. When Clement's professional career interfered, and later when he left Ashcroft to take up his duties as Lieutenant-Governor of B.C., Henry

The Cornwalls' "upper house", CA 1863. (COURTESY BCARS)

Cornwall took over the operation of the ranch, and the post office, which remained open until April 1, 1886.

Following his marriage to Charlotte Pemberton of Victoria in November 1870, Clement and his bride returned to Ashcroft farm where they resided at the "upper house". Over the years five children were born to Clement and Charlotte.

At this time Henry moved down to the "public" roadhouse, where he remained, even after his marriage in 1874 to Mary Josephine Eyre, a step-daughter of Captain Martley of Pavilion. As their family of four children grew up, the roadhouse continued operating with Chinese cooks in the kitchen and Indian girls from the nearby reserve to do the cleaning.

It was not until the late 1880s that the Cornwalls' roadhouse became known as "Ashcroft Manor". For many years it had been known simply as "Cornwall's", and "Ashcroft House". Following the survey of the railway town on the Thompson River six miles from the Cornwalls' ranch, the community was officially named "Ashcroft Station" in honour of Lieutenant-Governor Clement Cornwall. Gradually the word "Station" was dropped, and the town became just "Ashcroft". In order to avoid confusion between their ranch and the town, the Cornwalls renamed their lodge "Ashcroft Manor".

With Henry Cornwall's death in 1892 at age 54, his family moved to Cherry Creek near Kamloops, where Henry Jr. operated a ranch and guest lodge during the 1920s and '30s. Clement Cornwall, who lived with his family in Victoria for some years, died there in 1910. His remains were later interred in the family graveyard at Ashcroft Manor.

Over the years, and according to the needs of each family, various changes were made to Ashcroft Manor. During the early 1900s, when Clement's married daughter Caroline, her husband George Barclay and their four children lived there, they added a second storey to the roadhouse, which greatly increased the accommodation. Unfortunately, while at work in her flower garden Caroline was bitten by a rattlesnake, and died soon afterward. During the 1930s a granddaughter of Henry Cornwall, Gwendolyne Mary Parker and her husband J. Alan McLennan Parker, took over Ashcroft Manor with five acres of surrounding land. During their tenure the "upper house", rented at the time, burned down in a fire that consumed both the historic building and an original barn close by.

The last of the Cornwall family to live in Ashcroft Manor were Henry Cornwall's great granddaughter Vashti (Parker) Fisk, her husband T.C. "Trav" Fisk, and their three sons, who purchased the manor house property in 1972. By this time the old house, badly in need of restoration, was closed to the public. For some years the Fisks approached various agencies, including the provincial government, for assistance in a restoration project, but to no avail. As the years rolled by, the old house slowly deteriorated until 1981 when it was purchased by Tom and Susan Saunders of Prince George. Today the restored manor has become a visitor's delight, not only for its historical significance but also as a showplace for beautiful gifts and crafts. Built nearby and in keeping with the old roadhouse is a charming restaurant and tea house where refreshments are served within, or outside in the lovely English gardens surrounding the buildings.

ASHCROFT.

While the building of the Canadian Pacific Railway disrupted traffic on the road between Yale and Spence's Bridge in the mid-1880s, it brought new enterprise and employment to the interior through the development of the town of Ashcroft. The history of the town actually began with the building of a "hotel" beside a ferry landing on the east bank of the Thompson River in 1883.

BARNES AND BRINK.

During the 1860s two American adventurers, John Christopher Barnes and his partner, William Brink, earned a living packing on the trails between Lillooet and the Cariboo goldfields. By the end of the decade the partners had saved enough funds to settle down to farming. The land they chose, pre-empted by Barnes in 1868, a flat river bench on the southeast bank of the Thompson River, had been overlooked by earlier settlers due to its isolated location. During the 1870s these men both took native wives and raised families on their land, known as the Butte Ranch, where Brink did most of the farming and Barnes pursued his career as a pack-train operator. As the railroad was constructed west into B.C. in the early 1880s, it became apparent that a western station would be necessary somewhere north of Kamloops on the east bank of the Thompson River. The Butte Ranch property became the logical site. Unfortunately, Billy Brink did not live to appreciate the fact that their land, "on the wrong side of the river" had suddenly become prime real estate. Brink's son-in-law, Oliver Evans, however, could see the possibilities very clearly, and with John Barnes he made sure the opportunity did not escape. Acting quickly, the pair raised funds to construct a ferry on which they transported lumber and supplies across the river to the flat on the east bank.

THE THOMPSON RIVER HOTEL, 1883.

There they built a "hotel" not far from the surveyed track line. Named the "Thompson River Hotel", it contained a few rooms and a well-stocked saloon. Dr. Mark S. Wade, staff physician for C.P.R. construction crews in the early 1880s, made a trip to the site of Ashcroft in June 1884, when there were just two buildings there, one of which he referred to as a "wretched establishment dubbed as a hotel". [18] Upon entering the building Dr. Wade was asked by the proprietor to examine a man who was lying comatose in an upstairs bedroom. "He's been taking opium, and I can't wake him up," was the remark. Upon examining the man, Dr. Wade was unable to connect the opium story with his condition, but noticed a recent blow to his left temple. While the proprietor kept insisting that opium was the cause of the problem, Dr. Wade overheard a conversation between him and a man named William Abieshire, who had fought with the patient the previous evening, hitting him over the head with a shovel. The man died that night, and an inquest was held soon afterward, when the actual cause of death was determined. By this time Abieshire had fled the country, the provincial police hot on his trail. The proprietor of the Thompson River Hotel was charged with protecting a criminal, while Abieshire escaped to California, never to be heard from again.

By the time the railway arrived on the flats of the Butte Ranch, Barnes and Evans had surveyed a townsite around the hotel and were selling the first of many land lots.

THE ASHCROFT HOTEL, 1886.
With the railway station established on the flat, a new facility, the Ashcroft Hotel, built by Oliver Evans and financier E.E. Bligh, appeared across the street. The building of a bridge across the Thompson River in 1884 caused the little community on the east bank to more than double in size. At first it was known as Barnes Station, and then Ashcroft Station, but the name Ashcroft, after the Cornwall family, has survived. By 1886 many businesses formerly located in Yale had moved their operations to Ashcroft. With a population of over a hundred, the new community included four general stores, three blacksmith shops, a school, three transportation agencies, and two hotels. In opposition to the Ashcroft Hotel, the Cargile House was built by William Cargile in 1886.

By 1890 Oliver Evans had sold his interests in the Ashcroft Hotel to his associate, E.E. Bligh, who took on a new partner, William Lyne, formerly of the Pinchbeck and Lyne ranch at Williams Lake. Following his marriage to Mary Collingsworth of Wisconsin in 1887 Lyne had dissolved his alliance with Pinchbeck, and with his new wife moved to Ashcroft. By 1898 he had become sole owner of the Ashcroft Hotel. At this time the facility was considerably enlarged and completely refurbished. Prior to the re-opening in January 1898, the following advertisement appeared in the *B.C. Mining Journal*:

"ASHCROFT HOTEL,
WILLIAM LYNE PROP.

This hotel has recently been refitted and refurbished.
A new wing, 50' X 26'containing 19 rooms including
bath and sample rooms will be open by Oct 1.
Good table and good service.
THE ONLY 1st CLASS HOTEL IN TOWN." [19]

The additon of the new wing doubled the accommodations and completely changed the outward appearance of the hotel. From a single-roofed, nondescript, two-storey structure it became an imposing "L" shape, facing two streets. Broad, second-storey verandahs running along the sides of the building allowed guests the opportunity to enjoy

Ashcroft's pleasant climate without being exposed to the dust from the streets below. Many of the town's early outdoor events were viewed from these vantage points—horse racing down the middle of Railway Avenue, and in the winter, ice skating on an empty lot beside the railway station. Always painted white, the building stood out clean and distinct against a backdrop of bare brown hills. Equally distinctive was the hotel's interior. At a time when a large proportion of the population was single men, the hotel saloon with its swinging half-doors, long polished bar, plate-glass mirrors and framed lithographs of languishing buxom women, was crowded every night. In contrast to this, Protestant Church services were held in the dining room of the hotel, which at times were said to have emptied the bars. On occasion the hotel catered to special dinners. The *B.C. Mining Journal* of January 12, 1897, reported on the Annual Dinner of the Yale and Lillooet Pioneer Society, held at the Ashcroft Hotel a few nights before:

"Our host, William Lyne, had spared no pains in decorating the dining room, arranging the tables, and most important of all, in preparing the following excellent menu enjoyed by over thirty guests:

SOUP
OYSTER.
FISH
BOILED SALMON and EGG SAUCE.
ROAST
BEEF, MUTTON, TURKEY, CHICKEN.
ENTREE
OYSTER PATTIES.
VEGETABLES
MASHED POTATOES, GREEN PEAS, CORN.
PASTRY
PLUM PUDDING & BRANDY SAUCE.
BLANC MANGE, JELLY, JELLY PUFFS.
PIES
LEMON, CUSTARD, APPLE,
PUMPKIN.
CAKE
FRUIT CAKE, JELLY CAKE.
DESSERT
FRUIT, NUTS, RAISINS, ETC...
TEA, COFFEE, ETC." [20]

This extensive list of choices would please the most sophisticated tastes and bore no resemblance to the meals served at the first crude roadhouses of earlier years.

Following the death of William Lyne in 1903 the hotel was sold to William Thompson of Vancouver. Among later owners were Albert Johnson, James Veasey, and John McGillivray. On July 7, 1916, a devastating fire that began in the Ashcroft Hotel destroyed a large part of the town, costing the community an estimated $500,000. John McGillivray, owner of the hotel at the time, soon rebuilt a modern facility on the same site, before selling it to Oscar Olson. The lobby of this fine hotel, a spacious area filled with large potted plants and a distinctive floor covering of oversized black and white tiles, was also home to a gregarious parrot. Housed in a big metal cage the bird, with a large vocabulary of both pleasant and cheeky greetings, delighted and insulted guests and passersby for many years. Unfortunately this building also burned down, on November 8, 1974, and was not rebuilt.

CACHE CREEK, 1861.
Lot 104, G.2., Yale-Lytton.
The land on which the settlement of Cache Creek is located had, in 1861, been part of the pre-emptions of Donald McLean, retired Chief Trader of the Hudson's Bay Company, and his several sons. As F.W. Laing, in his report of 1939, pointed out:

"This land was referred to in other records as McLean's FARM as distinguished from McLean's Station, or restaurant, located just north of the mouth of Hat Creek." [21]

Following the death of Donald McLean in the Chilcotin War of 1864 these claims were abandoned until 1872, when more or less the same land was pre-empted again by James Campbell.

BONAPARTE HOUSE, 1862.
In anticipation of the building of a wagon road in 1862, James Orr opened a wayside house on top of Rattlesnake Hill, just south of the present village of Cache Creek. Known as Bonaparte House, it operated until the spring of 1865 when Orr sold out to Charles Semlin and Philip Parke, employees of the Cornwall brothers at Ashcroft House. That winter Semlin and Parke had Orr's building moved down to the foot of Rattlesnake Hill, to the

junction of the Cariboo Road with the new road to Savannah's Ferry. Prior to the opening of Bonaparte House in April 1866, an addition was built on, which almost doubled its capacity. An advertisement in *The Cariboo Sentinel* points out the strategic new location of the roadhouse:

> "Bonaparte House....Semlin & Parke, Proprietors.
> At the junction of the Cariboo and Big Bend Roads is now open for accommodation. Distance from Clinton 26 miles, from Savannah steamboat landing 22 miles, from Spence's Bridge 30 miles. Travellers will find prices and accommodation to suit the times. Give them a call. Stabling, hay and grain, attentive hostlers. Stage leaves here twice a week for Big Bend and Yale, and once a week for Cariboo." [22]

The short-lived Big Bend mines brought a great deal of business to Bonaparte House, where the saloon was a favourite watering hole for the crew working on G.B. Wright's wagon road to Savannah's Ferry.

CACHE CREEK HOUSE, 1868.

In 1868, anxious to develop his own ranch at Cache Creek, Philip Parke sold his interest in Bonaparte House to William H. Sanford, better known as "Boston" Sanford, who renamed the roadhouse "Cache Creek House". Sanford and Charles Semlin had been partners in the pre-emption of a large tract of land located in an area now known as Boston Flats. In 1870 while Sanford was busy financing an irrigation project to carry water to Boston Flats, he sold his interest in the roadhouse to Semlin. Semlin later gave up Cache Creek House, trading it to James Campbell in exchange for the Dominion Ranch, near Cache Creek. During Campbell's tenure of seven years the roadhouse was rented to J.T. Jones, former headmaster of the Cache Creek Boarding School, who enlarged and improved the building by raising the roof and adding dormer windows. By 1878 Cache Creek House was owned by James A. Newland, an agent for the B.C. Express Company, but not for long. On a return visit to Cache Creek on October 22, 1880, Sarah Crease mentioned Mr. Newland in her diary, saying that he was "giving up hotel and barkeeping for employment as storekeeper for Mr. Onderdonk, at Kamloops." [23]

In charge of Cache Creek House was Mrs. Uriah Nelson, wife of the new owner. Remaining overnight, the Creases "found a bright warm room waiting for our reception, and a more comfortable bedroom than before—which we took possession of after a good supper." [24]

The next morning however, Sarah Crease wrote:

"In the morning on my clothes I found a horrible—-, the first met with on our journey hitherto." [25]

Without mentioning the awful word, in the margin of her diary Mrs. Crease had drawn the outline of a bedbug, with a capital "B" on it.

THE 12 MILE HOUSE, (NORTH OF ASHCROFT) 1893.
Part of Lot 93, G.1., Lillooet.
Cole F. McDonald established the 12 Mile House in 1893, shortly after the arrival of the C.P.R. at Ashcroft, when the road teemed with freight wagons hauling machinery to the mines of the Cariboo. Situated on a pleasant flat beside the original wagon road, which at that time ran along the west side of the valley, the roadhouse was part of a small farm, 12 miles northwest of Ashcroft.

A native of eastern Canada, Cole McDonald had arrived in Ashcroft with a C.P.R. carpenter gang in 1888 where he and a partner operated McDonald and Rankin's blacksmith shop and wheelwright business for a few years. After his marriage to Rose Veasey in 1892 McDonald rented Hat Creek House for a year before establishing his own farm and roadhouse at the 12 Mile post.

Photographs of the 12 Mile House taken in 1912 show that the building had recently been enlarged to more than double its original size. An imposing, well-kept, white frame building with two dormer windows in the upper storey, it had at least a dozen rooms including a large, fully stocked saloon. During the 20 years of its operation, McDonald's 12 Mile House was a successful business. Its location, a full day's run from Ashcroft, the availability of McDonald's blacksmithing services, and the sociable neighbourhood pub, all contributed to its continued popularity, especially with the freighters. In the 1890s and early 1900s the schedules of the B. X. Stage included the 12 Mile House as the first stop-over point on the journey north of Ashcroft.

To provide an education for the ten McDonald children and several of the Robertson family from Upper Hat Creek, a school opened in 1907, close to the 12 Mile House. Nina Robertson, eldest daughter of Mr. and Mrs. John Robertson, remembered the McDonald family very well. The Robertson children who lived on a farm ten miles away drove themselves to school by horse and buggy every day. Occasionally, when one of them forgot to take lunch along, they would walk over to the roadhouse, where Mrs. McDonald fed them free of charge. Apparently Rose McDonald and her daughters did the housework at the roadhouse while a Chinese cook prepared the meals. The five McDonald boys did the outside chores and helped their father in the blacksmith shop.

In 1914, as abruptly as it had started, the operation of the 12 Mile House ended, when Cole McDonald, at 50 years of age, suffered a fatal heart attack. Following this Mrs. McDonald and her large family left the area to live in Victoria. Today, the land surrounding the 12 Mile House is part of the Hat Creek Ranch, but the site can still be seen. Winding through the front yard of Hat Creek House, the original road runs south for half a mile, past where the 12 Mile House once stood. From there the road continues on through the Cache Creek Indian Reserve, where it joins the present Highway 97.

HAT CREEK HOUSE.
Lots 93, 94, G.1., Lillooet.

In August 1860, shortly before his retirement from the Hudson's Bay Company, Chief Trader Donald McLean took up residence at Hat Creek. There, on an open flat near the junction of two trails to Lillooet and Fort Kamloops, McLean built several log buildings, one of which served as a roadhouse and store, where he catered to passing miners and pack-train operators. While "McLean's Station" was mentioned in the diaries of James Douglas and Bishop Hills in 1861, it was the Reverend Ebenezer Robson in 1862 who first mentioned any details about the roadhouse:

"I was interested in Mr. McLean, so decided to put up at his wayside House in the Bonaparte valley that night. When I arrived at the sprawling group of cabins, I was amazed, for never, since I started my journey, had I come across such a gathering of men, women, children, cattle, horses, dogs and insects. My horse was turned out to grass, and I waited long for my supper, being prepared by a Chinaman who was said to have graduated in the employ of the Shuswap Chief St. Paul. The meal when I got it was not inviting but which I ate as I felt I must fortify myself against the coming day's work....I did not take a bed, for the bunks were as hard as boards, the pillows seemed to be flour sacks filled with grass, and the dark looking blankets had enwrapped too many sweaty, unwashed bodies. So placing my Mexican saddle against the wall, and spreading my saddle cloth over it, I pulled off my boots, said my prayers, and using my coat as a blanket, slept the sleep of the weary....Poor McLean, I never saw him again for he was shot to death in the Chilcotin war in 1864....I met three of his sons later, as prisoners, convicted of murder and outlawry, for which they and one other paid the supreme penalty." [26]

Although the name "McLean" was not mentioned, R. Byron Johnson clearly described Donald McLean, his family, and the roadhouse at Hat Creek in 1863:

"We stopped on our third night from Lytton at the wayside House of an old Scotsman who had served the H.B.C., and whose strapping half breed sons came forth from the paternal roof-tree to welcome us to its shelter. We passed a merry evening with the old man who told us many stirring stories of his former wild life....As the aperture that served for a window was covered with a mosquito bar, we lay down in our blankets on the earthen floor in the hope of a comfortable rest. This was not to be, alas, for in the middle of the night the Irishman with whom we travelled felt the need to bathe his face in the creek, and going outside, left the door open. After this there was no sleep, the mosquitoes descending on us in swarms." [27]

In spite of his several enterprises at Hat Creek in the early 1860s, Donald McLean did not apply for legal tenure of the land, but instead pre-empted many acres at the junction of Cache Creek and the Bonaparte River, the later site of the settlement of Cache Creek.

Following McLean's untimely death in the Chilcotin War of 1864, his wife Sophia and her family remained at Hat Creek for several years. At this same time Neil McArthur, also a former Hudson's Bay Company employee, pre-empted 160 acres just south of McLean's, at the mouth of Hat Creek, on January 29, 1861. To this property he moved a log building and a barn abandoned by the fur traders from across the Bonaparte River.

R.D. Cumming, owner and editor of the *Ashcroft Journal,* wrote of these relics in April 1953:

"There is an historic barn at the mouth of Hat Creek where it enters the Bonaparte River, constructed of unbarked cotton-woods with roof supports of huge barked Fir or Pine, a foot or more in diameter. It was built by the Hudson's Bay Co in the 1840's, and beside it there used to stand a home for company employees when they came down from Hat Creek, which was the hunting grounds of the Company." [28]

On March 10, 1866, prior to his departure for the Big Bend gold mines, McArthur conveyed his land at Hat Creek to George Dunne, a teamster on the Cariboo Road. At this time a description of the improvements on the property included "a dwelling house, barn, six outbuildings, and fencing around the fields." [29] The following year Dunne acquired 50 acres of McLean's ranch from Sophia McLean. In his application of September 1871 for purchase of a final 20 acres between the 117 and 118 Mile posts on the west side of the Bonaparte River Dunne mentioned:

"The land is and has been occupied by me since 1866. I have expended a large sum of money in buildings and other improve-ments." [30]

By the close of 1871 Dunne had acquired all the land included in the later survey of Lots 93 and 94, G.1. Lillooet.

On January 10, 1873, these lands, with their improvements, were mortgaged to Jerome Harper of Clinton for $2,000. Hat Creek House was leased out to various entrepreneurs who paid an annual rent: in 1876 proprietor Gus Schubert paid $500. When Harper died in California before Dunne's mortgage was paid, his brother Thaddeus sold the property to William Cargile of Dog Creek on June 1, 1881, for $3,000. On receiving a Crown Grant for Lots 93 and 94, G.1. Lillooet in February 1887, Cargile sold Hat Creek House and ranch to Steven Tingley of the B.C. Express Company, who operated it as a stage stop and horse ranch. During his tenure Tingley built a barn large enough to accommodate 200 horses.

While general opinion concedes that a nucleus of McLean's road-house of 1860 exists within Hat Creek House, it is still not certain as to which of the owners or occupants of the land built the roadhouse that stands today. George Dunne's land application of September 1871 which stated that he had recently spent "a large sum of money in buildings", gives rise to the possibility that Dunne built the first stages of Hat Creek House. However, the 1870s were not a time of prosperity for the roadhouses. Hat Creek House, as it stands today, was probably a restoration and expansion of Dunne's building, by William Cargile in the mid-1880s. After the arrival of the C.P.R. at Ashcroft, many roadhouses north of there expanded their facilities. The full-length verandah and drop siding of Hat Creek House, indicative of the 1880s, may have been added by Steven Tingley.

Standing behind Hat Creek House today is the McLean cabin, said to be a relic from McLean's original ranch on the north side of Hat Creek. The small, squared-log building with dovetailed corners, quite different from the usual Hudson's Bay Company construction, was said to have been built in 1863. This building was mentioned by Sarah Crease in her diary of October 13, 1880:

> "In the valley of the Bonaparte, close to Hat Creek House, stands the cottage of old McLean whose three sons are now in prison at New Westminster for murder and horse stealing." [31]

By 1910, when Charles Doering, president of the B.C. Brewing Company, bought Hat Creek ranch as a retirement home, the road-house had reached the proportions of a hotel, with 20 rooms, a kitchen, a large sitting room and bar, and various store rooms, but no plumbing. The operation of a roadhouse was not a priority with Mr. Doering whose main interests were in raising fine thoroughbred horses and shorthorn cattle. While the Doerings lived in the drafty old building it was closed to the public.

The last private owner of Hat Creek House, J. Basil Jackson, stepson of Charles Doering, assumed control of the ranch following Doering's death in April 1927. Jackson and his wife, the former Dorothy Parke of Cache Creek, also lived in the rambling old road-house until 1952, when a new home was built nearby. After her husband's death in the 1970s, Mrs. Jackson sold Hat Creek ranch, less a few acres, to B.C. Hydro, in connection with the development of the Hat Creek Coal Company. At this time the preservation of the several historic buildings, including the roadhouse, barn and black-smith shop, a vintage smokehouse, and ancient bunkhouse, became a major concern of Mrs. Jackson and many residents of the area. Because of her insistence, and the support of the Cache Creek and Kamloops Historical Societies the new land owners co-operated, demonstrating their good intentions by re-roofing Hat Creek House. Later, when the Hat Creek Coal Company withdrew its proposals the ranch was sold again. In 1981, Hat Creek House and its adjacent buildings were purchased by the B.C. government as a heritage site. Restoration began soon afterward and was completed in 1987, when the building was opened to the public.

SCOTTY'S RESTAURANT, THE 121 MILE HOUSE FROM YALE.
Lot 468, G.1., Lillooet.

William Donaldson, popularly known as "Scotty", a colourful Orkney Islander, settled on the west bank of the Bonaparte River in 1860 where he built a log cabin, ran a few cattle, and kept a roadhouse beside the trail to the Cariboo. It was September 1862 before Donaldson made application to pre-empt 160 acres of land, about four miles north of McLean's. The property was Crown Granted in 1899.

The earliest documentation of Scotty's tenure at this site appears on Judge Begbie's map of 1861, just north of "MacDonald's", (Ranald and Allan McDonald, sons of Hudson's Bay Company factor Archibald McDonald). Built beside the old pack trail to the Cariboo via Loon Lake, a well-used route prior to 1864, Donaldson's roadhouse did a roaring business, as described in two separate accounts of 1862. The first of these, part of a report by engineer Walter Moberly, was not very complimentary:

> "Being hungry, I requested Scotty to provide us with a meal, whereupon he produced a frying pan of stale flap jacks and a pan of milk. Each flap jack was about 3 ins. in diameter, and ½ inch thick. Having demolished as many of the unsavoury cakes and drunk as many cups of milk as it took to appease our appetites, I asked what the charge would be. When Scotty demanded 50 cts. for each cake, and 50 cts. for each cup of milk, my packer was so enraged I had great difficulty in preventing a personal confrontation. We left this miserable hut as soon as possible, the packer vowing to get even later." [32]

While Moberly and his packer objected to the prices at Scotty's, the Englishman W. Champness and his party, having travelled south over the Loon Lake trail to Donaldson's roadhouse, made no such complaint:

> "On our arrival at Scotty's ranch we found a single wooden house with one small window. It is a much frequented place for rest and refreshment being on one of the main trails to and from

the diggings. Small as it is for a tavern, a large quantity of "Cobblers", "Streaks of Lightning" and other drinks are served. Most of the up-country whiskey is well vitrioled (caustic, or biting) and almost makes one's throat raw. Here a drink costs from one to two shillings. Whilst staying here we were very crowded as the small building was filled by miners both day and night, sleeping under the tables and benches as well as on top of them, and all over the floor." [33]

Apparently Donaldson was known to get very drunk on his homemade "Streaks of Lightning", and miners complained of being wakened in the middle of the night by an hallucinating Scotty who, convinced that he was about to be robbed and murdered, drove his guests out into the night.

On his departure from the Bonaparte in 1872 Donaldson spent the remainder of his days in the Okanagan where he died in 1882. Scotty Creek, or as it was first known, Scotty's Creek, a small stream flowing into the Bonaparte River, assumed the name of this pioneer in the mid-1860s.

MUNDORF'S ROADHOUSE, THE 20 MILE HOUSE FROM ASHCROFT.
Lot 42, G.1., Lillooet.
A roadhouse farm known first as "Fraser's Ranch" had a long and fascinating history. William Fraser, a miner on the Thompson River in 1858, pre-empted 160 acres of land at the junction of Grave, or Maiden Creek, as it is now known, with the Bonaparte River in October 1863. From a sketch drawn by Fraser as part of his application, the roadhouse is seen as a substantial, single-storey log dwelling on the north or upper side of the wagon road, beside the Hudson's Bay Company trail to Loon Lake. Undoubtedly William Fraser did well at his roadhouse farm during the height of the Cariboo gold rush and until 1870, when the enterprise was sold to Jacob Mundorf.

Mundorf, a native of Germany, had arrived in British Columbia from California in 1858. On settling at Williams Creek in the early 1860s Mundorf bought interests in several mining claims and by 1866 had acquired real estate in Cameronton where he and his associates, Mundorf & Co., operated the "Miners Bakery & Restaurant", and "Mundorf & Co. Livery Stables & Feed Shop". By August 1867 Mundorf had converted his livery stables into a saloon and entertainment centre known as "The Crystal Palace" where his sweetheart, "Katrina", danced and entertained the miners.

"Katrina", whose real name was Elisabeth Catherine Haub, was a young woman of Pennsylvania Dutch extraction, who had arrived in Barkerville in 1865 in the first of several groups of hurdy-gurdy dancers. Within the year Katrina was married to Jacob Mundorf and had a son, John, one of the first children born in Barkerville. The Crystal Palace Saloon had been operating for less than a year when on September 16, 1868, tragedy struck Barkerville. A fire, said to have started in an apartment above Adler and Barry's saloon, swept through the town, destroying almost every building. Although rebuilding began almost immediately, the fire dispersed large numbers of inhabitants, among whom were Jacob Mundorf and his little family.

By 1870 the Mundorfs had settled in the Bonaparte valley where they purchased William Fraser's property at the 124 Mile post on the Cariboo Road. Here they continued what Fraser had started, the operation of a roadhouse and small ranch. The family also kept a B.C. Express Company stables at the ranch until the mid-1880s, when the horses were moved to Hat Creek.

"Mundorf's" roadhouse is mentioned in a number of diaries, including those of George Sargison in 1871 and Arthur T. Bushby in March 1872. In both accounts this point, at the head of the Bonaparte valley, seemed to be where transportation methods changed twice a year. While stagecoach passengers enjoyed the amenities of the road-house, hostlers switched the horses from sleigh to stage or vice versa, depending on the season. Arthur Bushby wrote:

"At Mundorfs' changed sleigh for wagon, much too crowded for comfort. Cold and raw drive. On the road met a man wrapped in blankets, he had left Clinton the night before— drunk, thought he had frozen to death—but sobered up to find himself still alive." [34]

While the Mundorf family continued to use Fraser's single-storey roadhouse during the 1870s, by the mid-1880s increased business on the road from Ashcroft created a need for larger facilities. In 1886 a new, two-storey frame roadhouse was built beside the wagon road, directly in front of the original building.

A photograph dating from 1890, which turned up in the effects of a descendant of the Mundorf family, shows almost all the 20 Mile House buildings, including Fraser's original house, used at this time as a bunkhouse.

The 20 Mile House, CA 1890. (COURTESY MRS. LOTTIE CAMERON, VANCOUVER, BC)

Five children were born to Jacob and Elisabeth Mundorf, two sons and three daughters, one of which was Elisabeth, who died at age 14 in 1888 of "mountain fever". All the children worked hard on the ranch and helped their mother in the roadhouse, but according to those who knew them, they were not a happy family. Years later, after all the children were grown, Jacob and Elisabeth Mundorf obtained a legal separation. At that time Elisabeth left the 20 Mile ranch to live with her younger son, George, who had given up all his claims to the ranch. John Mundorf, the eldest son, had left home earlier for Victoria where he was employed as a blacksmith.

With the help of his daughters, Christine and Charlotte, Jacob Mundorf continued to operate the ranch and roadhouse at the 20 Mile until his death in 1903. Christine, now married to Edmond B. Ferguson, took over the operation. A tireless worker all her life Christine was also a hard taskmistress, criticizing and abusing all who worked for her, including her husband. Medical authorities later determined that Christine had suffered for years from a brain disease that affected her behaviour.

In 1910 when Roddy Moffat, a freighter from the Quesnel area, stopped by, he found the saloon at the 20 Mile roadhouse had been closed permanently. During the 1930s a niece of Christine Mundorf, Marion "Dandy" Mitchell, visited her, and later recalled her impressions. By this time cars were common along the Cariboo Road, reducing the need for the roadhouses. As this was Marion's first visit she was anxious to see the interior of the old house. Although many of the rooms were locked Christine opened them, selecting the keys from a large bundle hanging from a belt around her waist. In the saloon, a large room filled with small round tables and chairs, there was a remarkably handsome polished hardwood bar which ran the full length of one side of the room. The parlour, a seldom-used room even at the best of times, contained several pieces of expensive, upholstered furniture, and a large ornate wood-burning heater. Although Miss Mitchell did not stay long, Christine Ferguson would not let her leave without giving her some fresh fruit, picked from the orchard nearby.

In early September 1942, not long after the sale of the 20 Mile House to P.A. Woodward of Vancouver, caretakers Alex Morrison and his wife Harriet, absorbed in the process of fumigating the house with sulphur, were unaware that sparks from the chimney had set fire to the roof. The flames spread quickly and on reaching the sulphur became an inferno. When it was realized that the fire could not be put out, a few pieces of furniture were rescued, but almost all the valuable artifacts were lost; the fire also consumed two nearby barns. The several pieces of furniture saved from the fire were returned to the Mundorf family, and are still in use today. Over the years the 20 Mile ranch has changed hands several times. Today, across the busy highway from where the roadhouse once stood there is a restaurant and gas station known as "Jacob's Cafe".

DOUGHERTY'S ROADHOUSE FARM, 1869-1900.
THE 126 MILE HOUSE FROM YALE, (23 MILES FROM ASHCROFT).
Lot 8, G.1., Lillooet.

The Dougherty family, a fourth and fifth generation of whom still live and ranch at Maiden Creek, first settled there in 1869. Edward Dougherty, originally from the Isle of Man, emigrated to eastern Canada in the 1840s. As a young man he had worked in the goldfields of Australia but returned to Canada during the early days of the Fraser River gold rush. While passing through the interior a few years later Edward was impressed with the pleasant climate of the Bonaparte valley. At Barkerville in the 1860s he met Elizabeth Ebert, a young girl of Pennsylvania Dutch origin, from San Francisco. Like Elisabeth Mundorf, Miss Ebert had been a hurdy-gurdy girl in Barkerville in 1865. In fact, it is possible that the Mundorfs, Edward

Dougherty and Elizabeth Ebert, left together for the Bonaparte valley following the Barkerville fire of 1868.

While it appeared that all the arable land in the Bonaparte valley had been taken up by 1869, Edward was able to acquire an abandoned pre-emption of 160 acres on Grave (Maiden) Creek, through which passed the Cariboo Wagon Road. Elizabeth Ebert and Edward Dougherty were married in Clinton on December 16, 1871, by the Reverend J.B. Good of Lillooet, and made their home at the 126 Mile post where they kept a roadhouse. Typical of many pioneers, the Doughertys had a large family: nine children, four of whom were girls. Dougherty's roadhouse served the travelling public for many years and was well known for the sumptuous meals served there, which cost 50¢ each. Willis West, general manager of the B.C. Express Company from 1903 to 1919, who knew every roadhouse on the Cariboo Road, wrote that the meals at Doughherty's

> "always included three kinds of hot meat for a mid day meal, with vegetables and at least three kinds of pie and pudding, two kinds of cake, relish, cookies, and stewed fruit." [35]

Of this same roadhouse, West also mentioned Edward's youngest son, Charles Dougherty, as the "proprietor with five bouncing

Elizabeth Ebert Dougherty and Edward Dougherty. (COURTESY HELEN CADE, CLINTON, BC)

daughters" who, when an "extra" coach arrived late on a winter's night with a load of half-frozen passengers, made his children give up their warm beds to the travellers.

At a time when women were scarce, the Dougherty girls and their vivacious mother were always a welcome addition to any social function, especially the annual Clinton Ball. The orchestra had to devise ways of keeping girls from leaving the dance too early. Edward Dougherty, the father of four unmarried beauties, loved to dance "The Flying Dutchman Polka" and could be relied upon to remain at least until the orchestra had played this favourite piece. Aware of this, the four or five musicians, including Alphonse Hautier of Lytton, would postpone Dougherty's favourite dance as long as possible, or at least until he threatened to leave. Only then would the fiddlers tune up for "The Flying Dutchman". As the first strains were heard, the floor was cleared, and Edward Dougherty would take his wife in his arms and they would dance the polka as could no other couple in the Cariboo.

While only in his 58th year, Edward Dougherty contracted pneumonia and died at Maiden Creek in January 1897. Elizabeth Dougherty remained at Maiden Creek, assisting her son in the operation of the ranch before retiring to Clinton where she died in 1944 at the age of 92.

There have been at least three residences on the Dougherty ranch. A two-storey frame structure that was built in the 1880s burned down in 1951. A second small frame building still standing north of the present home served as a temporary dwelling after the fire. The present home, built in the 1950s on the original site by Charles Dougherty and his wife, Mary Jane Pollard, is now occupied by Ray Dougherty, grandson of Charles. Near the house is a gnarled old crab-apple tree planted in 1887 when the first Charles Dougherty was born. The temperate climate of the narrow valley has in the past nourished a fair-sized orchard, noticed particularly by a stagecoach passenger of 1912:

"We passed Maiden Creek Ranch, the home of Mr. and Mrs. Charles Dougherty, marked by an orchard. It was a flourishing ranch; haying in progress in the surrounding fields, and cattle pasturing in the hills." [36]

When drought and disease killed most of the orchard, the Doughertys concentrated on raising beef cattle.

Today, where once the wagon road passed beside the roadhouse, the present Highway 97 has been built on a higher level to the east of the house, offering some privacy to the Dougherty family living there now.

KAY'S HOUSE, THE 129 MILE HOUSE FROM YALE, 1862.

Lot 144, G.1., Kamloops.

In speculating on the building of the Cariboo Wagon Road through the Grave Creek valley in 1862, the partners William H. Kay, W.L. Brown and M.R. Lodge pre-empted 480 acres of land from the boundaries of the 124 Mile House ranch to within five miles of Clinton. The postponed completion date of the wagon road through that area may have put a wrench in the plans. By 1869 all but Kay's pre-emption had been abandoned.

On Kay's land at the 129 Mile post a roadhouse was built in the early 1860s where Mrs. Kay provided meals and accommodation to travellers during the early days of the Cariboo gold rush. In 1865 when Barnard's four-horse stagecoaches first travelled from Yale to Barkerville, a change of horses was made at the 129 Mile House before driver John Haskell continued on to Clinton, and in 1866 "Kay's House" was included in a list of approved accommodation on the wagon road.

By 1867 the Kays had a neighbour, Edward "Ned" Allen, who pre-empted land just south of Kay's property. Allen, an ex-prize fighter from England, was a quarrelsome individual who believed that any argument could be solved by intimidation and physical abuse. One day Allen took it upon himself to check the boundary line between his and Kay's land. Convinced that Kay's roadhouse was on his property Allen marched over to Kay's house armed with an axe and began to chop down the house. Kay's wife, the only person home at the time, pleaded with Allen to postpone the affront but Allen continued, even after Kay arrived on the scene, when a terrible fight broke out. Poor Kay was quite unable to handle the ex-fighter, and was almost killed. For these offences Allen was charged and tried in Clinton where he was found guilty and sentenced to a year in the New Westminster penitentiary. Following his incarceration Edward Allen returned to the interior where he entered provincial politics as member for Lillooet in 1882, a post he held for several terms. The 129 Mile roadhouse continued operation until 1870, when the land was sold and became part of the Spanish ranch, near Clinton.

BRIGADE AND SUPPLY ROUTES OF THE FUR TRADERS.
After the building of a new Fort Kamloops on the west side of the
Thompson River in 1842, the upper portion of the trail to Fort
Alexandria was relocated to follow the north side of Kamloops Lake,
and across the Deadman River to Brigade Creek and Loon Lake.
From there it proceeded north over the second crossing of the
Bonaparte River to the west end of Green Lake, where it joined the
original trail at the north end of Horse Lake. Travellers to the
Cariboo used the upper portion of this route from 1861 on, until
the completion of the wagon road between Cook's Ferry and
Clinton in 1864.

TRAVELLERS ON THE ROUTE TO THE CARIBOO, 1861 TO 1864.
Having reached the Bonaparte valley by either the Yale or the
Lillooet route, early travellers could get on to the brigade trail from
Scotty's Creek just north of Hat Creek, or from the junction of the
Bonaparte River and Grave (Maiden) Creek at Fraser's ranch. The
trail from Scotty's ran northwest, to meet the trail from the
Bonaparte at Loon Lake.

THE ROADHOUSE AT THE UPPER CROSSING.
Lot 786, G.1., Lillooet.
From between the two Loon Lakes the brigade trail continued
northwest until it crossed the Bonaparte River for a second time. At
this point on the high plateau, where Fly Creek flows into the
Bonaparte, there had been a roadhouse during the fur-trade era, kept
by a Mexican packer by the name of "Rebadand". By April 1861 the
land at the Upper Crossing had been pre-empted by John Allen.
In Walter Moberly's account of a journey he took in the summer of
1862, he found the roadhouse at the Upper Crossing had burned
down:

"I proceeded from Clinton by way of a small stream that falls
into the Bonaparte, and thence passing along the foot of Castle
Mountain I finally reached the Second Crossing of the
Bonaparte. There I had fully expected to recruit for a day at the
wayside House that in early days had been built there. The
weather for the past few days had been very rainy, with mosquitoes and horseflies in swarms. Sleeping or trying to sleep on the
wet ground made matters exceedingly unpleasant. As I had only
my horse for a companion, I also felt very lonely. My provisions

were all gone, and as I was very hungry I was anticipating the enjoyment of a good meal of bacon, beans, hot coffee and bread. I was woefully disappointed however, for when I arrived at the Second Crossing I found that the House had burned down, and the place completely deserted. Finding a few half grown onions in what had been a garden, I devoured them, then built a fire and dozed through a miserable night of drenching rain and vicious mosquitoes." [37]

HARRY GUILLOD, 1862.

Returning south from the Cariboo in October 1862 Harry Guillod took the old brigade route to Scotty's Creek. Leaving Bridge Creek [100 Mile] Harry and his friend walked 25 miles to Green Lake House. Sadly out of funds, they camped and made supper from two grouse Harry shot with his revolver. Fortunately they met the Methodist preacher, Dr. Evans, who lent them a sovereign to tide them over. The next day Harry and his companion ate dinner at the rebuilt Upper Crossing roadhouse where the proprietor was a married man with a baby:

> "We reached a House on the Buonaparte River having done 16 miles. My moccasins were coming to smash. The man there was very civil, giving us a turndown in a back room with a blanket or two—a partition, minus the door separated us from his bedroom, as was manifest from the fact of a baby making a dear little noise for its mama." [38]

On purchasing some flour from the store Harry and his companion left the Upper Crossing roadhouse the next morning, bound for Scotty's roadhouse. The journey took longer than anticipated when they took the wrong trail and spent the rest of the day lost among the rocks and cliffs of Castle Rock, far to the west of Loon Lake.

GREEN LAKE HOUSE, 1862.

Lot 728, G.1., Lillooet.

Travellers on the brigade trail between Scotty's Creek and Horse Lake usually reached Green Lake on the second night of the journey, where they camped at the northwestern end of the lake. By 1862 a settler, Robert. T. Graham, who later leased the 70 Mile House, was operating a roadhouse known as Green Lake House.

JAMES THOMSON, SEPTEMBER 1862.

Making their way south from the Cariboo in September 1862, James Thomson of Edwardsburgh, Upper Canada, and his two companions reached Green Lake:

> "Started at 8.00 a.m. [from Bridge Creek] Trail through green timber, showers of hail. Dinner in woods. Got to Green Lake House at 5.00 p.m. (25 miles) stayed all night, straw mattress. Stayed over Sunday at Green Lake. Snow on the mountains all around. Lake 300 ft. above sea level." [39]

THE CARIBOO MILE POSTS.

As the Cariboo wagon roads were being built between 1862 and 1865, wooden mile posts were erected by the road contractors, to indicate the distances from Lillooet and Yale, to Barkerville.

In spite of the fact that they had been built of 12- by 14-inch squared timbers with "housed" tops to shed the rain, the posts did not last more than 30 years, so that by the 1880s they had all but disappeared. In 1896 while Ashcroft was considered to be the centre of business in the interior, the government of the day decided to re-establish the mile posts. The job of marking the 280 miles from Ashcroft to Barkerville was awarded to Anson M. Bushnell, a horse-trading homesteader of the Clinton area. To a bicycle wheel, the axle of which was affixed to a cyclometer, "Old Bush" fastened a set of handles cut from a discarded bar-room chair, and on a small shelf erected in front of the wheel he kept a set of stencils, an axe, and a yellow rain slicker. Trundling the homemade barrow, his eyes glued to the cyclometer, Bushnell walked up the centre of the road. At each mile he cut and set up a small stake about 12 inches high, upon which he stencilled the distance from Ashcroft.

The town of Clinton, known historically as the 47 Mile post, (from Lillooet) was to be renumbered the 32 Mile, and at the famous old 70 Mile House Bushnell was heard to remark (loud enough for proprietor Bill Boyd to hear) "They'll be calling this the 55 Mile House". To this Boyd hotly replied, "Not as long as I live." As he continued up the road Old Bush, realizing how unpopular his task was, completed his contract under cover of darkness.

But this was not the end of it. Three or four years later the authorities noticed that very few of Bushnell's markers remained, and because only Bushnell knew the mileage points, he was given another contract to install a second set of markers, this time mounted on posts 42 inches tall. On each five- by ten-inch board the words "from Ashcroft" were to be lettered, with the mileage numbers below. But Old Bush had difficulty with the lettering. The stencils were a nuisance, and in desperation he cast them aside and resorted to free-hand printing. Frequently, in the first 50 miles before he became adept at lettering, he ran out of room and "Ashcroft" had to be hyphenated to make it fit. Later still, long after Bushnell had collected his pay for the job, the Public Works Department prepared a third set of mile markers, ten inches square, painted white with black lettering, to replace Bushnell's sloppy job. Ironically, after all the trouble and expense of replacing the markers, very few of the revised mileages were ever adopted. [40]

CHAPTER SEVEN

WILLIAMS LAKE TO QUESNELLE FORKS

RUMOURS of the rich diggings on the Quesnelle River in 1859 travelled like wildfire. Vague as they were, they were sufficient to start a fresh tide of gold seekers upriver and overland by way of the several trails. Gold on the Quesnelle was coarse, much coarser than on the Fraser, especially on the high benches above the river, where nuggets weighing six or eight ounces were found. By September there were reports of miners making up to $600 each in less than a month. Until the arrival of pack trains in the summer of 1860, food and supplies were very scarce, having to be packed in from Alexandria, a community on the east bank of the Fraser River many miles to the southwest. By early fall supplies at Quesnelle Forks were virtually exhausted by the steadily increasing population of prospectors. In October the weather turned nasty, sending hundreds of men scurrying south to avoid starvation in a land of deep snow.

There were, however, a few hardy men who remained to winter on a broad flat at the junction of the north and south branches of the

Quesnelle River. Among these were John McLean and his several companions. Occupied with the many exciting gold discoveries that summer, McLean decided late in the fall to make a trip out for supplies to last the winter. Taking one companion and two horses, he travelled south to Round Tent Lake, a camping ground about 30 miles south of the Quesnelle River. There they turned northwest on to "Dancing Bill's trail", leading to Alexandria. As described in the summer of 1860, the surveyed townsite of Alexandria was

"...situated on a bench about 30 or 40 ft. above the river, consisting of nine houses; immediately above it is a second bench which completely intercepts the buildings from the view of the traveller till he is close upon them.... Of the original two liquor saloons and restaurants, three trading posts and one storage building, there was now only two saloons and one store." [1]

On reaching Alexandria McLean and his companion found the trading post there completely without provisions, and were just about to start back empty-handed when the packer Joel Palmer and his men arrived, driving a herd of cattle and a mule-train load of stores from Oregon. From these McLean and his companion purchased all the supplies they could load onto the horses and, with their own packs full, returned to their camp at Quesnelle Forks.

QUESNEL, QUESNELLE, QUESNELLEMOUTH, AND QUESNELLE FORKS.
The spelling of the word Quesnel has been changed several times over the years. Honouring Lieutenant Jules Maurice Quesnel, who accompanied Simon Fraser on his journey to the coast in 1808, by 1860 the spelling had become "Quesnelle", as seen in the reports of Gold Commissioner P.H. Nind in 1860, and J. Boles Gaggin, the first appointed magistrate at Quesnel in 1864. Just why, and by whom the change was made, is not known; the only reasonable explanation is that it was a careless mistake made by a clerk.

With the discovery of gold on the Quesnel River in 1859, and the establishment of the first permanent mining camp at the confluence of the north and south forks of the river, the community there became known as Quesnelle Forks, or Quesnelle City. The little village at the mouth became, for many years, Quesnellemouth, to avoid confusion with Quesnelle Forks. By the 1870s, with the decline of Quesnelle Forks, the town at the mouth of the river became, once again, "Quesnelle", but not until 1900 was the spelling changed back to the original.

As the Cariboo gold rush increased in momentum in the spring of 1860 at least a thousand miners were reported to be working, not only on the Quesnelle River, but at many locations on the Fraser north of Williams Lake. In their frantic haste to work the ground, few miners had taken the time to register their claims at the nearest government agency in Lillooet, 200 miles south. As a result, many disputes arose among the miners of the Cariboo region. These were reported to Thomas Elwyn, magistrate at Lillooet, but even if he had been able to help, he had no jurisdiction that far north.

THE FIRST GOLD COMMISSIONER FOR THE CARIBOO, 1860.

By July 1860, Philip Henry Nind, an English lawyer with a Master's degree from Christ Church, Oxford, had been appointed the first government representative in the Cariboo district. At Fort Hope, where Nind joined a Hudson's Bay Company brigade to reach his northern post, he wrote to inform Governor Douglas that he had obtained the services of one William Pinchbeck as his chief constable, and a Mr. Seymour as his second, to assist him in his duties. Although officially appointed to the "district of Alexandria", Nind chose to make his headquarters at Williams Lake, the junction of several main routes to the mining areas of the Quesnelle, Horsefly, and Fraser rivers. On his arrival Nind set up his tent

Philip Henry Nind, first gold commissioner in the Cariboo, 1860. (COURTESY BCARS)

beside the brigade trail in a large open valley just north of the lake and close to a little log church.

This site, known for centuries as "Columnetza", or "meeting place of the princely ones", had been the gathering place for neighbouring tribes of Shuswap, Chilcotin and Carrier Indians. With the arrival of the white fur traders in the early 1800s this became a camping spot, used by the men of the brigade as they passed through on their annual trek. In 1841, under the command of Chief Trader Peter Skene Ogden, the returning brigade had included Father Modeste Demers, on his way to minister to the native tribes of New Caledonia. At Columnetza, where the missionary preached and baptized many native people, he supervised the building of a small church close to Mission Creek, named in memory of the visit.

DAVIDSON'S ROADHOUSE AT WILLIAMS LAKE, 1860 AND '61.
Lot 72, G.1., Cariboo.

By 1859 the village of Columnetza, with its church and gardens, had become the object of land development and private enterprise, sparked by the arrival of gold miners and business opportunists.

One of the first was Thomas W. Davidson, an experienced miner from Montecristo, California, who gained recognition in 1858 as the discoverer of a small gold strike on a creek 15 miles north of Victoria. Later that year he was a partner in a transportation agency at Port Douglas with entrepreneur Gustavus B. Wright. Although the alliance did not last long, these two men later played key roles in shaping the development of the Cariboo.

While transporting goods to Alexandria with packer Marion Woodward in 1859, Davidson located arable land at Williams Lake, where he began to develop a farm, roadhouse and store. With the introduction of the Pre-emption Act in 1860 Nind, who was also the district magistrate, took many applications for land, including 160 acres for Thomas Davidson, situated at the foot of Williams Lake. By gaining the co-operation of mining associates John Telfer and Moses Dancerault, Davidson acquired several additional parcels of land, and by 1861 had 720 acres in his name. Davidson's developments at Williams Lake were sufficiently outstanding to have prompted Nind to mention them in a letter to Governor Douglas:

> "Davidson's farm, where excellent crops of grain and vegetables have been harvested, and where a substantial and commodious roadhouse has been built." [2]

"Davidson's" roadhouse near Mission Creek, the only roadhouse for many miles, was indeed a popular place. The meals served, the result of Davidson's farming, were the delight of travellers, who enjoyed the change from the usual fare of bacon, beans and bannock. Liquor was also available, brought in by Davidson's pack trains, and where there was liquor, there was always gambling in the form of poker, monte, and billiards, all adding to the profits of the roadhouse.

THE FIRST OVERLAND ROUTES TO THE QUESNELLE RIVER, 1860. DAVIDSON'S TWO CUT-OFF TRAILS TO DEEP CREEK.

Following the rich discoveries of gold on the Quesnelle River and the emergence of Quesnelle Forks, it became the ambition of every packer, merchant and entrepreneur to find the safest and most direct overland route into the area. At that time the route north of Williams Lake was anything but direct. From Mud Lake, a pack trail built by Joel Palmer in 1859 turned east over the mountain to Beaver Lake, in a wide, fertile valley northeast of Williams Lake. Beyond this there was no definite route until 1860, when ferry operators on the Quesnelle River built pack trails south to Beaver Lake and Deep Creek, within ten miles of Williams Lake. On his return from inspecting the mining areas of Quesnelle Forks and Keithley Creek that summer, Gold Commissioner Nind wrote to Governor Douglas about the rapid developments taking place, and gave suggestions for the route of a wagon road to the goldfields. Nind stressed that these were not his own opinions, but those of the miners and settlers in the area.

Up to that time these were the only first-hand reports of the Cariboo region to reach Governor Douglas. In this way Nind played an important role in establishing the first access routes into the area, even to suggesting that steamships could be used on the upper Fraser. One of those settlers with whom Nind consulted was Thomas Davidson, whose name appears more than once in official letters. An opportunist, Davidson had by 1860 established a store at "the Forks", where he sold produce from his farm at Williams Lake. In a report of a return journey from Quesnelle Forks in November that year, Nind described "a new and shorter trail" [3] cut by Davidson that summer, from the Court House at Williams Lake, to Deep Creek, ten miles north. This trail bypassed Palmer's route of 1859, from Mud Lake.

MENEFEE'S MISSION CREEK ROADHOUSE, 1861.

By the fall of 1860 when most of the arable land at Williams Lake had been pre-empted or purchased, Thomas Davidson realized that if his ambition for a larger farm was to materialize, he would have to look elsewhere for sufficient land. He found it ten miles away, near the head of Williams Lake. In the meantime, with the steady demand for farm produce, and an increasing clientele frequenting the roadhouse, his enterprise at Mission Creek had become an attractive property.

Following two years of successful mining in the Horsefly area, Thomas Menefee of the Dunlevy party, with a partner, Dudley Moreland, made arrangements to purchase Davidson's farm at Williams Lake for $15,000, a worthwhile investment, or so they thought as they took over on September 23, 1861.

On vacating the Mission Creek property Davidson transferred his interests to his new "Lake Valley" farm where he developed the land and built a large, two-storey log roadhouse. In 1862 Davidson built another trail, this time from his new property directly north to Deep Creek farm, shortening the distance to the Quesnelle River by yet another nine miles. Little did the roadhouse-keepers at Williams Lake anticipate the effects this trail would have on their business in the very near future.

From a daybook kept at the Mission Creek roadhouse between September 24, 1861, and January 2, 1862, it appears that Marion Woodward, an associate of Davidson's, was managing the roadhouse, while his two brothers, James and Charles Woodward, worked on the farm. By the spring of 1862 Woodward had become part owner of the ranch, buying out Moreland's share for $8,000. The daybook also contains the names of many of the original miners and settlers of the Cariboo who purchased meals and drinks at the roadhouse, feed for their animals, and goods from the store. At this time customers paid $1.25 a meal, four dollars for a bottle of whisky, three dollars for champagne, and 30¢ a pound for beef.

That fall, a gambler, Gilchrist, shot and killed an innocent bystander during a quarrel over a poker game at the Mission Creek roadhouse. In an account of this event, written many years later, the interior of the roadhouse is described:

"...the large log building, not yet divided up into rooms or passages assumed a cavernous gloom in its nocturnal state, making it seem more vast than it really was. The only light came from a fireplace of pine logs stacked endwise up the chimney, where it flashed red and yellow lights upon a strange and numerous company." [4]

Thomas Menefee, who was seldom at Williams Lake, was more often attending to one or another of his many business interests within the Cariboo. Horse racing was his great love, and as the owner of several thoroughbreds brought in from Oregon, he was often seen with his trainer, B.F. English, at the races held in Barkerville, at Cornwall's ranch near Cache Creek, or at Williams Lake.

In an account of the first gold strike near Horsefly in 1859, historian Alex McInnes describes each of the five Dunlevy partners. Of Menefee he wrote:

> "A rather slight but wiry build he was the comic of the outfit, a born entertainer...song and dance emanated from him 'like scent from a woman', as Dunlevy would say, or 'like skunk pee', as Ira Crowe would snap, when Tom's antics exasperated him, but just the same they all liked him. A hat worn at a rakish angle on the back of his head gave him a devil-may-care air that suited him, and his close-set eyes, long lean face, jutting lower jaw and chin whiskers would at times give him a foxy appearance that also suited him, for he was by nature a foxy fellow." [5]

PINCHBECK'S "LOWER HOUSE", 1862.
Lot 72, G.1., Cariboo.

William Pinchbeck's arrival at Williams Lake with Gold Commissioner Philip H. Nind in July 1860, and his appointment as Nind's chief constable, gave him an immediate position of respect in the community. Originally from Yorkshire, England, Pinchbeck and his two brothers had been in California in 1849, where they mined, and later operated a hotel in San Francisco. A partner in their ventures was William Lyne, who became a lifelong associate of William Pinchbeck's. Among the hundreds to declare the lower Fraser River a mining "humbug" in 1858, the Pinchbeck brothers returned to Victoria, where William found work in the recently formed police force.

Once settled at Williams Lake, Pinchbeck was quick to realize the financial benefits of farming and roadhouse-keeping, and with a partner, Thomas Meldrum, took up land just one half mile south of Davidson's farm, where they built a roadhouse, and operated a store. With the arrival of William Lyne in 1861, the three partners formed an alliance known as Pinchbeck & Co. Pinchbeck's store and roadhouse was referred to as the "Lower House", due to its proximity to the Mission Creek roadhouse. In 1862, when it was expected that a

The Lower House, William Pinchbeck's first roadhouse, 1868. (Courtesy BCARS)

wagon road would soon reach Williams Lake, an advertisement for Pinchbeck's enterprises appeared in the *B.C. & Victoria Directory* of 1863:

"WILLIAMS LAKE. B.C. LOWER HOUSE.
PINCHBECK'S HOTEL & STORE.

The accommodation for travellers unsurpassed
by any Hotel in the country.
The table is constantly supplied with every
delicacy that money can purchase.

A LARGE STOCK OF
MINERS SUPPLIES OF EVERY DESCRIPTION
CONSTANTLY ON HAND.
THE CHOICEST BRANDS OF WINES, LIQUORS
AND CIGARS
TO BE HAD AT THE BAR.
PINCHBECK & CO.Props." [6]

SIGNS OF CHANGE, A FORECAST OF THE FUTURE.
By the fall of 1861 the seemingly endless duties of Gold Commissioner Philip Nind had taken their toll on him, both physi-

cally and mentally. During the summer he had suffered from insomnia, and an uncontrollable twitch in his face. In October, realizing that he was experiencing a nervous breakdown, Nind wrote for an official leave of absence, but it was December before he was able to depart for England. Earlier, Nind had received notice of a change in the location of government headquarters for the "Upper Country" from Alexandria to Quesnelle Forks, the centre of the mining activity. Williams Lake was to be the site of only occasional inspection. Following Nind's departure, the two constables, William Pinchbeck and Thomas Hankin, remained at Williams Lake to maintain the peace.

By 1862, the jurisdiction of "Cariboo", as it had become, was split into two sections, East and West, with Thomas Elwyn at Quesnelle Forks, and Peter O'Reilly at Alexandria. As O'Reilly's inspections at Williams Lake became less frequent, Constable G.R. Gompertz was posted there as jailer, postmaster, and magistrate's clerk. During the three years of his tenure Gompertz, the senior officer, appeared incapable of disciplining himself and was often found drunk and neglectful of his duties. This was noticed particularly by Dr. Cheadle as he and Lord Milton passed through the area late in 1863. The jailhouse, an insecure log building at best, was constantly being broken out of by prisoners who had nothing better to do than plan their escape.

A prime example of this occurred in October 1862, when Judge Begbie arrived to preside over the trial of a prisoner, "Connor", accused of assault with intent to kill. A grand jury had been chosen from among the large population of wintering miners. During the trial a horse race, in progress on a nearby track, so distracted the attention of the court that a temporary adjournment was ordered. At this time the prisoner, who had been left in the care of two temporary constables, escaped from the jail, hopped aboard a fast horse, and got clean away before the court could resume. Following several incidents of a similar nature Constable Gompertz was relieved of his post, and William Pinchbeck took on additional duties.

With the gold rush at its height in 1862, profits increased at the two roadhouses at Williams Lake. The sudden increase in the population of Cariboo had caused a virtual famine, everywhere except at the self-sufficient roadhouse farms. Bishop George Hills, who arrived at Williams Lake in July 1862, mentioned the Mission Creek roadhouse, "the former abode of Mr. Davidson, where all kinds of produce seem to flourish." [7] Here Hills and his party had enjoyed a delicious beef dinner, with a dessert of wild raspberries and fresh cream. Wages for good cooks were considerable. Hills mentioned that the cook at the roadhouse, an American black, was making $150 a month.

Following the very successful season of 1862 the roadhouse proprietors at Williams Lake looked forward to the next year when a wagon road was scheduled to be built through the area. Improved road conditions would reduce feight rates and lower the cost of goods, assuring them of even larger profits.

THE WAGON ROADS TO THE CARIBOO, 1862 AND '63.

By the spring of 1862, after the awarding of several contracts to Thomas Spence, Joseph Trutch, Charles Oppenheimer and Walter Moberly, the work of building a wagon road from Yale began. At this same time negotiations were completed with contractor Gustavus B. Wright for the building of a second route, an extension of the Harrison-Lillooet wagon road, from Lillooet to Cut-Off Valley, 47 miles north. On completion of his contract Wright was given the option to build a further 240 miles of road to Alexandria, on the Fraser River. While there was a desperate need to have a wagon road built to the goldfields, no one in the colonial government was familiar enough with the country north of Lillooet to be able to plan the actual route of such a road. Neither were they able to estimate the costs involved. With very little financial help from Great Britain, roads at this time were built by private contractors, who were paid only after the completed mileage was inspected and approved. Some profit was allowed the contractor through the collection of road tolls and special concessions.

Gustavus Blin Wright, born in Shoreham, Vermont, in 1832, had mined for gold in California prior to his arrival in British Columbia in 1858. Armed with some capital, some engineering experience, and a lot of energy and adventurous spirit, Wright and his partner, Thomas Davidson, operated a supply and transport company at Port Douglas. Wright's first association with the colonial government came in 1859 when Governor Douglas requested him, as a frequent traveller over the Harrison-to-Lillooet route, to give his professional appraisal of the trail. So impressed were the governor and his associates with Wright's knowledge and spirit of co-operation that in 1861 they asked him to submit a proposal for the building of a wagon road from Lillooet to Cut-Off Valley. When Wright's proposal of March 12, 1862, was accepted, he was given the authority to:

"Lay out and complete a wagon road of the uniform width of 18 feet, according to specifications and directions from time to time, and to the satisfaction of the Chief Commissioner of Lands, or his agents, along a route approved of by the said Chief Commissioner, but selected in the first instance, by the contractor." [8]

With the successful completion of his contract to Cut-Off Valley in August 1862, Wright signed another agreement to build a road to Alexandria. By November 9, 1862, the last day of road building that season, advance crews had reached the 127 Mile post, north of Lac La Hache. From that point on surveyors had planned for a road through the San Jose River valley to Williams Lake and the banks of the Fraser River, where it would turn north to Alexandria. On examination of the route, Wright realized there would be definite problems between the Mission Creek farm and Soda Creek. To build a road along the high cliffs and around the deep coulees of the river would require expensive blasting. Several bridges would also have to be built, all of which would postpone completion of the road, but those were not the only problems. For miles in that area, the only water for animals was down at the river, 500 feet below the cliffs. The alternative to this was a route from Davidson's Lake Valley farm, up Davidson's cut-off trail, built that summer, to Deep Creek. Wright, who had taken that route during a reconnaissance trip to Alexandria, knew it to be well used by the packers, with ample feed and water en route.

On weighing the merits of the two routes, Wright decided to build the road via Deep Creek. He and a partner, Franklin Way (formerly of Spuzzum) purchased Moses Dancerault's Deep Creek farm, past which the road would be built. Careful to keep this fact quiet, Wright realized he would have to alert Colonel Moody and his staff of Royal Engineers, including Sergeant McMurphy, of his change in plans. Early the next year, just as work began, Wright took McMurphy with him to inspect the two routes in question. During the five-day sojourn Wright and McMurphy visited the operators of the two roadhouses at Williams Lake. Legend has it that Wright requested of them a loan of $15,000, ostensibly to help pay off his road crew; in fact, it was to finance the particularly expensive piece of roadwork, should he take the road past Williams Lake. Unfortunately for them, they refused.

As the advance road crew reached Davidson's Lake Valley farm a short time later and turned north up the cut-off trail to Deep Creek,

The 127 Mile House, Lac La Hache. (COURTESY BCARS)

it became obvious to the Williams Lake roadhouse-keepers that Wright's road was going to bypass their community. News of Wright's half-interest in the Deep Creek farm made the situation even worse, prompting the belief that Wright had built the road merely to further his own interests. Summoning Captain John Grant of the Royal Engineers, Thomas Elwyn, recently resigned magistrate of Quesnelle Forks, and now part owner of the Mission Creek farm, tried to exert his influence over Wright to make him change his mind. At this same time Captain Grant, who had overseen the initial survey of the route to Williams Lake, was convinced of its merits, while Wright held fast to his decision to use the Deep Creek route.

For several weeks the battle raged on between the two factions, with Sergeant McMurphy receiving contravening orders almost daily. When Wright made a trip to Victoria to see his lawyer, Henry Crease, he was confronted by Colonel Moody, who was obviously in an awkward position. Wright argued that to go by Williams Lake would be "financially suicidal", and demanded his contractual rights. Moody, to convince himself of Wright's argument, despatched Sergeant James Lindsay to the scene of contention. On receiving Lindsay's report Colonel Moody conceded that Wright was correct, and gave his official approval to the road by way of Deep Creek.

To further justify Wright's decision to bypass Williams Lake, Lieutenant H.S. Palmer, following a survey in 1862, stated:

"Although the Western route from Lac La Hache to Alexandria via Williams Lake offers no serious impediment to roadmaking between the Court House [Williams Lake] and Soda Creek, there are some very sharp ascents and descents, so that with animals the detour from the head of Williams Lake [Davidson's cut off to Deep Creek] is preferable, and there is little doubt that a modification of this latter route will be adopted for the future wagon road." [9]

Wright's road to Soda Creek via Deep Creek was used until 1932 when an access was built from Soda Creek to Williams Lake. Earlier attempts to change the road were opposed by teamsters, who complained of the lack of water and feed along that route. For many years the uproar of protest over the building of Wright's bypass lingered on. Again and again, editorials appeared in newspapers and books, criticizing Governor Douglas and his government for their part in the scandal. In the meantime Wright's wagon road reached "Mr. Saunder's House" on the banks of the Fraser at Alexandria, on August 8, 1863. [10]

In spite of being off the road, the two roadhouse farms at Williams Lake continued to cater to farmers and miners along the Fraser River as far south as Dog Creek. A great disappointment was suffered in 1864 when the community was omitted from Barnard's stagecoach route, which made stops at the 150 Mile House and Deep Creek House, before continuing on to Soda Creek to connect with G.B. Wright's new steamer, the S.S. *Enterprise*. On the return trip the steamer reached Soda Creek late in the afternoon, with just enough time for the stage to deliver passengers to Deep Creek House, where they remained overnight. This was a bitter pill for the Williams Lake roadhouse-keepers to swallow.

As their roadhouse business declined, the owners of the two farms at Williams Lake concentrated on raising grain, vegetables, and beef for sale to the mining camps east of Quesnellemouth. Wheat grown on Pinchbeck's farm was processed into flour, and beer, manufactured on both farms, sold in the saloons at 25¢ a glass and 50¢ a jug. Hard liquor also, made from white wheat and distilled by Pinchbeck & Co., sold locally at four dollars a gallon. The boiler and worms used in Pinchbeck's distillery had been transported to the Cariboo on the backs of mules all the way from San Francisco. By the early 1870s Pinchbeck was paying an excise tax of one dollar a gallon to the government, which sent the occasional inspector to test the strength of the product. At this time Pinchbeck & Co. was also manufacturing adobe bricks in a kiln on the farm.

When Thomas Meldrum left Williams Lake to start a ranch in the Chilcotin in 1866, he sold back his interests in Pinchbeck & Co., leaving Pinchbeck and William Lyne to carry on. While the Cariboo was suffering through an economic depression at that time, the discovery of gold in the Omineca country northwest of Fort George in 1869 sent a stampede of miners and opportunists back into the country. As far south as Williams Lake, farmers such as William Pinchbeck, James M. Bohanon, and Peter Dunlevy of Soda Creek were shipping farm produce and liquor to the new, but short-lived, gold rush. Pinchbeck went so far as to have a 30-foot river boat built on his farm, which he had towed to Soda Creek. From there goods were loaded and taken upriver to Manson Creek, where Pinchbeck and his partner William Lyne operated a hotel and store for a few years. In the meantime the roadhouses at Williams Lake carried on. A page from the Pinchbeck & Co. daybook of April 1870 recorded a few of the many transactions taking place:

"Tommy Halfbreed, 1 black ankscheef...............$2.00
Memo. Chinee Cook commence to work April 2, at noon.
Whiley, Chimney Creek, 1 gal. whiskey..............$4.00
Scotty, 2 drinks...................................$1.00
Mexican packer, Fraser River, whiskey, tobacco....$2.00
Charles Argus, (carpenter) 1 pr. pants............$7.00
Cash for washing by chinee........................$1.50
James Thurber, supper, 50 cts., 4 drinks..........$4.50
B.F.English, by 1 yoke of oxen, credit..........$300.00
Ah Moon & Co., 10 lbs. beans, 10 lbs bacon, salt,
tea, 1 pr. drawers, 4 meals for Chineeman........$18.50
Peter Dunlevy & Co., 15 gals. whiskey @$4.00.....$60.00
Tommy Halfbreed, 1 pr.boots, socks...............$9.95." [11]

On July 4, 1873, while taking part in the annual celebrations in Barkerville, Thomas Menefee was taken ill and put to bed at the home of Mr. J. Newlands. Despite the good care he received, Menefee passed away three days later on July 7, of inflammation of the lung. For years Menefee had suffered from the effects of gunshot wounds he had received in 1858 while travelling with a party of American prospectors. At the mouth of the Okanagan Canyon, where they were attacked by Indians, three men were killed, and

Menefee, one of several wounded, was transported 250 miles by mule to Yale, and then by boat to Victoria, for medical aid. Following a partial recovery he met Peter Dunlevy on the lower Fraser, and became one of his four partners. A native of Missouri, U.S.A., Menefee was only 42 years of age at his death; he was buried at Soda Creek where he had resided for some years.

At an auction of Menefee's estate held soon after his funeral, the extent of his assets was revealed. Included in the sale were the Mission Creek farm, consisting of 1,000 acres of fenced land, 75 head of cattle, and 15 head of horses, and the well-known race horses Dexter and Dick. The estate also included Menefee's half interest in Dunlevy's Soda Creek farm, the Exchange Hotel, and a one-third interest in a flour mill known as "The Protection Mills", at Soda Creek. While the Mission Creek farm was not bought immediately, it was sold by Menefee's heirs the following spring, to William Pinchbeck. With the two ranches under their control, Pinchbeck and Lyne now owned close to 2,000 acres of land.

THE PINCHBECK RANCH, THE LATTER YEARS, 1884-1893.
Lots 71, 72, G.1., Cariboo.
Soon after settling in the Williams Lake valley, both Pinchbeck and Lyne had taken native wives, and both had families of several children. During the 1870s the eldest sons, William Pinchbeck Jr. and Billy and John Lyne attended the Cache Creek Boarding School. These boys were grown men working on the ranch when William Pinchbeck left home on a trip to England in the summer of 1884. On his return a few months later he was accompanied by several other people, including an English bride, Alice Kilham, 17 years his junior, his sister Annie and her husband William J. Anders, and a young niece, Emma Pinchbeck. En route from Europe the group had travelled to New York, Minneapolis and Chicago, where arrangements were made for several pieces of modern machinery, notably a portable sawmill, to be shipped to Williams Lake.

The arrival of the steam-powered sawmill triggered an extensive building program on the ranch, part of which was a new, two-storey, frame-built roadhouse on the upper ranch. In charge at the roadhouse was Annie Anders, assisted by Miss Angelique Dussault, and Annie's niece Emma. Annie's husband William managed the store, operated the saloon, and kept the books. Many years later Emma Pinchbeck recalled the unique system that supplied water to the kitchen of the roadhouse. From Mission Creek, a flume carried water into a barrel under the sink. Occasionally frogs got into the flume, and were known to jump out of the barrel onto the kitchen floor.

In the upper storey were eight bedrooms, one of which was reserved for Judge Begbie on his annual assize circuit through the Cariboo. During the 1870s and '80s rooms were rented in summer to commercial travellers, and in winter to seasonal boarders, usually miners, who lived on the Pinchbeck ranch. Those miners who could afford to, spent the several months of winter in San Francisco, while others who had not fared as well, went only as far south as Soda Creek, or Williams Lake where, compared with Snowshoe Mountain or Barkerville, the climate was mild. These men paid eight dollars a month for room and board while they drank, gambled, and socialized all winter. Upon their arrival in the fall they handed their gold over to the bar-keep at the roadhouse, who acted as banker, keeping a tally of their debts during the winter. If a man spent all his gold before spring he was given a chance to pay for his keep by working on the ranch. In the saloon a certain level of civility was maintained by a "bouncer", or strong man, who had the unenviable task of persuading the badly inebriated to leave. The miners had no love for them, and more than one was beaten up.

In addition to a new roadhouse at Mission Creek, or the upper farm, an elegant, two-storey frame residence known as "Lake House" was built on the lower end of the ranch, overlooking Williams Lake. Constructed expressly for Pinchbeck's new bride, the house contained an imposing entrance hall, and two reception rooms, or parlours, one on either side of

Lake House, William Pinchbeck's residence, built in 1886 overlooking the south end of Williams Lake. (COURTESY BCARS)

a wide staircase. Behind this were the dining room, kitchen, pantry, and dairy room. Upstairs were four bedrooms and a large attic.

During the winter of 1887 William Lyne, whose native wife had returned to her people years before, spent several months in Victoria where he married a former acquaintance, Mary Collingsworth of Wisconsin. They returned to the Cariboo the following spring, but less than a year later Lyne sold his interests in the farm back to Pinchbeck, and with his wife moved to Ashcroft, where he bought an interest in the Ashcroft Hotel.

At Lake House, three sons were born to William Pinchbeck and his wife Alice. Lonely for her family in England, Alice made several trips back home over the next few years, and in fact she and her sons were away at the time of her husband's death on July 30, 1893. Pinchbeck had been in poor health for several years, and never fully recovered from an operation performed in Victoria the winter before.

At the time of his death William Pinchbeck was in debt to the Western Ranching Company, the operators of the Gang Ranch, for the sum of $23,040.30. It had originated in 1887 when he borrowed $20,000 at nine percent interest over five years.[12] While rich in real estate and tangible assets Pinchbeck, like most farmers, suffered from a lack of ready cash. In September 1891 Pinchbeck had written to his creditors

William Lyne and his wife, the former Mary Collingsworth, May 1887.
(COURTESY BCARS)

apologizing for his inability to meet his payments, saying that he expected very shortly to have $1,000 from his interests in the Omineca, as well as the returns from a crop of grain not yet threshed. Obviously this income did not materialize, and the stress from his growing indebtedness may have hastened his death. He was only 62 when he died.

When Alice Pinchbeck and her boys returned home from England that summer, they found that the ranch, and even their own home, had been taken over by the creditors, whose only object was to regain their investment in the Pinchbeck farm. At an auction held shortly afterward, everything, including machinery, livestock, household furnishings and goods from Lake House and the upper farm roadhouse, was put up for sale, from which about $6,000 was realized. With hardly a penny Alice Pinchbeck and her sons left Williams Lake for Victoria in the spring of 1894.

For several years the operators of the Gang Ranch attempted to sell the Pinchbeck farm, but were unable to do so. In the meantime it was leased to Joseph Philip Patenaude, manager of the 150 Mile House hotel and store, who with his sons Albert and Ernest, a daughter Ida, his second wife Marie, and their young son Spencer Hope, lived on and worked the farm until 1889, when it was sold to Robert Borland, owner of the 150 Mile House ranch, for $17,000.

While occupying the "lower" ranch himself, Bob Borland leased the upper farm to Mike Minton, a Chilcotin rancher. On the property with Minton were his two orphaned nephews, Billy and Tommy Comer, and their sister Mamie. When Minton died in the early 1900s, the Comer brothers continued farming, and the land there became known as the Comer meadows, and the Comer Ranch. By 1910, with the departure of the Comers, the upper roadhouse was left empty. The end came in 1925 when it was torn down, its timbers used in the building of new homes in the Williams Lake area.

As owner of the Pinchbeck farm in 1899, Bob Borland occupied Lake House, which then became known as Borland House. Just prior to the First World War Borland sold the property, including Borland House, to the Pacific Great Eastern Railway. During the war while railway development stood still, an old Swede was hired as caretaker of the house. In 1919, as the tracks neared Williams Lake, Walter M. Slater and his wife Ethel managed the Borland ranch and lived in Borland House. For a year it became a boarding house, where various railway surveyors and engineers were housed. Still standing in 1930, this impressive landmark was eventually taken apart, its lumber used in the construction of several smaller buildings in Williams Lake.

CHAPTER EIGHT

MUD LAKE, QUESNELLE FORKS AND WILLIAMS CREEK

IN November 1860, Gold Commissioner Philip Nind wrote one of his long, informative reports to Governor Douglas, describing a journey he had made that fall to the mines in the Quesnelle River district. On this occasion Nind and his constable, William Pinchbeck, had accompanied Judge Begbie who, with his clerk, Arthur Bushby, was on his first annual circuit "to look over the gold regions". [1] Travelling on horseback the party left Williams Lake on September 20, taking the brigade trail to Mud Lake, "a sheet of water prettily situated in a valley" 20 miles to the north "where General Joel Palmer had established a store and pastured one hundred and fifty head of cattle". [2]

MUD LAKE HOUSE, 1861.
Lot 59, G.1., Cariboo.
Late in 1860 the prospectors John Rose, Benjamin MacDonald, Fred Black, and W.R. "Doc" Keithley discovered the richest gold-

bearing creeks of the Cariboo, northeast of Quesnelle Forks. With those first adventurers were several others, among them George Weaver and James May.

Heading south for the winter after a profitable season in the mines, Weaver and May speculated in land at Mud Lake in November 1861, at the junction of the brigade trail and Palmer's route to Beaver Lake. Here they staked out two pre-emptions of 160 acres each on the "south eastern end of Mud Lake". [3] That Weaver built a house on his land is noted in the description of another pre-emption recorded that year by John Thomas, "situated at Mud Lake, about one and a half miles from Weaver's House". [4] These properties were transferred in 1862 to James Sellers and Peter C. Dunlevy, who developed a farm and built a large log roadhouse. As the second of several roadhouses operated by the Dunlevy consortium, Mud Lake House, on the direct route to the Quesnelle River, was most strategically located.

By pooling their various talents the four partners made an unbeatable team in the operation of the roadhouse, with Sellers supervising the cooking, Thomas Moffitt, the arch gambler, in the saloon, and Peter Dunlevy operating the store. Only Ira Crow, the miner of the group, was absent, overseeing Dunlevy's and Sellers' several claims at Antler Creek. An advertisement for Mud Lake House appeared in the *B.C. & Victoria Directory* of 1863:

"THE MUD LAKE RANCH,

Situated On The Direct Road
to the
PEACE RIVER & CARIBOO MINES.
The accommodation for TRAVELLERS is not
surpassed by any House in the country.
CHOICE WINES, LIQUORS, & CIGARS.
The cooking Department is under the
superintendence of the best COOK
in British Columbia.
J. SELLERS, P.DUNLEVY, Props." [5]

Mud Lake House was well patronized, at least for a few years, as seen in the diaries of a number of travellers, particularly those of the "Overlander" groups on their arrival at Quesnellemouth in the fall of 1862. From John Hunniford's diary:

"Left on the raft for Mud Lake in company of 7 California miners and 16 of our own company. Ran four hours then ran the raft against a snag and stuck fast, had to give an Indian most of my clothes, to take me off. Camped in the bush with wet clothes, had no dinner, or supper.

"Sunday Sept. 14. The Ottawa raft came down and took us all on board to Alexandria, there had dinner, had nothing more to eat today. Travelled sixteen miles to Mud Lake House and carried my clothes, very tiresome work, slept on the Bar room floor all night in company with Packers and Miners." [6]

Having arrived at Quesnelle on September 11, three members of the Queenston party, including their leader, Robert. B. McMicking, took the trail to the goldfields. On reaching Cottonwood, they realized the futility of travelling to Williams Creek so late in the season. Leaving Quesnelle in a canoe on the 17th, they travelled south and reached Alexandria that afternoon. From there they walked to Mud Lake House, where they met with one of their party employed as a cook for $40 a month and board. Remaining all night, McMicking wrote of Mud Lake House: "Fine good House, the best log House I have ever seen, good garden and splendid water." [7]

Having established a farm and roadhouse at Soda Creek in 1863, Peter Dunlevy sold Mud Lake House the following year to entrepreneur Frederick Black, who in turn sold it to John Peebles. While it is not known how long Mud Lake House continued as a roadhouse, by 1877 the land had been purchased by Robert Ashmore Collins, a miller from Soda Creek, where he and his family lived and farmed on Lots 58, 59, and 60, G.1. Cariboo. Following the death of Robert Collins in 1908 his family fell on hard times, and borrowed money against the farm from Samuel H. Bohanon, a retired businessman in Quesnel. When the mortgage was left unpaid, Bohanon foreclosed. Flora Fuller of Quesnel, and her sister Josephine Guy of Minneapolis, heirs to the Bohanon estate, sold the farm in 1937 to Alexander Robertson, a rancher from the Chilcotin. This property, now off the main highway, is still held by the Robertson family.

It is assumed from a survey map of 1885 that the Mud Lake roadhouse was one of four buildings located on the lower side of the original wagon road that winds through Lot 59, Weaver's preemption of 1861. These buildings were still standing in the 1930s, close to Melinda Creek, which runs through the property. When the buildings were dismantled, a number of the best logs were saved and stacked in a small enclosure nearby. The logs, local to the site, were an enormous size, about 22 inches by 10 inches by 40 feet in length, whip sawn and squared on all sides.

BEAVER LAKE HOUSE, 1860.
Lot 160, G.1., Cariboo.

Continuing on with his report to Governor Douglas in November 1860, Gold Commissioner Nind described his journey from Mud Lake, where he and constable Pinchbeck turned east and rode for 28 miles "over high rolling woodland and prairie" [8] to Beaver Lake, at the northwestern end of a wide, fertile valley. On a camping ground there Nind noticed that

> "D'Orsey and Deschilles have built a good sized log House, and cultivated a garden." [9]

Here three sections of land of 160 acres each were pre-empted by Richard D'Orsey and the two Deschilles brothers on October 13, 1860, making these the first registered pre-emptions of the Cariboo region.

Within the next year Beaver Lake, at the junction of several trails to the Quesnelle and Fraser rivers, had become an important animal market for pack-train operators. At this site mule teams and horses were traded and sold at high prices, with single animals sometimes bringing as much as $300. With its distinct agricultural advantages the area had also become the last feed-supply point for packers facing the bleak, desolate mountains to the northeast. These attractions drew many speculators to Beaver Lake, and by the close of 1860 all the arable land had changed hands more than once. Such was the case with the Frenchmen D'Orsey and the Deschilles brothers, who sold their property to Peter Dunlevy and his partner James Sellers.

On taking over from D'Orsey and the Deschilles, Dunlevy and Sellers refurbished the roadhouse and opened a store, one of the first independent trading posts in the country, where Dunlevy sold miners' supplies and traded goods with the Indians.

The roadhouse, known generally as "Sellers", was situated beside the trail, on the right or north bank, downstream from where a bridge spanned Beaver Creek. Meals prepared by a hired cook, and supervised by James Sellers sold for $1.50 each. Unsurpassed in quality and variety, the menu was described in the diary of a traveller of 1862:

"Had dinner at Sellers—had been living on bacon, beans and bread. Had fresh trout delicately fried, roast beef, mutton, roll of veal, potatoes, turnips, cabbage, lettuce and radishes. For dessert there were two kinds of pudding, cream, cheese, rolls of bread and large draughts of fresh milk." [10]

Of equal popularity was Thomas Moffitt's saloon, where the "finest of wines and liquors" were served, and where fabulous amounts of gold were said to have changed hands over the gambling tables. Ready to exchange their gold for an evening's relaxation at the roadhouse, the miners were easy prey for professional gamblers. One such victim arrived with a gold poke worth $2,000, played all night, lost all his gold, and ended up owing the house a further $6,000. James Sellers, the tall, brawny Texan who was the host at the road-house, discouraged the bad losers from physical violence with his good-natured remark, "Now don't you start sumthin ya cain't stop", and if that was not sufficient, he roughed them up just enough to end the confrontation. [11]

Peter Dunlevy, known as a shrewd businessman, was also possessed of a generous philosophy of life, "grubstaking" many a prospector, believing that life itself was a gamble. Born in Pittsburgh, Pennsylvania, on Ocober 21, 1834, of Irish parents, Dunlevy was only 18 when he went to the California gold rush and met two of his lifelong friends, James Sellers and Ira Crow. As a rule Dunlevy hated violence, leaving all such matters to Sellers, but on one occasion while Sellers was away, Dunlevy was forced to handle a delicate situation on his own.

Father Charles Grandidier, a Catholic missionary stationed at Fort Hope, left there early in the summer of 1861 for the goldfields of the Cariboo, where he intended to minister to the miners. Carrying only his mass kit, a few dollars, and some slices of bread and cheese, the priest travelled by way of the Harrison-to-Lillooet route, and the Bonaparte River. Plodding along in the rain near Hat Creek he chanced to meet the retired Hudson's Bay Company trader Donald McLean, who had recently settled there. The plight of the ardent missionary so touched the dour Scotsman that he took the priest home, fed him, and lent him a horse. Many miles to the north, at Beaver Lake, Grandidier sought shelter overnight at the local road-house. There he was ushered into a single common room filled with miners. Placing his blanket beside the roaring fireplace, Grandidier knelt to say his prayers, which immediately prompted gales of laughter from the miners. Hearing the disturbance, Peter Dunlevy rushed in from the kitchen, revolver in hand. Recognizing the problem immediately, he threatened to put a bullet through the next man who dared to mock the priest. Known to be a man of his word, Dunlevy was not challenged, and peace reigned all night.

In 1865, when Dunlevy and Sellers sold the Beaver Lake property to Anthony Buckner and Elias Hemenover, the new owners amalgamated all the arable land there into one large holding. Following the completion of the wagon road to Barkerville in 1865, traffic through Beaver Lake lessened, and while Buckner and Hemenover continued to operate a roadhouse, they looked for an alternate source of income. On finding a market for butter, cheese and milk in the populated areas of Quesnelle Forks and Williams Creek, they invested in a large herd of purebred dairy cows. For a few years the venture proved successful, but when too many of the valuable animals died during a series of long, hard winters, the business failed. By October 1870 the Beaver Lake ranch, advertised as one of the finest in the country, was sold for $6,000 to the French-Canadian packer Frank Guy and his associate Ah Tom, an employee of the large Chinese firm of Kwong Lee and Company, of Victoria. Over the next 20 years the Beaver Lake ranch, often employing Chinese labour, became a profitable enterprise. For a few years the partners swapped interests back and forth until 1889, when Frank Guy became the sole owner.

During the 1890s the roadhouses north of the 150 Mile post enjoyed a profitable period due to a resurgence of mining in the Horsefly and Quesnel Dam areas. In an article describing new developments in the area during the summer of 1895 a reporter mentioned Beaver Lake:

> "...where Frank Guy has a ranch and stopping place. In earlier days it had been kept by Peter Dunlevy. Mr. Guy intends building a new House." [12]

The "new House" started in 1896 was of frame construction, located on the south side of Beaver Creek, several hundred yards east of the original roadhouse site.

As old age and illness overtook him, Frank Guy left Beaver Lake for the 150 Mile House where he spent his last days with his old friends George Vieth and Bob Borland. Prior to his death in September 1898 Guy sold his ranch and roadhouse to Clifford W.

Cariboo pioneers. Back row, l. to r.: Fred Rose, Bob Cummings, Gassy Shaw. Front row, l. to r.: Mr. Thompson, Bob Borland, Frank Guy. CA 1895. (COURTESY EMILY PRIOR)

Eagle, of the firm of Eagle and Paxton, near Williams Lake. Since Guy left no will, his estate was handled by an appointed administrator, John A. Fraser of Quesnel, who worked hard to obtain a Crown Grant for the new owner. Due to its complicated history, the line of ownership was difficult to prove. Fortunately Peter Dunlevy was still living at Soda Creek, and through his testimony the several confusions were cleared up. A certificate of clear title was issued on August 12, 1902.

In purchasing the Beaver Lake ranch, "Toppy" Eagle intended to use it as a link in a relay of freight-wagon stations between Ashcroft and the recent mining developments on the Quesnel and Horsefly rivers. Occupied with other business interests, Eagle arranged for his newly married sister Christine and her husband, Gavin Hamilton, son of the well-known Hudson's Bay Company factor of the same name, to live and work at Beaver Lake. When Toppy was killed in the First World War, Christine Hamilton inherited the property. Nine children were born to the Hamiltons, each of whom worked on the ranch and assisted in the operation of the popular roadhouse. During the 1950s Gavin Hamilton and his sons became well known as big-game guides in the area, catering to wealthy American tourists who enjoyed the home-cooked meals and friendly atmosphere of the roadhouse. Following the deaths of their parents the family continued to operate the ranch and roadhouse. On February 28, 1971, while Tom, Pete, and Ethel Hamilton sat listening to a hockey game on the radio, a fire started in the attic of the old house, and by the time it was discovered the second storey was engulfed in flames. While some possessions were saved, most of the treasured family pictures, ledgers, and valuable documents were lost in the fire that completely demolished the house.

LITTLE LAKE HOUSE, 1860.
Lot 394, G.1., Cariboo.
Past Beaver Lake the trail to Quesnelle Forks rose sharply for several miles, veering to the northeast through forests of pine, patches of meadow and small swampy lakes. At Little Lake, 16 miles north of Beaver Lake, Commissioner Nind made note of another campground:

"where a House has been built for the accommodation of travellers." [13]

Nind also noticed several pastures close to the shores of Little Lake, the only feed in the vicinity.

During the summer of 1859 as miners began their explorations north of Quesnelle Forks, two ferries were established, one on each of the two forks of the Quesnelle River. The first to operate on the south fork were Robert Smith and his partner Edward Champlain, who ran a ferry prior to any government authority. By 1861 the trail by way of the North Fork, or Cariboo River had become the more popular, and for this reason Smith gave up the ferry, and with another partner, O'Brian, began to develop a small farm and road-house at Little Lake, the start of a new trail to Quesnelle Forks. A year later Smith made application for 160 acres of land "at Little Lake, near Quesnelle River" and advertised his roadhouse in the *B.C. & Victoria Directory*:

"LITTLE LAKE HOUSE.
Situated eight miles from the Forks of Quesnelle
and sixteen from Beaver Lake, on the direct
route to CARIBOO.

———————

First class accommodations for Travellers.
THE CHOICEST WINES, LIQUORS, and CIGARS,
GOOD FEED FOR ANIMALS.
SMITH & O'BRIAN, Proprietors." [14]

Smith's pre-emption of 1861 was never completed, and by 1865 it was considered abandoned.

VIETH AND BORLAND, 1890.

During the early 1890s when mining operations took on new life in the Quesnelle River and Horsefly areas, George Vieth and Robert Borland, pioneers of the Keithley area, accepted contracts to supply fresh beef to the new mines from their 150 Mile House ranch. At this time Borland applied for a pre-emption on the abandoned land of the Little Lake ranch, where he established a roadhouse, slaughterhouse and two barns. To ensure a steady supply of meats, about a dozen steers were driven in every few days from the ranch to Little Lake. A cowboy on those cattle drives in 1893, Albert J. Patenaude, later recalled:

"On long drives the cowboys used a 'belled' white cow, also known as a 'Judas' cow, to lead the nervous steers through difficult areas of creek or clime. Having reached their destination the belled cow was turned loose to find her own way home. When the cow reached the 150 mile ranch, it was time to start another several steers on their way to market. Once the cows were slaughtered the meat was hung for several days, and then sewn up in cheesecloth bags, and packed in ice." [15]

In charge of the slaughterhouse for many years was Samuel Crabtree Prior, who had left England for Canada as a boy of 13 to join an uncle in Bowmanville, Ontario. Fascinated by accounts of life in the west, Prior soon made his way to the Cariboo, arriving in 1891. At first he tried mining, but quickly realized he could make more money butchering cows.

On receiving a Crown Grant in 1900, Borland sold the Little Lake property to Sam Prior. A few years later Prior became an important witness in a bizarre murder case.

The Chinese cook at Little Lake House was a good friend of Sam Lock's, cook at the nearby Bullion Mine. Sam had worked for the owner, John B. Hobson, in California, and when Hobson moved his business interests to the Cariboo in 1893, the faithful servant followed. It was the practice at this time, for Chinese working in foreign lands, to have most of their wages collected by an educated representative or local Tong man, who saw to it that their families back in China were adequately provided for. Sam Lock had been sending money home for some time through Chew Hong, the Tong man at Quesnelle Forks. In 1906 Sam heard from a fellow Oriental, just returned from a trip to China, that his family was in dire financial straits, and that his wife was failing from lack of medical attention. Sam was beside himself at the news, and sent immediately for Chew Hong.

That afternoon as the miners returned from their work in the pit, they could hear the shouting and cursing in Chinese coming from the cookhouse. Then, as blood-curdling screams filled the air, the men rushed into the kitchen where they found Sam Lock, bloodied cleaver in hand, shrieking curses over the mutilated body of Chew Hong. "May your worthy ancestors deal with you in eternal fire forever," screamed Sam over and over, as the men pulled him away from the gory scene. Hobson was away at the time, but in regard for Sam, he dropped everything and returned to the Cariboo. By this time Sam had gone into hiding in the deep woods near Little Lake, where Prior's cook fed him for some time. While many people knew where Sam was hiding, their lips were sealed, even after a reward of $300 was posted by the provincial police. Sam Prior of Little Lake, who knew it was only a matter of time before the fugitive was found, persuaded Sam Lock that his life might be spared if he gave himself up. At the trial held in Clinton, despite the testimonials presented on Sam's behalf, Hobson's cook paid for his crime on the gallows on December 6, 1907.

PRIOR'S LITTLE LAKE HOUSE.

Romance came into Sam Prior's life when he met Emily Eholt, daughter of the foreman at the Bullion Mine. Married in 1910, the happy couple returned from their honeymoon to find their home at Little Lake burned to the ground. Rumour had it that the fire was started in revenge for Prior's involvement in Sam Lock's capture. A new, two-storey log house, built on the same site, soon replaced the original. Situated at the junction of two roads to the Quesnel River, the home became a roadhouse, serving the travelling public for many years. As business increased in 1913, a program of expansion on the ranch included a large addition to the roadhouse, with a dining room, living room and pantry on the main floor, and four bedrooms upstairs. A post office, operated by Sam Prior, also opened that year. Known as Hydraulic, after a post office previously located on the Quesnel River, the office continued at Little Lake for over 47 years. Following Prior's death in 1960, a Certificate of

Appreciation for his work was received from the postmaster general in Ottawa. Emily Prior continued to reside at the Little Lake ranch until her death in 1981.

QUESNELLE FORKS, 1860.

From Little Lake House to Quesnelle Forks, a poor trail of eight miles led through mosquito-laden swamps and burnt and fallen trees to where it descended a precipitous bank to the Quesnelle River. From this point a rope ferry, established by Benjamin Harte and James Locke, carried passengers and freight to the opposite bank.

By the spring of 1861 an improved trail had been built from Little Lake to Quesnelle Forks, where a toll bridge across the river at the townsite had replaced the ferry. Financed by Samuel Adler and his partner Tom Barry, the 200-foot structure, "of workmanlike and substantial appearance" [16] had cost the builders $5,000, a fortune at the time. While it was a great convenience, the bridge did not pay for itself. In 1862 the bridge-keeper's account estimated that although 6,000 people had used it, most had not paid the toll.

BRIDGE HOUSE SALOON AND ROADHOUSE, 1860.

Situated on the north end of the bridge was Adler and Barry's Bridge House, the gayest spot in Quesnelle Forks during the early 1860s. Here was offered a variety of entertainment, from billiards to theatrical performances, put on by wandering actors and musicians. While the cost of food and alcoholic beverages was high at Bridge House, accommodation was free, down on the floor, wrapped in one's own blanket. Adler and Barry continued to operate at Quesnelle Forks for a few years, but when business faded in 1865 they transferred their interests to Barkerville.

By 1861 Quesnelle Forks, or Quesnelle City, as it was known for a while, had doubled in size and tripled in population to become the largest supply depot of the region. While in 1860 only limited supplies had reached the community, by the following season several pack trains arrived, including those of Thomas Davidson of Williams Lake. Other roadhouses and stores were operated by Fred Black and his partner William Carlyle, William Morehead, and the Chinese merchant Ah Tom, agent of the firm of Kwong Lee and Company, of Victoria. Although the importance of Quesnelle Forks faded as other centres rose, the town was sufficiently established to support, until 1875, three well-filled stores, several hotels, and two butcher shops. By this time most of the mining claims abandoned by

Europeans on the Quesnelle River had been taken over by a population of Chinese miners. During the winter of 1875 as many as 200 occupied the abandoned buildings of Quesnelle Forks. For nearly 40 years they continued to live there, practising their own culture and religion, until the 1920s, when most had left. One of the last Chinese merchants at Quesnelle Forks was Lim Sing who sold his store in the 1940s, to the miner Herman Neilson and his wife. From time to time during a resurgence of mining activity, Europeans returned to live at "The Forks", where they operated stores and hotels.

McRae's Hotel, Quesnelle Forks, 1895.
Lot 3, Townsite of Quesnelle Forks.
During the 1890s, while big hydraulic mining companies operated on the Quesnelle River, John McRae and his wife kept a hotel and general store at Quesnelle Forks, where they maintained a successful business for some time.

James Sellers's Hotel at Cedar City, 1865.
Cedar Creek, close to Quesnelle Lake, usually associated with the rich "Nugget Patch" of gold discovered by John Lyne and Edward Platt in 1921, had in fact been the site of a growing community in the mid-1860s. Among the residents there was James Sellers, a partner of Peter Dunlevy's. Having sold his interests at Beaver Lake in 1865, Sellers was investing in another potentially strategic location:

> "A new town has sprung up a few hundred yards from Quesnelle Lake. It contains two stores, one kept by Mr. Isaac Lipsett, and another by Mr. Gibson. A restaurant and a butcher shop are kept by a son of the Flowery Kingdom. Mr. Sellers, formerly of Beaver Lake, is putting up the most substantial building in camp, which will open as a hotel in a week or two." [17]

Cedar City was virtually destroyed two years later by the great fire of 1869.

Davis's Roadhouse and Store, Keithley Creek, 1860.
Having registered many claims and collected a number of annual mining fees, Gold Commissioner Nind left Quesnelle Forks and rode north to Keithley Creek where in July, William R. "Doc" Keithley and his partners had discovered rich deposits of gold on the hillside

60 feet above Cariboo Lake. At that time the trail from Quesnelle Forks ran directly uphill and across country, through dense forests and across gravelly, quartz-bearing creeks for 25 miles, to an open hillside overlooking a range of rugged, snow-capped mountains. From this viewpoint the valley of Keithley Creek could be seen, where extensive mining was taking place. On his arrival Nind was most suprised to see the amount of labour expended in the building of enormous water wheels, pumps, and flumes, working in the bed of the creek. While Keithley and his associates made the initial strike of gold, they soon sold out, leaving it for others to mine. In their search for the "Mother Lode" they believed that while Keithley Creek was rich, even richer ground was not far away. It was a year later when the real wealth of Keithley Creek was dug. One of the first to work the ground was the Slide Company, a consortium of miners that included William Hazeltine and George Weaver, who recovered a pound of gold per man for many months. Located five miles up the creek, at the junction of two trails, the Slide Company's operations were soon surrounded by a number of buildings that included "Red Headed Davis's" roadhouse, store and saloon. To this establishment flocked the miners, rejoicing in their new-found wealth, followed closely by the gamblers and prostitutes, ever ready to extract a share. In addition to the usual amenities of this early roadhouse the proprietor had installed a billiard table and a piano, packed in on mules from San Francisco.

THE ANTLER CREEK DISCOVERIES, OCTOBER 1860.

In a letter to Governor Douglas dated March 27, 1861, Commissioner Nind excitedly reported the rich discoveries of gold on Antler Creek late in 1860, and his journey the following February to the site:

"Sir, I have the honor to inform you that during the winter great excitement has prevailed respecting the discovery of rich diggings on Antler Creek. The secrecy observed by the discoverers of the large prospects they were reputed to have found, together with the subsequent announcement of the situation of the creek, tended to so inflame the minds of all, that a new rush of staking took place in the dead of winter to this El Dorado. Many claims were staked, and in several instances the same ground was taken up by different parties. This led to contention, and almost to violence—with deadly weapons being drawn, but happily with no evil result. Shortly afterwards an appeal having been made for my appearance, I determined to proceed to Antler Creek." [18]

Accompanied by Constable Pinchbeck and two Indian packers Nind left Williams Lake on February 27, 1861. Severe winter conditions made travelling slow, and it was five days before they reached Davis's roadhouse up Keithley Creek. A storm raging on the mountain delayed the journey for another day, but when at last the weather cleared they proceeded north, up Snowshoe and Little Snowshoe Creeks to Antler, a distance of 20 miles:

> "There I found one log cabin built by the discoverers Rose and MacDonald, and the rest of the miners living in holes dug out of the snow which was six or seven feet deep. There I remained fully occupied for nearly six days, settling disputes and other transactions." [19]

CAPTAIN MITCHELL'S BRIDGE, 1861.
The following spring when Nind once again made his way to the goldfields he used a new, more direct route to Keithley Creek, by way of a toll bridge across the North Fork of the Quesnelle River. The builder, Captain Josiah E. Mitchell, had constructed the piers, blocks and windlass at his own expense, from local timber. At the north end of the bridge was a store, saloon, and roadhouse.

LAKE HOUSE, CARIBOO LAKE.
A roadhouse situated at the western end of the narrows between the lesser and main Cariboo Lakes was built in 1860 by Joseph Rawley, ferryman on Cariboo Lake. From this point passengers and freight were transported to various locations around the lake where mining was in progress. By 1861 a miner, L.D. Loucks, had taken over the enterprise, where he remained for several years.

KEITHLEY TOWN, 1861.
As a result of the Antler Creek discoveries and the new trail to Keithley by way of the North Fork, a small settlement emerged on a pleasant flat of land below the mouth of Keithley Creek. Among the miners' tents were half a dozen log buildings, including three general stores, a butcher shop, a blacksmith shop, and a roadhouse advertised as the

"CARIBOO RESTAURANT
KEITHLEY CREEK.
GEORGE TEAS & D.MCKEON, PROPS.
THE CHOICEST BRANDS OF WINES, LIQUORS
and CIGARS.
MEALS AT ALL HOURS.
PIES, BREAD, CAKE & CONFECTIONERY." [20]

SAM BRILEY'S ROADHOUSE AND STORE, LITTLE SNOWSHOE CREEK, 1861.
News of the Antler Creek mines set off fresh waves of migration to the Cariboo area in 1861, leaving the communities on the lower Fraser virtually deserted. Where the first prospectors had carried in their own supplies, by the summer of 1861 pack trains of goods were reaching Antler Creek over a trail built and paid for by the merchants of Antler and Keithley creeks.

Along this well-used route a miner, Samuel Briley, built a road-house and store at the mouth of Little Snowshoe Creek in the summer of 1861. While Davis's enterprise on Keithley Creek lasted only a short time, the location of Briley's camp, a few miles farther up the mountain, lasted for years and proved to be a boon to miners of that remote area. At his store Briley established a reputation for honest dealing, giving the miners fair exchange for their gold. An advertisement of Briley's establishment appeared in the *B.C. & Victoria Directory* of 1863:

"SAMUEL BRILEY,
Eight miles above Keithley's Creek, on the Direct Route
to Antler, Williams, and Lightning Creeks.

Every accommodation for Travellers.
MEALS AT ALL HOURS.
The TABLE supplied with everything the market affords.
WINES, LIQUORS and CIGARS,
of the best quality, to be had at the Bar." [21]

During the late 1860s this establishment was sold to local entrepreneurs George Vieth and Robert Borland, who continued to operate the store until the turn of the century. While it is not known how long Sam Briley remained in the Cariboo, it is apparent that he spent his last years on the coast. An obituary in the *Colonist* of June 9, 1886, mentioned:

"Sam Briley, an old Cariboo miner staying at the Colonial Hotel died of a heart attack. He was over fifty, unmarried, an industrious and sober man. Of late he had been working as a cook at Gillespie's camp." [22]

THE KEITHLEY CREEK RANCH, 1869.
Lot 349, G.1., Cariboo.
George Augustus Vieth and Robert Borland had arrived in the Cariboo in the early days of the gold rush. Both had tried mining, but without much success, and by 1867 they had formed a partnership in the packing and supply business which, up until that time, had been slow and unreliable. It was their belief that with their own pack trains and a few contracts, they could build a profitable business while being of service in the development of the country. Over the next 40 years they accomplished both these aims. On purchasing two freight wagons and 64 hand-picked mules, they obtained two contracts, one to carry mail to the goldfields, and the other to deliver supplies to the northern posts of the Hudson's Bay Company. These were the first of many enterprises that included three ranches, several stopping houses and stores, and various gold mines.

In 1869, they pre-empted 160 acres of land on the delta of Keithley Creek, where they kept a popular roadhouse and store. A

Vieth and Borland ranch at Keithley Creek, CA 1895. George Vieth, second from right, Bob Borland, fourth from right. (COURTESY BCARS)

post office opened there in 1873. In the store the miners exchanged their gold for goods, and in later years Borland claimed to have handled at least five tons of gold over the counter.

Over a period of 60 years three roadhouses have been built on the Keithley ranch. The original, a single-storey log building containing a store and post office, burned down in the 1890s. The second road-house, a two-storey log structure built on the same site, also burned down, in 1935. Fortunately the second store and post office were housed in a separate log building, which still exists. The present house, also a two-storey frame structure, was built on the original site in 1937 by a ship's carpenter, Wilkene, and a local man, Ole Sanburg. By 1886, when Vieth and Borland acquired the 150 Mile House ranch, they had reached the height of their careers. The next decade saw most of their interests sold, and the partnership dissolved in 1899. Despite their advancing years, for both were past the age of 70, they continued to be active. While George Vieth pursued his mining interests until his death in 1906, Bob Borland retained the Keithley Creek ranch, and in 1897 acquired the Pinchbeck farm at Williams Lake. At this time Borland's niece, Mabel Borland, arrived from Ontario. While her uncle spent most of his last years at Williams Lake, Miss Borland ran the Keithley ranch, where she was postmistress and government agent for the area. After the death of Bob Borland in 1923, Miss Borland returned to eastern Canada, but not before she had placed a granite headstone on her uncle's grave in the little cemetery close by the ranch. Sold in 1935 to Wiff Rae and his wife Betty Gorrie, the Keithley ranch became a hunting and fishing resort.

Among the many people who spent their holidays at the ranch during the 1940s were John Crittenden and Robert Conn, Seattle-based businessmen, who bought the ranch and guiding franchise in 1952. John's wife Bernice ran the kitchen of the roadhouse for many years, until she burned her hand severely, and had to retire.

In 1953 the Keithley ranch received an interesting visitor, a Mrs. McAllister of Saskatchewan who said she had been born on the ranch in a little cabin where her mother, a native woman known only as "Saltchuck", had lived with Bob Borland for many years. On a tour of the ranch Mrs. McAllister recognized the store and post office building, part of the barn, and the little cabin where she was born. The original barn, added to later, had been built of logs that ran the full length of the building, reinforced in the middle by two sets of cross logs. The cross logs created partitions, or rooms, in the barn, which for many years housed ancient sets of harness, carpenters' tools, and outmoded ranch implements, each one stamped with the identifying mark of V & B. An old wooden packing case, still used to store grain, bears the label: "Mrs. H.J. Vieth, Downsville, Rhode Island"; it was left there from a time when George Vieth's sister-in-law lived on the ranch.

Bob Conn, in addition to his fishing and hunting, had a sincere interest in the history of the area, and did a lot of exploring in the mountains behind the ranch. There he found a wide variety of Chinese and Caucasian artifacts, including a number of wooden grave markers, which he housed for years in the old post office cabin. The lettering on the headboards was worn and almost indecipherable, but on two of them were the words: "In memory of Joseph Rawley, native of New York, died October 4, 1881" and "John Olmere, native of Devonshire, England, died May 6, 1882."

Bob Conn died suddenly in the 1980s, after which his wife Betty sold most of the artifacts before returning to Seattle.

THE LIVE YANK'S HOTEL, LITTLE SNOWSHOE MOUNTAIN, 1863.

Not far from the site of Vieth and Borland's store is Luce Creek, a tributary of Snowshoe Creek, lying in the shadow of Yank's Peak, the highest in the area. Both these names are in memory of the pioneer William Luce, a prospector from Maine, U.S.A., who arrived in the Cariboo in the early 1860s. By 1863 Luce had staked a claim on Little Snowshoe Creek, where he mined and built a cabin beside the trail. Many travellers on the way to Antler Creek passed by Luce's cabin, and it became a well-known stopping house. During the heyday of his career Luce hired a Chinese miner to do the cooking at the roadhouse, while Luce, when he was not mining, loaded up his trusty Kentucky rifle to hunt grouse, grizzly bears, or anything else that turned up. The nickname "Live Yank" was given Luce by a reporter from *The Cariboo Sentinel*, who more than once wrote articles about Luce's progress in mining, and his hunting exploits. On one occasion while Luce was shooting into a flock of Franklin grouse, his rifle exploded and fell apart in seven pieces, leaving only the stock in his hands. Miraculously Luce was not injured, although several birds were killed. Most of all Luce loved to hunt grizzly bears, and in the evenings beside the fireplace of his roadhouse he would spin many an exciting tale of his escapades. One of these occurred in 1862, when Luce and his associates recovered over 30 mule carcasses off the mountain.

It had been a warm day in September when Michael Brown's pack train left Antler town, heading south for Keithley Creek. As they started down the mountain a short time later the sun clouded over, the wind grew cold, and the temperature fell dramatically. Over the high plateau a blizzard came down, the snow so thick and heavy that progress became impossible. With the storm increasing, the packers, concerned for their own survival, shot the fear-crazed mules as they floundered around in the deep drifts. Fashioning makeshift snow-shoes they descended to lower altitudes where they found Luce's cabin. When Luce heard of the amount of edible meat left frozen under the snow, he decided it was too precious to waste. With the help of several men at the camp, he brought most of the meat out on hand sleighs and distributed it among the miners of the area.

With the establishment of more accessible routes to the goldfields by the mid-1860s, Luce's stopping house became less frequented. The packers had also changed their route, making supplies less available. Continuing on with his mining for many years, William Luce, the "Live Yank", died in his cabin on a spring day in May 1881, and was buried nearby. The site of "Yank's old cabin" at the head of Luce Creek is clearly seen on a map drawn by Amos Bowman, a mining engineer who made a report on the area for the Geological Survey of Canada in 1885. At the site, the outline of Luce's cabin is still visible; built facing the south, it had been a large structure measuring 20 by 40 feet, half of which were add-ons and lean-tos. A pile of uniformly sized rocks in the northeast corner suggests a fireplace, or stone chimney. Among the rubble left by artifact hunters are quantities of metal "Bell & Black" matchboxes in varying stages of disintegration. Half hidden in the deep moss close by are shards of champagne, gin, and whisky glasses, the remnants of a well-stocked saloon.

BARR'S HOUSE, 1880s.

Robert Barr, a miner of the 1880s, kept a roadhouse, the remains of which can still be seen, beside the trail and a little downstream from the mouth of Luce Creek. In later years Barr worked with George Vieth and J. Severwright in a hydraulic mine known as "The Golden Gate".

THE COLOURED MAN'S HOUSE, NIGGER CREEK, 1862.

During the gold rush there were a number of American blacks in the Cariboo. Some had arrived with the Californians in 1858, but stronger than their desire for gold was their hope for a new life, free from slavery and oppression. During the 1860s at least two road-houses were known to have been operated by black men. One of these, situated at the junction of Jack of Clubs and Lightning creeks was run by two men, while the other, known as "the Coloured Man's House", and sometimes "The Nigger's," was located at the upper end of Nigger Creek, at the junction of the trails to Antler and Keithley creeks. In an account from 1862 the cabin in the latter location proved to be a lifesaving factor in the rescue of a group of residents of Antler Creek who became lost in an early snowfall on Bald Mountain. Another reference to this roadhouse, also in 1862, but not nearly as flattering, appeared in Reverend R.J. Dundas's account of a journey to Antler Creek:

> "...as to our poor pack horse, it gave out completely, and we had to leave it on the ridges of the Bald Mountains over which the trail passes between the Forks of the Quesnelle and Antler Creek. We sought shelter in a filthy cabin kept by a black man, and known as the "Niggers"—the only house of refuge within many miles. We resolved that one of us should push on next morning alone for Antler Creek. (17 miles distant and a good stiff walk) Another man at the "Niggers", also on his way to Antler Creek with two or three unloaded animals, consented to take the heaviest part of our pack." [23]

ANTLER CREEK, 1861-'62.

In February 1861 Gold Commissioner Nind had reported seeing only one cabin on Antler Creek, but by June ten log buildings, a sawmill, and a sea of tents had appeared along the creek. One of these, a large log house 35 by 50 feet, built by Messrs. Norris and Kane, served as a boarding house for the men working in their mine. Where only a few months earlier there had been absolute silence, the noise from 11 companies of miners at work could be heard up and down the creek. By August the number of buildings had doubled again, comprised of stores, roadhouses, saloons, and log dwellings, surrounded by an even larger number of canvas tents. Judge Begbie, who first visited the town in the summer of 1861, remarked that in comparison to similar communities in the California rush, the miners of Antler were a sober and law-abiding lot. Nevertheless, as Begbie also remarked, wherever gold was found, and liquor sold, professional gamblers followed, "as the carrion crow scents the dead on a battlefield", and Antler Creek was no exception. Merchants also took advantage of the free-spending miners, providing luxuries not usually seen north of New Westminster, and charging exorbitant prices.

PORTER'S HOUSE AND STORE, 1861.
Alexander Porter of Porter and Company, miners at Antler Creek, also had a roadhouse, store, and saloon beside the trail just south of the town, where champagne sold for $12 a bottle, and an ordinary meal of flapjacks and bacon cost $2.50.

During the summer of 1862, while the Reverend R.J. Dundas resided at Antler Creek, he gathered some very realistic impressions of the roaring gold camp, which later appeared in an Anglican Church missionary magazine. Travelling on foot over Bald Mountain, Dundas first realized he was close to Antler when he heard the creaking and groaning of the enormous wooden water wheels in operation along the creek. He also noticed the absence of trees on the hillside, cut down to make mine pit props and lumber for the 60-odd buildings that stood facing each other on the east side of the creek. Between the buildings a wide plank walkway ran intermittently along a perennially muddy street. Permeating the whole area was the terrible stench of rotting carcasses from the slaughter-houses at each end of the town.

CUSHEON'S HOTEL, ANTLER CREEK, 1861.
Upon his arrival Reverend Dundas was offered accommodation in what was said to be the best "digs" in Antler town, a hotel operated by James Cusheon and his wife. The "hotel", built of rough lumber, consisted of a large entrance room, bar-room, lounge, and dining room. Behind the kitchen was a lean-to, containing an apartment occupied by the Cusheons, and Mrs. Cusheon's mother and sister. On inspecting the general sleeping area, an open loft in the attic, Dundas explained:

> "I looked for a corner in which to lay my blankets, but found it dirty, swarming with lice and bedbugs." [24]

Fortunately he was allowed to sleep on the dining-room floor which, by comparison, was clean. In contrast to his remarks concerning the accommodations, Dundas found the meals to his satisfaction:

> "Enjoyed a good supper, cooked by Mrs. Cusheon—good bread, fresh beefsteak, beans, dried apples, and tea." [25]

Louse Racing.

While lice and bedbugs were the curse of most roadhouses, the miners made use of the "wee buggies" in a form of entertainment known as "louse racing". Lice or bedbugs, whichever were the handiest, were placed in competition on plates, the winner being the first to cross from one side to the other. A heated plate speeded up the action considerably and allowed a greater number of races to be run in an evening. Betting was heavy, and much gold changed hands.

The Destruction of Antler Town.

At Antler Creek, where the valley was very narrow, the town was built on ground that had been staked for mining. In August 1861, much to the consternation of the merchants, a miner, Joseph Patterson, began sluicing away the road through the town, under-mining some of the buildings. Not long afterward, the gold commissioner ruled that all the buildings of Antler town were to be removed to Sawmill Flat, three miles south. Obviously, from Dundas's description of 1862, the ruling had not yet been carried out. While some residents did move their buildings, most abandoned them and left for Williams Creek.

Sawmill Flat, 1861.

Named for R.P. Baylor's sawmill operating just south of Rose and McDonald's discovery claim, Sawmill Flat, at the junction of the trails to Keithley and Williams creeks was a logical site for a town, but apparently too far from the mining, which was farther down the creek.

Musgrave Arms, Sawmill Flat, 1869.

Suprisingly, after most of the population had left the Antler area, a new "hotel" was being built at Sawmill Flat in 1869, when this announcement appeared in *The Cariboo Sentinel*:

> "In consequence of the increasing travel between Barkerville and Keithley Creek, Mr. J. G. Jennings, [the owner of a store there] has commenced putting up a large hotel on Sawmill Flat. It is to be named the Musgrave Arms, in honour of our new Governor." [26]

Nothing more was heard of the Musgrave Arms project, possibly due to the exodus of the population to the Omineca gold rush in 1870. Still visible across Sawmill Flat today are the deep wagon ruts in the grass along the original trail from Keithley Creek, a reminder of the heavy traffic moving along that route 130 years ago.

LITTLER'S HOUSE, 1880s.

"Littler's", a wayside house beside the trail to Keithley Creek, was situated at the southern end of Sawmill Flat. Built in the early 1880s by Frederick Littler, expressman and mailman on the Keithley-to-Williams Creek run, it was a natural setting for a roadhouse, close to good water and pasture. Today the outlines of Littler's large cabin and adjoining blacksmith shop are still visible, despite the debris left scattered over the site by artifact hunters.

Fred Littler, an ex-boxer from London, England, was said to have been Billy Barker's bodyguard after his big strike in 1862. It was well known that Littler did a lot of drinking, and during one of his binges he challenged Judge Begbie to a boxing match. When Begbie declined, in consideration of Littler's inebriated condition, Littler continued to insist on the match, and Begbie, tired of Littler's nagging, let him have it on the chin, knocking him out with one swift blow.

MALONEY'S ROADHOUSE, 1861.

In their search for gold in the area adjacent to Antler Creek early in 1861, miners followed the creek to its source on Bald Mountain, above which they came across the headwaters of Williams Creek. In a small valley at the foot of the mountain, where a little creek meanders through a sunny alpine meadow, the miner Thomas Maloney built a cabin beside the trail, eight miles from Williams Creek. By October 1861, Maloney had applied to pre-empt 80 acres of land at this site, where his cabin had become a popular roadhouse.

Among the great population in the Cariboo in 1862 there were many classes of men with contrasting ideologies and morals. Providing religious guidance and comfort to the miners was the aim of the Anglican Bishop George Hills and his clerics, the Reverends Dundas and Sheepshanks, who spent the summer in the goldfields. Early one morning while walking from Antler Creek to Richfield, Dundas called in at Maloney's roadhouse for a bite of breakfast.

As he sat eating a plate of fried beef and bacon, a sullen-looking individual sat down at the table with him. Dundas attempted to engage him in conversation, and while he ate voraciously, the man remained silent. Just as they had finished eating, another man suddenly shot through the door of the roadhouse. "Look out," he called, and before anyone could move, the silent stranger was up and running, out of the house and into the woods. A few moments later two constables from Richfield arrived, puffing up the trail. They had heard that the noted gambler and outlaw "Liverpool Jack", who had shot a man in a saloon in Richfield the night before, was there, at Maloney's. Dundas was quite shaken to think that he had eaten breakfast in company with such a man.

During the summer Bishop Hills had been visiting a terminally ill miner, John Emmory, one of two brothers mining on a nearby creek. Hearing of Emmory's death on August 19, Hills made arrangements for the funeral, which was to be held, at Emmory's request, beside the grave of a dear friend who had died the year before "close to Maloney's roadhouse". In his diary Bishop Hills described the details of the event:

> "...the procession of some forty miners, who had given up their valuable time to bear the corpse eight long miles up the Bald Mountain from Williams Creek, to show respect for their departed comrade....I had visited him for near a month before he died. Truly will his aged parents in New Brunswick be consoled to hear of his last month on earth and how happy he was to be buried amidst the respect and regrets of many friends." [27]

The Reverend Dundas, in his account of the funeral, mentions "the brother of the deceased, who stood forward and thanked the Bishop for his kindness." The two graves at Maloney's are still to be found "on a grassy flat, up a bank by which the trail ran, some little way in the rear of a settler's House." [28]

Although extensive efforts have been made to discover the identity of Emmory's graveside companion, nothing has come of them. Church records do not go back that far, and graves outside a cemetery, unless they are registered, are hard to verify.

The outlines of Tom Maloney's roadhouse, which operated between 1861 and 1866, are still visible. It had been a large building, but all that remains today are piles of rock from two stone fireplaces, one at each end. Close by the house is the outline of a four-furlong racetrack, marked with rocks. Though the creek at Maloney's flat is named Racetrack Creek, nowhere are there any accounts of races held there.

With the completion of the wagon road from Quesnellemouth to Barkerville in 1865, traffic along the Antler trail declined, and Tom Maloney left the area in search of greener fields.

WILLIAMS CREEK, 1860.

William Dietz, after whom Williams Creek was named, was one of several prospectors on the creek in February 1861. While this became the richest and longest-worked creek of any in the Cariboo, Dietz was said to have staked the poorest claim of all.

By the close of 1862 there were three distinct communities on Williams Creek, the result of three separate strikes of gold in different locations up and down the creek. The first community, known as Williams Creek, soon became Richfield, a name suggested by Lieutenant H.S. Palmer of the Royal Engineers when he surveyed the townsite. When a third layer of pre-glacial gold was discovered on a tributary of the creek in 1862, by Ned Stout, it encouraged the men of the Barker Company, and John "Cariboo" Cameron, to dig deeper on their claims below the canyon. As activity increased around those two claims, about half a mile apart, cabins and small shops located around them. On the lower end the community became known as Cameronton, while around the Barker Company claims the name remained indefinite for some time, being alternately Middleton, Centreville, and finally Barkerville.

At first the miners on Williams Creek lived in tents, but by winter most of them had built log cabins, close to their claims. Even at that

Cameronton, or lower Barkerville, on Williams Creek, photographed by Charles Gentile. (COURTESY BCARS)

time buildings were not cheap. A log cabin with two rooms cost $600, and with a stone fireplace it was $800. For this reason most mine owners built boarding houses, which operated like roadhouses, to accommodate their employees.

CAMERON'S HOTEL AND SALOON, 1863.
One of the earliest boarding houses was operated by Mr. and Mrs. J. Cameron, (no relation to Cariboo Cameron) who had moved from their roadhouse at the 15 Mile point on the trail from Quesnellemouth, to Williams Creek in 1862. The business was sold in 1865 to Janet Morris, who moved it down the creek to Cameronton, renaming it the Pioneer Hotel. Widowed soon after, Janet married miner William Allen, and became quite successful as the proprietor of several roadhouses in the vicinity. Janet was killed in September 1870, when her carriage went over the bank at Black Jack Canyon.

THE CARIBOO EXCHANGE HOTEL, 1867.
An interesting and overlooked character in Barkerville's early history was Elizabeth Ord, an unattached and spunky woman from California. In July 1867 Miss Ord had advertised her hotel on Williams Creek:

"CARIBOO EXCHANGE HOTEL, BARKERVILLE, B.C.
Is now open for the accommodation of the mining community and the general public. No expense has been spared to render the House all that could be desired for comfort and convenience. The Bar is supplied with a complete stock of wines, liquors, and Cigars. Well aired beds may be had at moderate charge. E. Ord. Prop." [29]

A few months prior to this Miss Ord had published a "NOTICE" in *The Cariboo Sentinel* saying that "certain malicious persons" had circulated reports to the effect that she did not own the hotel, which in the Notice, she flatly denied, inviting anyone to see her title deed.
That this poor woman was continually harassed in her efforts to have a business career in the Cariboo goldfields is obvious from the reports of many court cases held at Barkerville between 1867 and 1872. On these occasions she appeared as both defendant and plaintiff, concerning mining claims, property damage suits, proofs of ownership, and even a breach of promise involving her engagement

to Robert Drinkall. At the hearing of this particular suit several witnesses portrayed Miss Ord as having a creditable character, until someone accused her of having been "a bilk", or a cheat, in the California gold camps. This condemned her, and she lost the case. Of course, this witness could have been paid. Was Miss Ord the paranoiac female she appeared to be, or was she the victim of male dominance and jealousy? These stressful events soon led her to financial ruin, disrepute, and suspected insanity. In October 1889, having been escorted to New Westminster as a likely patient for the insane asylum, she was examined by two doctors and declared to be sane.

"They Don't Agree.

A woman named Elizabeth Ord was brought down from Barkerville by Constable Lindsay, on the plea that she was insane and a fit subject for the lunatic asylum, where it was intended she should be domiciled for an undetermined time. Mr. Chas. Warick, Gov. Agent at New Westminster had her examined by Dr. I.M. McLean, and Dr. Cooper, who have declared her to be sane. Accordingly she has been liberated, and will be allowed to return to her home in a few days. It appears that the medical men in New Westminster differ in opinion from their fellows in the upper country." [30]

Roadhouses and boarding places advertised in *The Cariboo Sentinel* between 1865 and the mid-1870s included these five:

The Forest Hill Restaurant in Richfield where "Miss Hickman has opened her old stand again and is prepared to furnish single meals at $1.00, and board at $12.00 a week."

Miners Boarding House. Pearson & Carter, Props, whose house was located on the Crittenden claim, on Lowhee Creek.

"Miners' Boarding House and General Store. Edward Shearer, Prop."

Miners' Home. S.T. Wilcox, Prop. Free lodging, meals $16.00 a week.

Miss Parker's Boarding House in Barkerville, opposite The Cariboo Sentinel Office, "where meals are served from 5.30 a.m. to 9.00 p.m. Board $12.00 a week." [31]

STOUT'S GULCH HOUSE, 1868.

At Stout's Gulch, Alexander Douglas McInnes and his wife Mary Roddy McInnes operated a boarding house for the men of the Taff Vale, a company of Welsh miners. Earlier McInnes had helped to run a home for the men of Cameron's claim. Mrs. McInnes was a sister of Richard Cameron's wife, and had been on Williams Creek since 1862.

THE STOUT'S GULCH HOTEL, 1869.

Situated on the left side of the gulch was the Stout's Gulch Hotel, where the proprietor, Fred Rose, advertised board at $12 a week and single meals at a dollar. Rose, born in Buenos Aires, Argentina, and his wife, Emma Marguerite Otmiller, a Prussian, arrived on Williams Creek with Edward (Ned) Stout, the discoverer of rich diggings on what became Stout's Gulch, where they operated a boarding house for the men of Stout's mine.

THE BOWDEN HOTEL, MARYSVILLE, 1863.

As a result of the workings of the Marysville Company claims across Williams Creek from Cameronton, a community known as Marysville flourished for a few years. Among the several buildings was the Bowden Hotel, named for Nicolas Bowden, one of the mine owners. When several cases of typhoid and scurvy broke out on Williams Creek in 1863, the community, with some government help, raised the money for a hospital, which was built that year at Marysville.

LANE AND KURTZ COMPANY BOARDING HOUSE, 1870s.

For a few years this boarding house, located near the Lane and Kurtz Company mine on "the meadows" north of Cameronton, was operated by Joseph Huot de St. Laurent, a miner from Trois

Joseph St. Laurent. (COURTESY QUESNEL AND DISTRICT MUSEUM)

Rivieres, Quebec, and his wife, Georgina Wilhemina Nachtingal, a former hurdy-gurdy dancing girl in Barkerville in the 1860s. Joseph, who was well educated, was also the bookkeeper for the Lane and Kurtz Company, while Wilhemina, a girl of German extraction, was an excellent cook. This capable pair later ran a boarding house on Lowhee Creek, where both St. Laurent and John Bowron had mining interests.

CONKLIN GULCH, 1865.

Mrs. F.W. Dustin kept a boarding house on Conklin Gulch, a tributary of Williams Creek, where in 1874 the Erricson Company sank shafts into rich diggings below Williams Creek.

FORREST HOUSE, 1870s.

A hotel located at "the meadows", close to the workings of the Lane and Kurtz Company mine, was purchased and refurbished by Mr. W. Forrest in 1873. The hotel closed a year later when the mine failed and Mr. Forrest declared bankruptcy.

MADAME BENDIXON'S BOARDING HOUSE, 1880-1898.

While Fanny Bendixon operated a number of saloons in Barkerville from the time of her arrival in 1866, by 1880 she had become the owner of a boarding house located on Main Street, which she maintained until her death in 1898.

THE KELLY HOTEL.

Andrew Kelly, who staked a claim near Richfield in 1862, was a man of talent and ingenuity. While operating the Wake-Up Jake mine in 1863 he opened a bake shop and coffee bar on Williams Creek, a great boon to the busy miners. For two years both the mine and the bake shop were very successful, but by 1866 the gold in the mine was worked out. Early that spring Kelly was married in Victoria to Elizabeth Hastie of Ayrshire, Scotland, and in March, when the couple returned to the Cariboo, they moved to nearby Grouse Creek, where two communities had sprung up as a result of the Heron claim discoveries of 1864. Once again Kelly staked a claim and, with his wife, operated a boarding house and bake shop until 1870, when they and their two children returned to Barkerville. There they bought what had been the Hotel de France, renaming it the Kelly Hotel. The hotel operated for many years, and after Andrew and Elizabeth retired to Victoria in 1910, their son William Kelly took over the family

Andrew Kelly and Elizabeth Hastie Kelly. (COURTESY BCARS)

business. William married Lottie Brown, daughter of a pioneer family, and following William's death in 1917, Lottie carried on with the task of raising their four boys, and managing the Kelly Hotel and store. In 1919 Lottie married Malcolm McKinnon, a mining man. The hotel burned down in 1949.

AUSTIN'S HOTEL, RICHFIELD, 1880.

While residing temporarily in Barkerville in 1880, Sarah Crease and her husband, Judge Henry Crease, "put up" at Austin's Hotel where they occupied "two airy private rooms with clean bed and hangings", but where "the bed was very hard and narrow, and the floor very dirty". Before leaving Barkerville Mrs. Crease also objected to being charged $2.50 for "a little bit of laundry". [32]

FOOTNOTES

CHAPTER 1.

1. H.H. Bancroft, *History of British Columbia*, Volume 32, p.54.
2. *British Columbia Gazette*, July 25, 1858.
3. *Ibid.*
4. W. Champness, *To Cariboo and Back in 1862*, pp.94,95.
5. Sarah Crease, "Diary", September 4, 1880.
6. Viscount Milton, and Dr. W.B. Cheadle, *North-west Passage by Land*. 1865. p.347.
7. F.W. Howay, *The Early History of the Fraser River Mines*, p.89, Footnote #57.
8. Bishop Hills, "Diary", June 15, 1860.
9. Victoria *Colonist,* July 31, 1863, p.3.
10. James Douglas, Private Papers, 1861.
11. Bishop Hills, "Diary", June 25, 1863.
12. *Ibid.*
13. *Ibid.*
14. David W. Higgins, *The Mystic Spring*, p.98.
15. Bishop Hills, "Diary", June 12, 1860.
16. Simon Fraser, *Letters and Journals*, June 26, 1808.

CHAPTER 2.

1. James Douglas, letter to Lord Lytton, November 9, 1858.
2. Lieutenant R.C. Mayne, R.N. *Four Years in British Columbia*, p.137.
3. Dr. W.B. Cheadle, "Journal", October 2, 1863.
4. *Ibid*, October 4, 1863.
5. *Ibid.*
6. W. Champness, *To Cariboo And Back in 1862*, p.50.
7. Louis LeBourdais, "Harry Jones Story", p.6.

8. *British Colonist*, March 9, 1863, p.2.

9. *The Cariboo Sentinel*, May 7, 1866, p.3.

10. Dr. W.B. Cheadle, "Journal", October 6, 1863.

11. Arthur Bushby, "Diary", April, 1859.

12. Victoria *Gazette*, April, 1860.

13. *New Westminster British Columbian*, March 28, 1862.

14. Rev. M. McFie, *Vancouver Island and British Columbia*, p.225.

15. Arthur Bushby, "Diary", April 1859.

16. F. W. Laing, *Colonial Farm Settlers*, p.247.

17. Victoria *Colonist*, April 7, 1861, p.2.

18. Dr. W.B. Cheadle, "Journal", October 7, 1863.

19. *Ibid*.

20. *New Westminster British Columbian*, December 12, 1866.

21. Dr. W.B. Cheadle, "Journal", October 8, 1863.

22. Bishop Hills, "Diary", June 13, 1861.

CHAPTER 3.

1. Walter Moberly, "History of the Cariboo Wagon Road", p.26.

2. Bishop Hills, "Diary", June 26, 1860.

3. *Ibid*.

4. F.W. Laing, *Colonial Farm Settlers*, p.230.

5. *British Columbia Tribune*, June 4, 1866,. p.3.

6. Victoria *Colonist*, January 22, 1873, p.3.

7. *Kamloops Sentinel*, August 26, 1880, p.3.

8. Bishop Hills, "Diary", September 5, 1880.

9. *British Columbia Examiner*, December 7, 1868, p.2.

10. Sarah Crease, "Diary", September 5, 1880.

11. Bishop Hills, "Diary", June 28, 1860.

12. *Ibid*, June 29, 1860.

13. Alfred R.C. Selwyn, Geological Survey of Canada, *Report of 1874*, p.22.

14. B.C. Land Titles, Victoria, B.C., *Book of Mortgages and Conveyances*, October 14, 1862.

15. *British Columbia Examiner*, November 27, 1866, p.4.

16. *Mainland Guardian*, March 15, 1876, p.2.

17. Victoria *Colonist*, December 1, 1862, p.3.

18. Bishop Hills, "Diary", June 20, 1861.

19. *Ibid*, June 27, 1862.

20. Victoria *Gazette*, September 29, 1859, p.3.

21. F.W. Laing, *Colonial Farm Settlers*, p.234.

22. Vancouver *Sun*, 1940. "The Old 50 Mile House".

23. Lieutenant R.C. Mayne, R.N., *Four Years in British Columbia*, p.109.
24. *New Westminster British Columbian*, July 9, 1866.
25. Sarah Crease, "Diary", September 6, 1880.
26. *Ibid*, October 26, 1880.
27. *Ibid*.
28. Victoria *Gazette*, May 17, 1859, p.3.
29. Judge M.B. Begbie, letter, June 24, 1862.
30. Quoted in *New Westminster British Columbian*, January 23, 1864, p.2.
31. Dr. M.S. Wade, *Overlanders of '62*, p.155.
32. *Ibid*.
33. Bishop Hills, "Diary", July 7, 1860.
34. *Ibid*, July 12, 1860.
35. *The Cariboo Sentinel*, May 7, 1866, p.3.
36. Victoria *Colonist*, January 4, 1889, p.5.

CHAPTER 4.
1. Alexander P. McInnes, *Chronicles of the Cariboo*, p.2.
2. *British Colonist*, September 30, 1859, p.2.
3. Reverend Robert C. Lundin Brown, *British Columbia, An Essay*.
4. Harry Guillod, "Diary", August, 8, 1862.
5. *The B.C. & Victoria Directory*, 1862, p.156.
6. Henry M. Ball, "Diary", September 3, 1865.
7. Harry Guillod, "Diary", August 8, 1862.
8. Bishop Hills, "Diary", September 8, 1862.
9. Victoria *Colonist*, January 27, 1863, p.2.
10. Arthur Crease, "Diary", August 1901.
11. F.W. Laing, *Colonial Farm Settlers*, p.314.

CHAPTER 5.
1. Victoria *Colonist*, March 24, 1862, p.2.
2. Victoria *Colonist*, April 23, 1862, p.3.
3. Dr. W.B. Cheadle, "Journal", October 10, 1863.
4. Sergeant John McMurphy, "Diary", June 25, 26, 1862.
5. *Ibid*.
6. Lieutenant R.C. Mayne, R.N., *Four Years in British Columbia*, p.385.
7. James Douglas, Private Papers, June 8, 1861.
8. Bishop Hills, "Diary", June 18, 1862.
9. Dr. M.S. Wade, *The Cariboo Road*, p.146.

10. Victoria *Colonist*, May 22, 1861, p.2.
11. Bishop Hills "Diary", July 3, 1862.
12. Dr. W.B. Cheadle, "Journal", October 11, 1863.
13. Bruce Hutchison, *The Fraser*, p.210.
14. *Ibid*, p.212.
15. Clement Cornwall, "Diary", June 21, 1863.
16. Sergeant John McMurphy, "Diary", July 21, 1862.
17. *Ibid*, September 25, 1862.
18. Dr. M.S. Wade, *Overlanders of '62*. p.155.
19. R.H. Alexander, "Diary", October 22, 1862.
20. Sergeant John McMurphy, "Diary", August 27, 1862.
21. Victoria *Colonist*, August 31, 1863, p.2.
22. Sarah Crease, "Diary", September 9, 1880.

CHAPTER 6.
1. Dr. W.B. Cheadle, "Journal", September 13, 1863.
2. *Ibid*, September 15, 1862.
3. Sarah Crease, "Diary", October 22, 1880.
4. Henry P. Cornwall, "Diary", January 15, 1865.
5. *Ibid*, July 1, 1862.
6. *Ibid*, December 25, 1864.
7. Clement F. Cornwall, "Diary", February 26, 1863.
8. *Ibid*, May 7, 1863.
9. *Ibid*, October 13, 1863.
10. *Ibid*, November 30, 1863.
11. Dr. W.B. Cheadle, "Journal", November 20, 1863.
12. Clement F. Cornwall, "Journal", February 24, 1864.
13. *Ibid*, February 27, 1864.
14. *Ibid*, March 5, 1864.
15. *Ibid*.
16. *Ibid*, March 19, 1864.
17. *The Cariboo Sentinel*, May 21, 1866, p.4.
18. Dr. M.S. Wade, *The Cariboo Road*, p.254.
19. *B.C. Mining Journal*, January 22, 1898, p.4.
20. *Ibid*, January 12, 1897.
21. F.W. Laing, *Colonial Farm Settlers*, pp.352,353.
22. *The Cariboo Sentinel*, May 7, 1866, p.4.
23. Sarah Crease, "Diary", October 22, 1880.
24. *Ibid*.
25. *Ibid*, October 22, 1880.
26. *Western Methodist Recorder*, December 1904, p.2.

27. R. Byron Johnson, *Very Far West Indeed*, 1872, p.199.

28. *Ashcroft Journal*, April 30, 1953.

29. B.C.Land Titles, Legal Surveys Branch, Victoria, B.C. Crown Grant #3068/19.

30. *Ibid*.

31. Sarah Crease, "Diary", October 13, 1880.

32. Walter Moberly, "History of the Cariboo Wagon Road", pp.33, 34.

33. W. Champness, *To Cariboo and Back in 1862*, pp.84-86.

34. Arthur Bushby, "Diary", March 15, 1872.

35. Willis West, "Staging and Stage Holdups", p.199.

36. Laura McNeil, "Diary", August 22, 1901.

37. Walter Moberly, "History of the Cariboo Wagon Road", p.32.

38. Harry Guillod, "Diary", October 2, 1862.

39. James Thomson, *For Friends at Home*, p.309.

40. Hugh Reid, "Mileposts on the Cariboo Highway", p.5.

CHAPTER 7.

1. P.H. Nind, letter of October 17, 1860.

2. *Ibid*.

3. P.H. Nind, letter of November 9, 1860.

4. *The Toronto Mail*, Saturday, November 5, 1887, p.3.

5. Alexander P. McInnes, *Chronicles of the Cariboo*, p.6.

6. *B.C. & Victoria Directory*, 1863, p.158.

7. Bishop Hills, "Diary", July 15, 1862.

8. Gustavus B. Wright, letter to Henry Crease, March 17, 1862.

9. Lieutenant H.S. Palmer, R.E., Report of March, 1863, pp.2,4.

10. Sergeant John McMurphy, "Diary", August 8, 1863.

11. Pinchbeck & Co., Daybook, April, 1870.

12. Western Canada Ranching Company, Account books, 1890-1893.

CHAPTER 8.

1. P.H. Nind, letter to Colonial Secretary, October 17, 1860.

2. *Ibid*.

3. Cariboo Pre-emptions, 1860-'69, November 25, 1861.

4. F.W. Laing. *Colonial Farm Settlers*, p.316.

5. *B.C. & Victoria Directory*, 1863, p.157.

6. Dr. M.S. Wade, *Overlanders of '62*, p.139.

7. *Ibid*, p.141.

8. P.H. Nind, letter of November 9, 1860.

9. *Ibid.*
10. Captain C.W. Buckley, R.N., "Diary", April-August, 1862.
11. Alexander P. McInnes, *Chronicles of the Cariboo*, p.5.
12. *B.C. Mining Journal*, July 4, 1895, p.2.
13. P.H. Nind, letter of Ocober 9, 1860.
14. *B.C. & Victoria Directory*, 1863, p.158.
15. Conversation with Albert Patenaude, 1948.
16. P.H. Nind, letter of October 24, 1860.
17. *The Cariboo Sentinel*, July 18, 1867, p.3.
18. P.H. Nind, letter of March 27, 1861.
19. *Ibid.*
20. *B.C. & Victoria Directory*, 1863, p.160.
21. *Ibid*, p.153.
22. Victoria *Colonist*, June 9, 1886, p.3.
23. Reverend R.J. Dundas, *Sketches of Missionary Life*, p.2
24. *Ibid*, p.197.
25. *Ibid.*
26. *The Cariboo Sentinel*, July 21, 1869, p.3.
27. Bishop Hills, "Diary", August 19, 1862.
28. Reverend R.J. Dundas, *Sketches of Missionary Life*, pp.154-159.
29. *The Cariboo Sentinel*, July 1, 1867, p.2.
30. *Vancouver Daily World*, October 25, 1889, p.1.
31. *The Cariboo Sentinel*, June 17, 1865.
32. Sarah Crease, "Diary", September 18 and 24, 1880.

BIBLIOGRAPHY

PUBLISHED SOURCES

Akrigg, G.P.V. and Helen B. *British Columbia Chronicle, 1778-1846: Adventures by Sea and Land.* Vancouver, B.C. Discovery Press. 1975.

Akrigg, G.P.V. and Helen B. *British Columbia Chronicle, 1847-1871: Gold and Colonists.* Vancouver, B.C. Discovery Press. 1977.

Akrigg, G.P.V. and Helen B. *British Columbia Place Names.* Victoria, B.C. Sono Nis Press. 1986.

Anderson, James. *Sawney's Letters and Cariboo Rhymes.* Barkerville Restoration Advisory Committee of B.C. 1962.

Bancroft, H.H. *Bancroft's Works Volume XXXII. History of British Columbia. 1792-1887.* San Francisco. The History Company, Publishers. 1886.

Bancroft, H.H. *Bancroft's Works Volume XXVIII. History of the Northwest Coast Volume 11. 1800-1846.* San Francisco. The History Company, Publishers. 1886.

Binns, Archie. *Peter Skene Ogden: Fur Trader.* Portland, Oregon. Binfords and Mort, 1967.

Boam, A.J. and Brown, A.G. *British Columbia, 1912.* London, England. Sells Ltd.

Brown, R.C. Lundin. *British Columbia, An Essay.* New Westminster, B.C. The Royal Engineers Press. 1863.

Buckland, F.M. "Building The Cariboo Road." 6th Annual Report of Okanagan Historical Society.

Champness, W. *To Cariboo and Back in 1862.* Fairfield, Washington. Ye Galleon Press. 1972.

Craig, Andy A. *Trucking: British Columbia's Trucking History.* Saanichton, B.C. Hancock House. 1977.

Cornwallis, Kinahan. *The New Eldorado, or British Columbia.* London, England. T.C. Newby. 1858.

E.P. Creech. "Brigade Trails of B.C.". *The Beaver*, March, 1953.

Cronin, Kay. *Cross In The Wilderness.* Vancouver, B.C. Mitchell Press. 1960.

Decker, Frances. *Pemberton: The History of a Settlement.* Pemberton Pioneer Women. Pemberton, B.C. 1977.

Downs, Art. "The Road North". *Cariboo and Northern B.C.Digest.* Winter, 1947.

Downs, Art. *Paddlewheels on the Frontier, the Story of B.C. Sternwheel Steamers.* Cloverdale, B.C. Heritage House. 1967.

Edwards, Irene. *Short Portage to Lillooet.* Lillooet, B.C. 1978.

Elliot, Gordon R. *Quesnel, Commercial Centre of the Cariboo Gold Rush.* Quesnel Cariboo Observer. 1958.

Ferris, J.E. "Ranald MacDonald." *Pacific Northwest Quarterly* 48 (1957) 13-16.

Forbes, Molly. *Lac La Hache.* Quesnel, B.C. 1970.

Forbes, Molly, "Alex Meiss and His Wooden Leg." *Clinton Cache Creek Pioneer.* March 11, 1970.

Fraser, Simon. *Letters and Journals, 1806-1808.* Edited by W.K. Lamb. Toronto. Macmillan. 1960.

Gosnell, R.E. *The Year Book of British Columbia and Manual of Provincial Information.* 1903.

Halcome, Rev. J.J. *The Emigrant and The Heathen. Sketches of Missionary Life.* 1874.

Harris, Lorraine, *Halfway To The Goldfields. A History of Lillooet.* Vancouver, B.C. J.J.Douglas Ltd. 1977.

Higgins, D.W. *The Mystic Spring and other Tales of Western Life.* Toronto. Briggs. 1904.

Hong, William M. *And So That's How It Happened.* Recollections Of Stanley-Barkerville, Edited by Gary and Eileen Seale. Quesnel, B.C. Spartan Printing. 1978.

Horsefly Historial Society. *Horsefly, Its Early History, 1858-1915.* Revised Edition.1981.

Howay, F.W. *The Early History of the Fraser River Mines.* Archives of British Columbia, Memoir #6.

Hutchison, Bruce. *The Fraser. The Great Rivers of Canada.* Toronto and Vancouver, B.C. Clarke Irwin & Co. Ltd. 1982.

Johnson. E.P. "The Early Years of Ashcroft Manor." *B.C.Studies* #5. Vancouver, B.C. U.B.C.Press. 1970.

Johnson, R. Byron. *Very Far West Indeed.* London, England. Marsdon, Lowe and Searle. 1872.

Laing, F.W. *Colonial Farm Settlers on the Mainland of British Columbia, 1858-1871.* Victoria, B.C. 1939.

Laing, F.W. "Some Pioneers of the Cattle Industry." *B.C. Historical Quarterly*, Vol.6. October 1942.

LeBourdais, Louis, "The Famous Keithley Trail." *Vancouver Province*, August 29, 1926.

Lewis, William S. and Murakami, Naojiro, Editors. *Ranald MacDonald, 1824-1849* Eastern Washington State Historical Society. Spokane, Washington. 1923.

Lindley, Joe. *Three Years In Cariboo.* San Francisco. A. Rosenfield, Publishers. 1862.

Ludditt, F.W. *Barkerville Days.* Vancouver, B.C. Mitchell Press. 1969.

Lyons, C.P. *Milestones on the Mighty Fraser.* Vancouver, B.C. 1956.

MacDonald, Ranald. *Ranald MacDonald, the narrative of his early life on the Columbia.* Spokane, Washington. Eastern Washington State Historical Society, 1923.

Macfie, Matthew. *Vancouver Island and British Columbia, Their History, Resources and Prospects.* London, England. Longmans, Green & Co. 1865.

McInnes, Alexander P. *Chronicles of the Cariboo.* Dunlevy's Discovery of Gold on the Horsefly. Lillooet, B.C. Lillooet Publishers Limited. 1938.

McNeil, Laura. "Diary" *Big Country Cariboo.* Fall/Winter, 1978.

Martin's Mining Cases and Statutes of B.C. 1853-1902. Toronto. B.C. Carswell Co. Ltd. 1903.

Mayne, Lieutenant R.C. *Four Years in British Columbia and Vancouver Island.* London. John Murray. 1862.

Melvin, G.H. *Post Offices of British Columbia 1858-1970.* Vernon, B.C. 1972.

Milton, Viscount, and Cheadle, Dr. W.B. *North-West Passage by Land 1865.* Coles Canadian Collection. Toronto, Canada. Coles Publishing. 1970.

Moberly, Walter. "The History of the Cariboo Wagon Road." Art, Historical and Scientific Association of Vancouver, B.C. Papers. (1908).

Moore, James. "The Discovery of Hill's Bar in 1858." *British Columbia Historical Quarterly.* 3 (1939).

Morice, Adrien Gabriel. *The History of the Northern Interior of British Columbia, formerly New Caledonia.* Toronto. 1904.

Margaret Ormsby. *British Columbia, A History.* Toronto. The MacMillan Company of Canada Ltd. 1958.

Old Age Pensioners' Organization, Branch #77, Quesnel, B.C. *A Tribute to the Past.* 1808-1908. Quesnel, B.C. Spartan Printers.

Patenaude, Branwen C. *Because of Gold.* Quesnel, B.C. 1982.

Pettit, Sydney G. "His Honour's Honour." *British Columbia Historical Quarterly.* Vol. X1, No.3 July, 1947.

Ramsey, Bruce. *Ghost Towns of British Columbia.* Vancouver, B.C. Mitchell Press. 1963.

Ramsay, Bruce. *Inn-side British Columbia by Automobile.* Standard Oil of B.C. and B.C.Hotels Association. n.d.

Reid, Hugh. "Mileposts on the Cariboo Highway". *The Shoulder Strap.* Vertical Files, BCARS.

Rothenburger, Mel. *We've Killed Johnny Ussher.* Vancouver, B.C. Mitchell Press. 1973.

Smyth, Lindsay E. "The Origins of the Fraser River Gold Rush." *British Columbia Historical News.* Vol.25, No.4. Fall, 1992.

Splawn, A.J. *Ka-mi-akin, the Last Hero of the Yakimas.* Portland, Oregon. 1917.

Thomas, Emelene. "Cherished Memories." *North West Cariboo Digest*. January 1950.

Thomson, James. *For Friends At Home. A Scottish Emigrant's Letters from Canada, California and the Cariboo 1844-1864*. Edited by R.A. Preston. Montreal and London. McGill-Queen's University Press. 1974.

Topping, William. Editor, and Associate Editor, Bill Robinson. *British Columbia Post Offices*. Vancouver, B.C. 1983.

Touche, Rodger. "Frontier Inns." *B.C. Motorist*. May-June 1974.

Wade, Dr. Mark S. *The Overlanders of '62*. Victoria. Memoir No.IX, Provincial Archives of B.C. 1931.

Wade, Dr. Mark S. *The Cariboo Road*. Edited by Eleanor A. Eastick. Victoria, B.C. Haunted Bookshop. 1979.

Walkem, W.W. *Stories of Early British Columbia*. Vancouver, B.C. 1914.

West, Willis. "Staging and Stage Holdups". *British Columbia Historical Quarterly*. Vol.12, No.3, July,1948.

Williams, David R. *The Man for a New Country: Sir Matthew Baillie Begbie*. Sidney, B.C. Gray's Publishing. 1977.

Whitehead, Margaret. *The Cariboo Mission: A History of the Oblates*. Victoria, B.C. Sono Nis Press. 1981.

Woolliams, Nina. *Cattle Ranch*. Vancouver, B.C. Douglas & McIntyre. 1982.

UNPUBLISHED SOURCES.

Alexander, Richard H., "Diary", April, 1863. E/B/A1 3.2A British Columbia Archives and Records Service, Victoria, B.C.

Ball, Henry M., "Diary", August, 1864-Oct., 1865. Add.Mss. 681 BCARS.

Blair, George, "Diary", Jan.1862-Dec. 1863. Add.Mss. 187.BCARS.

Boss, Martha W. "A Tale of Northern B.C. to Cassiar." Add.Mss.771. BCARS.

Bowron, Lottie, M., Scrapbook, Reminiscences of Barkerville. Add.Mss. 44. BCARS.

Boyd, Archie. "Memoirs of Cottonwood House." Barkerville Historic Park, Barkerville, B.C.

Boyd, John C. Daybooks, Cold Spring House, May,1866-May,1886. Howay Collection, Special Collections Library, U.B.C., Vancouver, B.C.

Boyd, John C. Daybooks, Cottonwood House, 1874-1901. Quesnel and District Museum, Quesnel, B.C.

Buckley, Captain C.W.,"Diary", July, 1862. E/B/B85. BCARS.

Bushby, Arthur, "Diary", December 1858-April, 1859. Add. Mss.809. BCARS.

Cheadle, Dr. W.B., "Journal", 1863. E/B/C42.1. Parts 3 and 4. BCARS.

Clapperton, John, "Diary", 1862-1864. E/C/c53.3 BCARS.

Cornwall, Clement F., "Diary", 1862-1873. Add. Mss.759. BCARS.

Cornwall, Henry P., "Diary", December 1864-June 1865. Add. Mss.758. BCARS.

Courtney, Henry C., Manuscript, "Mines and Miners of British Columbia." 1878. Bancroft Library, Berkeley, California.

Crease, Arthur, Diary, "Bicycle Trip to Cariboo." August-September 1901. A/E/C86/C863.2 BCARS.

Crease, Sarah. "Diary of a Trip to Cariboo, Kamloops and New Westminster, Sept.1-Dec.7, 1880". A/E/C86 BCARS.

Currie, Vera Baker, Manuscript, "Susie", the life and times of Cecilia Elmore Baker. 1867-1958. Quesnel and District Museum.

Darlington, Esther, Ashcroft, B.C., Manuscript, "The Fabulous Fanny Faucault", 1988.

De Beck, Edward. Add.Mss.346. BCARS.

DeWees, Dick, Transcribed tapes, August 1977. Accession #142. Horsefly Historical Society, Horsefly, B.C.

Douglas, James, Private letters, 1827-1861. B.C.Papers, 11.29. B/20/1858 BCARS.

Douglas, James, Private papers, 1860. Bancroft Library, Berkeley, California.

Drinkell, A.J., Manuscript, "Cariboo Chatelaine", NW/P69D, BCARS.

Evans, Chad, Thesis, "Theatre In The Cariboo", Barkerville Historic Park. Barkerville, B.C., 1980.

Evans, Captain John, Diary, "British Columbia Mining Adventure, 1862-1864." Add. Mss.2111 BCARS.

Garrett, Reverend A.C., "Diary", June 3-10, 1865. Anglican Provincial Synod of B.C.Archives, Vancouver, B.C.

Guillod, Harry, Reminiscence, "Journal of a Trip to Cariboo." 1862. E/B/G94A. BCARS.

Gurney, William H., Reminiscence, "My First School, Cariboo Style." 1971. BCARS.

Haller, Joseph. Letters, 1858-1866. Lillooet Museum, Lillooet, B.C.

Hargreaves, Katherine G. Reminiscences. E/E/H221 BCARS.

Hills, Bishop George, "Diaries", 1860-1862. Anglican Provincial Synod of B.C. Archives, Vancouver, B.C.

Johnston, W. Alvin, Manuscript, "Birchbark to Steel", H. Albert Johnston family, Quesnel, B.C.

LeBourdais, Louis. "Harry Jones Story." Add. Mss. 676, Vol.7. BCARS.

Lyne, William Jr., 1890-1891. Account books, blacksmith. Add. Mss. 417.BCARS.

McColl, Sergeant William, "Diary", September 26-November 23, 1861. C/AB/30.6/M13. BCARS.

McKinlay, Duncan, "Memoirs", Vertical Files, BCARS.

McMicking, Robert B., "Diary",1862. Special Collections Library, U.B.C., Vancouver, B.C.

McMurphy, Sergeant John, "Diary", May 1862-August 1863. E/B/M221 BCARS.

Martley, Arthur H.J., "Reminiscences", Add.Mss.E/E/M363. BCARS.

Mission Ranch Daybook. September 24, 1861-January 2, 1862. 74A-365. BCARS.

Mitchell, Thomas R., "Diary", Add.Mss.838. BCARS.

Moffat House, Alexandria, B.C. "Diaries" 1891-1940s. Originals, Moffat family, Private collection.

O'Reilly, Peter, "Diary", 1858-1905. A/E/or3/Or3.BCARS.

Parsons, Otis, "Diary", 1858. E/B/P25 BCARS.

Phair, Arthur W.A., "History of Lillooet, B.C." Add.Mss. 275., BCARS.

Pinchbeck and Company. Daybook, 1870. Add.Mss.688. BCARS.

Pinchbeck, William Jr., "Notes on William Pinchbeck", 1930s. E/E/P65. BCARS.

Roeder, Henry, "Letters", E/B/R62cA. BCARS.

Rose, Frederick, Family history, ongoing genealogical study. Private collection.

Ryder, Angus G., "Recollections of Four Years at the 59 Mile House, Cariboo Road. 1910-1914", Add.Mss.1069, BCARS.

Sargison, George, "Diary", "A Trip To Williams Creek", December 1871. E/C/Sa7 BCARS.

Scholefield, Ethelbert O.S. Interview with John McLean of Quesnel, B.C. 1910. Add. Mss. 491, BCARS.

Slater, Ethel. "A Town Is Born." Vertical Files, BCARS.

Sylvester, Frank, "Memorandum of a Trip to Cariboo Via Douglas. July, 1864." E/B/Sy5.1A. BCARS.

Thomas, Father Francois M. T., "An Account of the Missionary Work done by the Oblates of Mary Immaculate in St. Joseph's District, Cariboo, B.C." Vertical Files, BCARS.

Trueman, Allen S., Thesis, "Placer Gold Mining in Northern B.C." University of B.C. Ch.5. 1935.

Trutch, Sir Joseph W., Daybook and ledger, 1862. Add.Mss.1184, BCARS.

Voorhis, Ernest, "Historical Forts and Trading Posts of the French regime and of the English Fur Trading Co's." NW971.F Vol.951. BCARS.

Wade & Co., Daybook, June 1863-December 1864. Howay Collection. Special Collections Library, U.B.C., Vancouver, B.C.

Walters, Glen, Transcribed tapes, July 1977. Accession #1-6, Side 1,2. Horsefly Historical Society, Horsefly, B.C.

Wardrop, J.R., "Gustavus Blin Wright, Colonial Entrepreneur." Victoria, B.C. 1876. BCARS.

Williams, Agnes, Transcribed tapes, September 1977. Horsefly Historical Society, Horsefly, B.C.

PUBLIC DOCUMENTS AND RECORDS.

Colonial Government Correspondence, 1858-1880. BCARS.

Begbie, Matthew Baillie, Supreme Court Bench Books, 1858-1879. BCARS.

Begbie, M.B., Colonial Correspondence, GR. 1372, F142-E. BCARS.

Cariboo Government Agency Letterbook, GR216, 1864-1880. BCARS.

Nind, Philip H., Colonial Correspondence, F1255. BCARS.

Palmer, Henry Spencer. Report of a Survey from Victoria to Fort Alexander via North Bentinck Arm, New Westminster, 1863. BCARS.

Department of Public Works, Notes on the Road History of British Columbia, 1853-1918. BCARS.

Colonial Secretary, Miscellaneous Official Correspondence. 1858-1900.BCARS.

B.C. Ministry of Provincial Secretary. Planning & Interpretation Division, Heritage Conservation, Victoria, B.C. assorted historical material, including "Cottonwood House, a documented history." by Judy Stricker, 1982.

Lists of Pre-empted Lands in Yale, Lillooet and Cariboo districts, 1859-1920. BCARS.

Lists of Certificates of Improvement, (Pre-empted Lands) 1865-1900. BCARS.

GR216, Mining Records 1860-1900. BCARS.

Geological Survey of Canada, Report of 1874. University of British Columbia. Vancouver, B.C.

Geological Survey of Canada. Memoir #149, Johnston & Uglow, 1925.

B.C. Department of Mines, Annual Reports, 1874-1940.

B.C. Department of Mines, Bulletin 34. Stuart Holland. 1954.

B.C. Land Titles, Victoria, B.C. Books of Mortgages and Conveyances, 1860-1868.

B.C. Department of Lands, Victoria, B.C. Legal Surveys Department Crown Grant Registry.

British Columbia Directories, 1863-1900.

PUBLISHED MAPS.

Western Union Telegraph, 1866. 3 Sheets. Drawn by J.C. White, from notes by J.Maclure. 17B8. 1866. Map Collection, Bancroft Library, Berkeley, California.

Pre-emptors Map, Quesnel Sheet, 1921. B.C. Department of Lands, Victoria, B.C.

Palmer, Lieutenant H. S., Sketch of Part of British Columbia. To accompany Report of Feb. 21, 1863.

Palmer, Lieutenant H. S. Sketch of Forks of Quesnel. Sept. 4, 1862. Land Reserves. 16T1, 17T1, Legal Surveys, Vault, Victoria, B.C.

Palmer, Lieutenant H. S. Plan of Route from New Westminster to Fountaine, B.C 1859.

Bowman, Amos, 9 Maps of Cariboo Mining District for Geological Survey of Canada, 1885, 1886. Little Snowshoe and Keithley Creek. Antler Creek. Lightning Creek. Williams Creek.

Begbie, Matthew B. Sketch of B.C. & Cariboo Country, 1861. Engineer's Camp, New Westminster, B.C.

Begbie, Matthew B. Discovery Route over Snowshoe Plateau. From Begbie's notes. Drawn by J.B.Launders, Oct. 1869.

MAGAZINES, PERIODICALS.

Western Methodist Recorder, Victoria, B.C.

Big Country Cariboo. Heldor Schafer. Quesnel, B.C. 1976-1978.

NEWSPAPERS.

B.C. Mining Journal, later known as the *Ashcroft Journal*

Bridge River-Lillooet News

British Colonist, later known as the Victoria *Colonist*

New Westminster British Columbian
British Columbia Gazette
British Columbia Examiner
British Columbia Tribune
The Cariboo Miner
The Cariboo Sentinel
Clinton Cache Creek Pioneer
Daily News Advertiser
Mainland Guardian
The New Westminster Times
100 Mile Free Press
The Quesnel Cariboo Observer
The Toronto Mail
Vancouver *Province*
Vancouver *Sun*
Williams Lake Tribune
Yale British Columbia Tribune
Kamloops Sentinel

TAPE RECORDINGS.
     Selected tapes from Aural History Department BCARS.
Pinchbeck, Fred. Tape No.FT17
Porter, Isobel. Tape No.495
Yorston, Janet. Tape No.380.

     Author's tape recordings, Private collection.
Barlow, Alex. Quesnel, B.C. 1982
Barlow, Anne. Quesnel, B.C. 1982
Beath, Charles. Quesnel, B.C.
Cook, Florence. Quesnel, B.C. 1982
Conn, Robert. Keithley Creek, B.C. 1979

Forbes, Molly. Lac La Hache, B.C. 1986

Hilborn, Gordon. Quesnel, B.C. 1976

Jackson, Dorothy. Hat Creek, B.C. 1978

Lyne, Georgina. Lac La Hache. B.C. 1983

Moffat, Roddy R. Alexandria, B.C. 1976

Parke, Sybil. Cache Creek, B.C. 1978

Petrowitz, Dolly. Williams Lake, B.C. 1977

Rankin, Gerald, Mary and Joan. Soda Creek, B.C. 1983

Rankin, Nellie. Morgan Creek, B.C. 1984

Rankin, Jim. Soda Creek, B.C. 1984

Watson, Jean. Quesnel, B.C., 1978

Windt, Tom. Alexandria, B.C. 1980

Yorston, Jack. Australian Ranch, B.C.

Yorston, Katherine. Australian Ranch, B.C.